T0168291

And Then There Were Nine

And Then There Were Nine . . .
More Women of Mystery

Jane S. Bakerman

Bowling Green State University Popular Press
Bowling Green, Ohio 43403

Library of Congress Catalogue Card No.: 84-72822

ISBN: 0-87972-319-X Clothbound
0-87972-320-3 Paperback

For Ruth Rendell

Contents

Foreword

Many people have contributed their time, efforts and skills to the development of this essay collection. To the scholars who prepared the studies of our subject-authors, to Pat Browne of the Bowling Green State University Popular Press, to Earl Bargainnier, who initiated this series with *Ten Women of Mystery*, and to Sonia Martin, Mary Ann Wallace and Betty Harstad, who are the staff and support of the Indiana State University Department of English, I owe—and give—heartfelt thanks. To Ted Bakerman, who thought this book could and should be done, I extend, as always, deep appreciation.

Jane S. Bakerman

Introduction

In discussing and evaluating those examples of popular fiction which are also categorized as formula fiction, it is easy to overlook the fact that one of the chief pleasures of reading formulaic works stems from the presence of the formula itself. The formula suggests to the reader that certain expectations will be fulfilled, that familiar patterns will be reintroduced, that no matter what entanglements of plot or characterization may be explored, certain basic, well-known factors of structure (and sometimes of character and setting) will appear. The familiar is comfortable because it is known—having enjoyed other examples of the formula in the past, readers anticipate enjoying the example currently in hand.

Further, though the immediate details of individual plots differ, the general thrust of all the stories is familiar and that familiarity of structure posits an imagined universe which is essentially orderly, logical and reliable. By implication, since fiction is often considered to be a reflection of (as well as reflections upon) life, formula fiction generally suggests that the real world in which readers live also functions according to sensible, perceivable rules, that there are certain basic patterns and codes of behavior which readers can come to understand, appreciate and perhaps, to live by.

The attraction of the formula is nowhere more important or more potent than in traditional crime fiction, a genre which allows its readers and fans to make safe forays into fictional worlds disordered by fictional crimes, to enjoy the dangers of the disruptions and the thrills of the chase while simultaneously enjoying the assurance and confidence which the formula offers—no matter how complex, disquieting, or even terrifying the plot complications or the characters' behavior may be, readers can be certain that, in the end, all will be set right. The detective—amateur, professional private eye, or police officer—will uncover the cause of the disorder, assign blame properly, remove the criminal (disrupter), and the story's little world will return to normalcy, to orderliness.

But readers and writers are never quite satisfied with any single tradition or formula; they always want more of a good thing. Another kind of gratification and interest which stems from formulaic writing derives, then, from the variety of ways in which skillful craftspersons manipulate the familiar, the elements of a formula. This impulse to experiment within the boundaries of a genre accounts, in part, for the many satisfying subgenres of crime fiction—the country-house mystery, the mean streets detective story, the modern gothic, the suspense novel, the caper plot and the spy story are some obvious and important examples. These important subgenres make artistic demands of their own upon their creators, and conventions which apply to each subgenre singly appear in conjunction with the basic, general conventions of the crime story genre.

Still other experiments, however, can be made. Because of the desire to improve (or at least *change*) any good thing and because the impulse to experiment is, happily, central to the consciousnesses of many writers, novels which are clearly within the realm of crime fiction but which deliberately break or bend or set aside some of the "rules" central to the formulae appear and are greeted by many readers with enthusiasm and a yen for more. Agatha Christie's *The Murder of Roger Ackroyd,* that classic of crime and controversy, is surely the best-known example. The subgenre most commonly associated with the rules-are-made-to-be-broken patterns of creativity, though, is the inverted mystery in which the perpetrator is known to readers from the outset and the suspense arises from the thrill of open competition between criminal and detective or from the fascination of watching a deviant or disintegrating personality struggle with itself and with outside forces. Ruth Rendell, with such novels as *A Demon in My View* and *A Judgement in Stone,* is one of the most distinguished practitioners of this art. Most inverted mysteries, however, are still firmly grounded on the premise that the fictional world can and will be restored to order through the good offices of a redemptive character (still often the detective) or of fate.

In the hands of some writers, the impulse to break the rules goes one step further and their fiction examines worlds in which order is not the governing principle and where justice may well be only a myth or, at best, a misguided or inadequate instrument of civilization. In the minds of some critics, these experiments tend to move the resultant novels beyond the farther boundaries of "popular fiction" and across the nearer boundaries of "serious fiction," and examples ranging from Dostoyevsky's *Crime and Punishment* to very recent studies of women victimized by crime such as Diane Johnson's *The Shadow Knows* or Beth Gutcheon's *Still Missing* spring readily to mind.

Though it is not the purpose of *And Then There Were Nine...More Women of Mystery* to resolve the question of what constitutes "serious" or "popular" fiction, it is, in part, the purpose of the essayists who contributed to this volume to explore some examples of the variety within unity which is so apparent in and life-giving to crime fiction. This collection, then, ranges from such writers as Daphne du Maurier and Margery Allingham, whose names are taken as synonymous with conventional subgenres of crime fiction, through Patricia Highsmith and Shirley Jackson, who deliberately set conventions aside or who move those conventions into other realms. Most importantly, perhaps, Jackson, Highsmith and E.X. Ferrars depict civilizations which are not essentially orderly, which are not founded upon a commonly understood concept of justice—where one must make her own order if, indeed, order is to exist at all.

In du Maurier's and Allingham's works, however, traditional as they may seem to be, experimentation and development are obvious. Du Maurier blends numerous conventions and genres in her fiction and Allingham creates novels which do not fit into her standard patterns. Craig Rice—in her various guises—also tries her hand at several subgenres, and, refusing to be very tightly bound by the hard-boiled school to which she is most frequently assigned, introduces hilarity into the mean streets down which her characters carom in pursuit of justice.

The other "conventional" writers also offer considerable variety within unity. Anne Morice exploits a telling device becoming ever more common and more popular in crime fiction—the special milieu and/or the special expertise of the detective; in Morice's case, the milieu is the theater and the expertise is Tessa Crichton's skills as actress-observer of the passing scene. Lillian O'Donnell also brings her knowledge of the theater to bear upon her crime fiction and Dorothy Uhnak's experiences as an officer of the law illuminate her novels convincingly and effectively. All these factors enlarge and enrich the authors' work.

Other factors besides experimentation also bind together the work of the subject-authors under study here. Morice, Allingham and du Maurier are particularly interested in class structure and they reflect this interest in their works. The later novels of O'Donnell and Uhnak seem to suggest a darkening world view on the part of their authors, a serious, sometimes sad, almost—at times—despairing, concept of the human condition in contemporary America where shifting standards of behavior and of civil codes call accepted conduct into question and may even allow for the abandonment of some codes altogether. These novels are, of course, very modern in tone and theme, yet, they are not so very different, perhaps, from du Maurier's studies of the price of upward mobility or Allingham's considerations of the impact World War II made upon those forms of English life she so prized.

The studies of the nine authors whose works form the subject matter of this book, then, indicate that in the hands of the thoughtful writer rule-following and rule-breaking are both worthy approaches to the creation of gripping fiction; that serious social commentary can spring fruitfully from entertaining escapist fiction, and that the most absorbing of all human questions—the presence of evil and the human propensity to engage in evil—are ever new, ever fresh, ever present.

The final qualities these Nine More Women of Mystery share are their skill and our admiration of it. They are talented artists who write compelling fiction, and it is the happy good fortune of those of us who studied their work and who contributed these essays to have had the pleasure of their company throughout the period during which this book was created.

Jane S. Bakerman
Indiana State University

Contributors

Martha Alderson is an editor for Webster Division of McGraw-Hill Book Company in Manchester, Missouri. She has contributed essays to the reference volumes *Twentieth Century Crime and Mystery Writers* and *Adolescent Female Portraits in the American Novel, 1961-1981: An Annotated Bibliography* and articles and reviews to *The Mystery Fancier, Reading in Virginia* and *Clues.*

Susan Baker received her B.A. from Rice University, her M.A. and Ph. D. from the University of Texas at Austin. She is an Associate Professor of English and Director of Freshman English at the University of Nevada, Reno, where she teaches an annual course in mystery and detective fiction. She has published articles on Shakespeare and Webster and was a contributor to *Twentieth Century Crime and Mystery Writers.*

Jane S. Bakerman, Professor of English at Indiana State University, is the author of articles, interviews and reviews and is co-editor of *Adolescent Female Portraits in the American Novel, 1961-1981: An Annotated Bibliography*. She served as adviser and contributor to *Twentieth Century Crime and Mystery Writers* and *American Women Writers, I-IV*. Her essay, "Ruth Rendell," appeared in *Ten Women of Mystery.*

Neysa Chouteau is a senior editor for Webster Division of McGraw-Hill Book Company in Manchester, Missouri. She contributed to the reference volumes *Twentieth Century Crime and Mystery Writers* and *Adolescent Female Portraits in the American Novel, 1961-1981: An Annotated Bibliography* and to periodicals such as *The Mystery Fancier* and *Grassroots Editor.* She has co-authored a series of mathematics textbooks and written programmed instructional materials for industry. Currently, she is editing a set of family letters for publication.

Carol Cleveland, a contributor to *Twentieth Century Crime and Mystery Writers,* is also a college professor, free lance writer and businesswoman who is currently practicing all these professions.

George N. Dove, Dean and Professor of English Emeritus of East Tennessee State University, has published criticism of detective fiction in several journals. An active member of the Popular Culture Association, he also served as adviser and contributor to *Twentieth Century Crime and Mystery Writers,* and his book, *The Police Procedural* was nominated for an Edgar by the Mystery Writers of America. His book on Ed McBain will be published by the Popular Press.

Rex William Gaskill is Associate Dean of Instruction at Normandale Community College in Minneapolis, Minnesota. He is a Ph.D. candidate in Speech Communication and English history at the University of

Minnesota. Besides administrative memos he is the author of a number of convention papers. Reading English detective fiction and rereading Jane Austen are his favorite forms of recreation. His current research is on Charles Gore and the Christian Socialist Movement in England.

Kathleen Gregory Klein is an Associate Professor of English and Co-ordinator of the Women's Studies Program at Indiana University at Indianapolis. She has published articles on twentieth century women writers, has contributed to *Twentieth Century Crime and Mystery Writers* and has written "Dorothy L. Sayers" for *Ten Women of Mystery*. She is currently writing a study of the professional female detective in British and American mystery fiction, 1864-1980.

Peggy Moran is Associate Professor of English at Purdue-Calumet, specializing in such popular culture courses as Science Fiction and the Detective Novel. She lectures frequently on film and literature and has written and presented numerous convention papers.

Daphne du Maurier
(Photo courtesy: Jane Bakerman)

Daphne du Maurier (Lady Browning)

1907	Born 13 May to Sir Gerald and Muriel (Beaumont) du Maurier in London. Gerald du Maurier was a very prominent actor-manager; Muriel Beaumont du Maurier was a well-recognized actress. George du Maurier, her paternal grandfather, was a famous artist-illustrator and author. Daphne du Maurier was privately educated in England and France.
1931	*The Loving Spirit,* first novel
1932	Married Lieutenant-General Sir Frederick A. M. Browning (d. 14 March 1965), two daughters, one son
1934	*Gerald: A Portrait* (biography of father)
1937	*The du Mauriers* (family history)
1940	Play *Rebecca* (which she adapted from her own novel) first produced; Alfred Hitchcock film *Rebecca* (Academy Award for Best Picture) adapted from novel first released
1945	*Hungry Hill*
1946	*The King's General*
1952	Fellow, Royal Society of Literature
1954	*Mary Anne* (based on family history)
1963	*The Glass-Blowers* (based on family history)
1967	*Vanishing Cornwall* with her son, Christian Browning, photographer
1969	Dame Comander, Order of the British Empire (D.B.E.); *The House on the Strand*
1975	*Golden Lads: Sir Francis Bacon, Anthony Bacon and Their Friends*
1976	*The Winding Stair: Francis Bacon, His Rise and Fall*
1977	Grand Master Award, Mystery Writers of America; *Growing Pains: The Shaping of a Writer* (autobiography)
1979	Television adaptation of *Rebecca* by British Broadcasting Corporation first released
1981	*The Rebecca Notebook and Other Memories* (memoir)

Daphne du Maurier

Jane S. Bakerman

During her long, distinguished career, Daphne du Maurier has tried her hand successfully at both fiction and nonfiction—biography, autobiography, historical romance, short stories and celebrations of place—but her auctorial reputation rests most firmly upon six romantic suspense novels whose plots stem from some crime or crimes. The novels are *Jamaica Inn, Rebecca, Frenchman's Creek, My Cousin Rachel, The Scapegoat,* and *The Flight of the Falcon.*[1] Not only have these works frequently put du Maurier's name on best-seller lists, but also they have contributed to a new reading of an old saying.

Among publishers, "One good turn deserves another," has been revised to "One good book can sell another." Du Maurier's enormously popular novels have not only themselves sold in vast numbers but also, for at least a generation, have helped vend books by association. Titles by other authors are advertised, displayed and sold by capitalizing upon du Maurier's reputation. Phrases such as "In the Tradition of *Rebecca,*" "In the Tradition of *Jamaica Inn,*" and "In the Tradition of Daphne du Maurier," for instance, blaze across countless book covers and advertisements.

Little attention, however, has been given to exactly what that tradition encompasses. Central to the du Maurier tradition are sound, exciting, workable plots: an orphan seeks refuge in her aunt's home only to find it the center of a smuggling ring; a young wife lives under the shadow of her predecessor and of her husband's secret; a noblewoman abandons family responsibilities to become lover and cohort of a pirate; a youth falls in love with a distant relative who is not only his beloved cousin's widow but also a suspected poisoner; an Englishman exchanges identities with a Frenchman and lives his double's life for a time; and an aimless young man finds his long-lost brother who is engaged in what may be a diabolical scheme. All of these basic plots are thrilling, all allow for abundant complication and all offer good possibilities for quick pace and great suspense.

Though even so swift a summary of the plots reveals variety, there are elements of commonality shared by all six titles under discussion here. For critics, that commonality has sometimes been dismissed as "formula fiction," and this term (often perceived as demeaning) has contributed to some misapprehension of the skill with which the author combines formulaic elements with experiments in established literary forms, especially variations of the *Bildungsroman,* to create the freshness and innovation which account for so much of her appeal. Indeed, the many, many modern gothics which echo *Rebecca* are good evidence that du Maurier tends to set trends rather than to follow them.

Certainly, it is no disgrace either to establish or to follow a popular, even beloved, literary formula. Du Maurier has done both; she tends to capitalize on some very old, established patterns (some reaching back into folk literature)—the worried, self-conscious second wife,[2] the dangerous dark-haired beauty, the ineffectual male seeking self-definition and power, the dark, mysterious male—and bend them to her will and to her skill. In doing so, she has created novels which strikingly match John Cawelti's description of successful formula fiction:

> popular story patterns are embodiments of archetypal story forms in terms of specific cultural materials. To create a western involves not only some understanding of how to construct an exciting adventure story, but also how to use certain nineteenth- and twentieth-century images and symbols such as cowboys, pioneers, outlaws, frontier towns and saloons along with appropriate cultural themes or myths—such as nature vs. civilization, the code of the West, or law and order vs. outlawry—to support and give significance to the action. Thus formulas are ways in which specific cultural themes and stereotypes become embodied in more universal story archetypes.[3]

The cultural images and symbols du Maurier employs in her romantic adventures are very closely allied with the cultural myths or themes which she explores. *Rebecca,* for instance, opens with one of English fiction's most famous lines, "Last night I dreamt I went to Manderley again." Manderley, the named house[4] which has become so indispensable to modern gothic fiction, is a very important socio-cultural symbol in the novel, for it represents all the pleasures, perquisites, comfort and standing of the powerful upper class to which Maxim de Winter belongs. Manderley is Maxim's heritage both in fact and in symbol and he will do almost anything to protect it.

Similarly yet differently, Jamaica Inn is the central socio-cultural symbol of the novel named after it. Normally, an inn represents a safe harbor for the weary traveler. Jamaica Inn, however, is an ironic symbol: there, plans for theft and bloodshed are laid; there, the spoils of shipwreckers (criminals of the lowest class) are stored. Not only the seat of criminal activity, the inn is also personally dangerous for Mary Yellan, the young woman who seeks refuge there. The emotional impact of both Manderley and Jamaica Inn is very great, for one represents a form of "the good life" any reader can recognize (and many desire) and the other represents all the false hopes and failed refuges most human beings encounter during the short journey between the cradle and the grave.

The cultural materials du Maurier most frequently employs in her romantic crime fiction also indicate elements of social convention. The British class system conflicting with the concept of upward mobility (for females via marriage; for males by assertion of control over lands and money); the idea that outside marriage a young woman has almost no identity; and the importance of retaining one's good name (no matter what reputation one deserves) are all central to these works. In *Rebecca,* for example, Maxim de Winter resorts to extreme violence to preserve his reputation and it is the consensus among those of his peers privy to his secret that he acted properly in doing so. Mrs. de Winter and Mary Yellan desire upward mobility and believe that marriage is their vehicle to security and status. Philip Ashley, the narrator of *My Cousin Rachel,* genuinely mourns Ambrose, the cousin from whom he inherits a vast estate, yet Philip is aware that as the master of the family holding, he enjoys power and position which would have been unattainable in a secondary or even a shared mastery.

Beyond those socio-cultural images and symbols lie others, even more pervasive and more powerful than those based upon class, property and reputation. Du Maurier also explores universal problems which take on the aura of cultural myth. The difficulty of distinguishing between good and evil and the impossibility of purging certain kinds of guilt are important in almost every story. Mary Yellan nearly falls prey to a very wicked man because she mistakes cultural trappings for his real nature. Armino Donati (*The Flight of the Falcon*) wants to trust his brother's charm, poise and attractiveness, but he suspects that vicious intent lies beneath Aldo's attractive exterior, and John, the protagonist-narrator of *The Scapegoat,* must learn that even the most crass codes of behavior can generate redemptive action.

Maxim de Winter not only hides his crime successfully but also involves his current wife and others in the concealment; he pays with years of misery, the loss of almost everything he sought to protect, yet guilt remains a constant in his life. Philip Ashley weighs the evidence against Rachel, his beloved, judges her—and lives out his years pondering his own guiltiness. Like Maxim de Winter, he has been both judge and jury; like Maxim, he must forever bear the memory and the weight of his actions.

The universal, mythically proportioned problems lying at the heart of du Maurier's most important novels are, indeed, basic. They are also, however, problems with which most human beings are expected to make their peace fairly early in life. One of the most important lessons learned by the very young is the ability to look behind disguise and to discover the essential decency or corruption of others, and very early on, people generally learn to assuage, ignore, or expiate guilt. Though these lessons may well have to be relearned or modified as maturing individuals confront new problems, people and situations, the groundwork, the basic principles of choice and evaluation, ought to be established during adolescence.

Though the du Maurier characters are no longer teenagers, they are, nevertheless, curiously immature for their years. Preoccupied by hard work and secluded in a small, friendly community, Mary Yellan has missed the experiences she needs to develop her judgment. Carefully protected, Philip Ashley has depended upon his cousin Ambrose for guidance. Both Armino Donati and John, the surnameless hero of *The Scapegoat,* have simply abdicated responsibility; they refuse to act. Maxim de Winter, seemingly an adult in full control of his powers, is caught in the grip of an obsession, Manderley and all it stands for, and is actually the most immature character of the lot. And Dona St. Columb, protagonist of *Frenchman's Creek,* a wife, mother, noblewoman, is frozen into immaturity, for she has substituted social activity and petulant rebellion for awareness and growth. Thus, these important characters are, for all narrative purposes, youngsters, and in her stories, du Maurier exposes them and many of their fellows to the maturation tests and experiences most commonly found in stories about adolescents. This device adds considerably to the novels' suspense, for it is, in a sense, a plot within a plot. Not only do readers wonder when and if the dangers and courtships will be resolved happpily, but they also wonder if the characters will be able to come to terms with the worlds in which they must live. Readers are keenly interested in discovering whether or not the characters will ever resolve the question of who they really are.

This question is also linked to another cultural artifact du Maurier exploits widely. She uses one of the oldest of western European tales, the Cinderella story,[5] in various ways throughout these six novels. Almost mythic itself, it becomes the vehicle for the ethical questions (of good and evil, of guilt) upon which the plot complications turn. Various elements of the Cinderella story appear in each of the novels under discussion here and all of them hinge upon the character's discovery of who he or she really is, the discovery at the heart of Cinderella's adventures.

Several situations are readily identifiable in *Cinderella*. The protagonist is an imposed-upon person who is trapped by fate, the ill will of others and the lack of property (which almost always stands for independence in these stories) in circumstances which belittle her, keep her dependent, prevent her from displaying her true beauty, intelligence, maturity and capacity for living a better (monied, socially prominent, powerful) life. Various elements of disguise are also notable. Initially, the protagonist is, in effect, disguised as an unworthy person, even as a scullery maid, for example. She then assumes a second disguise: she dresses and behaves as a princess, demonstrating what her true powers and position should be—but must return to her lowly life. After a series of dramatic events (including various tests, trials, journeys), Cinderella emerges into her proper identity. She is rescued. Cinderella is "saved" by the semi-effective magic of her fairy godmother, but, even more importantly, she is rescued by her lover, the prince, who raises her to her rightful place at his side. Though, by exhibiting proper behavior at the ball, she has acted in her own behalf, the most important redemptive actions are imposed upon her (like her initial passivity) by stronger, more active characters.

Ancient, powerful, extremely appealing to readers, the Cinderella story resolves itself into three basic elements: repression of the protagonist; action by the protagonist while disguised; and rescue of the protagonist by others, usually others who care for her. Traditionally, the newly crowned princess rides away with her prince to live happily ever after, exercising the power of her newly found wealth and position just enough to demonstrate how well she deserves it. She has escaped from the immaturity of social imprisonment and into the reality of life as an adult; she has passed her various tests and trials and been allowed to grow up. Society has accepted her because she has survived difficulties, because she has demonstrated that she can behave in socially acceptable ways and because someone else values her.

For the original Cinderella, the triumph is very nearly complete and she emerges into the highest of social classes. Du Maurier's Cinderella figures are seldom so fortunate, for irony informs the resolution of each of these novels and thus, in a very real sense, the author bridges the gap between fairy tale (or myth) and social realism even in her most romantic ficitons. Realism through irony is central to the conclusion of *Rebecca*, for example, when Mrs. de Winter, the most obvious Cinderella figure among the characters under study here, achieves her stated goal—she is all and everything to her husband, sure of his love, secure in their marriage—but loses all else she has dreamed of possessing through that marriage. Variations of this pattern also appear in the other five novels.

Clearly, then, du Maurier demonstrates a solid grasp of how to use basic formulae and traditional cultural elements in her work. In addition to these factors, however, useful, well-established literary patterns also appear, and they, too, indicate du Maurier's ability to blend old concepts into fresh, exciting new tales. Du Maurier capitalizes, for instance, upon the British preoccupation with the crime novel, a fact that, in 1977, won her the Grand Master award from the Mystery Writers of America.

In du Maurier's romantic suspense novels, as in *Cinderella,* the major question is not detection but justice. It is important that Cinderella's triumph include the public humiliation of her wicked relatives because, in the eyes of many people, public punishment is equated with justice. Because the evils which Cinderella confronts, overt cruelty, jealousy and selfishness, are easy to identify and are subject to social disapproval, the wicked are punished; justice, seemingly, is served.

But the evils which the du Maurier protagonists confront are more complex; simple, obvious punishment is not always meted out. Instead, the irony which colors du Maurier's social commentary also affects her portrayal of justice, for while justice is always imposed, it is often served secretly, privately. To du Maurier, the impact of a crime is of far greater interest than the solution of a puzzle and this interest demands sophisticated modes of punishment.

The crime motif in du Maurier's novels is also enriched by another element of the Cinderella story, the disguise pattern. Frequently, the novels' protagonists appear in disguise; Lady Dona St. Columb, for instance, dresses as a boy when committing piracy. To her bitter dismay, Mrs. de Winter unwittingly disguises herself as Rebecca, her predecessor, for she is tricked into duplicating the costume Rebecca once wore to a fancy-dress ball and this scene lays the groundwork for the revelation of Maxim's crime. These disguises are fascinating and useful plot complications, lending action, adventure, or ironic foreshadowing to the stories.

Even more useful, however, are the disguises worn by the other characters, and these disguises exacerbate the difficulty of separating evil from goodness, one of the mythic themes which pervades these works. In each of the novels, at least one very powerful personality is examined and explored; these characters are charismatic, mysterious, disguised. Several are not what they seem to be and are unmasked. Frances Davey, the Vicar of

Altarnum (*Jamaica Inn*), is not really a devout pastor ministering wholeheartedly to his flock but a dangerous criminal. Maxim de Winter is not a man emotionally crippled by the death of his beloved but rather a man tortured by guilt and the refusal to pay for his crime.

Others among these disguised charismatics are better than they first seem. Jean-Benoit Aubéry, the French pirate, *is* actually a criminal, but he is more decent, caring and nurturing than all the nobles among whom Dona St. Columb has lived. Jem Merlyn (*Jamaica Inn*) who makes no attempt to hide his career as petty criminal and horse thief, is far more honest with Mary Yellan than are the other inhabitants of the Bodmin area.

A third group, most notably Rebecca de Winter and Rachel Sangalletti Ashley, are essentially unknowable—one is never sure just which guise is mask, which reality. The world perceived Rebecca as the epitome of feminine grace and beauty, the perfect mistress for Manderley. To Maxim, her husband, she seemed a corrupt monster. To Mrs. Danvers, the housekeeper, and to Jack Favell, Rebecca's lover and cousin, she appeared to be a free spirit, capable of commanding devotion even from beyond the grave. Though most of the characters choose to believe Maxim's interpretation of Rebecca's character, the puzzle is never resolved. Nor is the mystery surrounding Rachel's character dispelled; she may be tragically accused of and punished for a crime she did not commit, a crime which was, indeed, never committed by anyone, or she may be a grasping poisoner who kills for wealth and position. These characters not only drive foward the action, but they also complicate the process of distinguishing between good and evil, sometimes beyond the capacity of the protagonists (and some readers). Unlike the disguises of the Cinderella figures, these enigmatic masks are meant to be impenetrable.

The disguise motif, then, establishes the most difficult tests the Cinderella figures must pass in order to win better lives. Further, because the enigmatic figures may mislead the protagonists, the element of disguise also strengthens the other fictional pattern du Maurier exploits. The education or maturation novel, the *Bildungsroman* (for which *Cinderella* is one of several important prototypes), is deeply embedded in both "serious" and popular fiction throughout western culture. Itself enormously popular, it is prime material for a writer like du Maurier who seeks a very wide audience.

In the traditional *Bildungsroman,* a young person who has great faith in his own power and potential tests his mettle as a means of initiation into maturity. He often takes a journey, acquires mentors of varying levels of reliability and engages in dangerous adventures. Ultimately, he emerges sadder but wiser, ready to take his place in adult society. He has compromised with the ideal and settled for pragmatism. Du Maurier uses this treatment of the *Bildungsroman,* most commonly found in "high culture" novels, very successfully in both *Jamaica Inn* and *Frenchman's Creek.*

In *Jamaica Inn,* Mary Yellan dreams of security and hopes to find peace and opportunity living with her aunt and uncle at the inn. Instead, she finds danger to her life and honor and a host of false mentors. Among them is her criminal uncle, Joss Merlyn, who presents a sexual threat; he finds Mary attractive and to her dismay, she is somewhat drawn to him. For relief, advice and comfort, Mary turns to a local minister, one of du Maurier's masters of disguise, who does, indeed, advise her but who is actually also a false mentor.

Because of his abusive treatment of her aunt and because of his criminal activity, which she slowly comes to recognize, Mary has little trouble recognizing Joss as an evil person; indeed, he represents the worst that life can offer her: sexual excess, constant danger, shared criminal behavior. Dark, mysterious, violent, Joss symbolizes trouble and degeneration. The Reverend Mr. Davey, however, seems to represent redemption until his mask is finally stripped away during a melodramatic series of events that include an abduction and wild chase over the moors.

Not only does the final unmasking of Davey leave Mary without a functioning mentor, it also forces her to question the basic rules of social convention. She has hoped to establish a very normal, secure life on the Cornish coast, and obviously one means of doing so would have been to marry well, preferably, like most of the Cinderellas, to marry *up.* The revelation of Davey as villain and exploiter removes him from the ranks of potential mates and also, importantly, calls into question the viability of Mary's dreams of security and status.

A poor girl with modest dreams, Mary is barred, finally, from upward mobility by the rules of the class system. Tainted by her low birth, her poverty, her association with criminals (she is even an unwilling spectator and thus marginally a participant in one raid), Mary cannot change her status. She shares in the guilt for this last raid because she was there and because willful blindness as well as circumstance have stopped her from preventing it.

Though Mary has learned not to trust outward appearances, her fate lies, finally, in the hands of yet another masquerader. Jem Merlyn, Joss' younger brother, is an enigmatic man who reveals little of his true emotion, a sexually attractive person who prefers liason (when he can get it) to marriage. Nevertheless he loves Mary and is the only individual who acts effectively to save her from rape or murder. Despite the tensions which exist between them in the early days of their acquaintance, Mary "believes" that she loves Jem, that he is her true mate and she rides off with him, " 'Because I want to: because I must; because now and for ever more this is where I belong to be' " (332).

The real world for which Mary, chastened and tempered, settles is a marginal world in which she will always hover between poverty and security, social acceptance and rejection, love and danger. Ironist that she is, du Maurier gives no guarantees that for this young woman there will be any "happily ever after." Though Mary is a successful *Bildungsroman* protagonist (she has learned, she has matured, she has compromised), she is a failed Cinderella; the class sytem prevails and Mary Yellan is frozen into the fringes of accepted society. She has love but little else, and du Maurier refuses to promise that that will be enough.

On the surface of her life, Dona St. Columb is, at the opening of *Frenchman's Creek,* Cinderella leading an enchanted life after the glass slipper has slid smoothly onto her foot. Chronologically an adult, Dona is nevertheless a rebellious child. Disgusted with her dull husband, often irritated by the demands of motherhood, and bored with London life, Dona disguises herself and engages in dangerous, illegal pranks, "playing at" highway robbery, until, restless and annoyed with herself as much as with her world, she runs away to Navron House, the family estate, fleeing both her obligations and her escapades.

There, however, she moves even more deeply into disguise and danger, for she comes to love a French pirate who is raiding the Cornish coast. A kind of nautical Robin Hood, Aubéry, the Frenchman of the title, teaches Dona what love and sexual satisfaction really are, and she revels in the relationship. Initially disguised as chic matron, polished noblewoman, Dona believes she has found her true nature when disguised as a thieving boy or sensual lover and she discovers that she is not only a competent thief but also a clever schemer when she undertakes to save her lover from imprisonment and death. During this period, Navron House continues to stand for the positive qualities of whatever is decent in Dona's public life, everything opposed to the corruption symbolized by London. The nearby creek where the Frenchman moors his ship and *La Mouette* itself symbolize freedom, love, the right to break social codes in order to achieve happiness—everything children imagine that adulthood allows.

Eventually, Dona must choose between life with the Frenchman and life as Lady St. Columb and in the end, social convention and family obligation claim her. For her, life as a constrained, post-ball Cinderella *is* reality whereas life on the fringes of society is dream. Except in memory, she will truly become,

> a gracious matron, and smile upon her servants, and her tenants, and the village folk, and one day she will have grandchildren about her knee, and will tell them the story of a pirate who escpaed (306-7).

Dona will not live happily ever after, but she will live responsibly.

She, too, has been tempered and chastened and like Mary, she responds, however hesitantly, to the lessons she has learned. If Mary Yellan cannot penetrate respectable levels of English society, no more can Dona St. Columb abdicate the upper classes. These young women come to know themselves very well; they find out precisely who they are, but they are, finally, defined by the social roles assigned by birth. Their very traditional *Bildungsroman* journeys, culminating in compromise and pragmatic acceptance, are complete.

The crimes in which Mary Yellan and Dona St. Columb participate differ from the crimes which are central to *Rebecca, My Cousin Rachel, The Scapegoat,* and *The Flight of the Falcon,* for though both young women are technically guilty of crimes, they are distanced from them by circumstances: Mary is an unwilling witness-participant and Dona pillages her neighbors while living an enchanted, dreamlike life. Also, each can expiate her guilt and both do so by surrendering to the behavior dictated by society. They will pay the price of their crimes over a very long term and they will forever remain aware that a part of the price is the destruction of their hopes, but they will not be riddled with guilt. Significantly, perhaps, their stories are told in the third person and this device also—like the distant times in which the novels are set—helps to undercut the impact of their protagonists' criminality.

Even though *My Cousin Rachel,* like *Jamaica Inn* and *Frenchman's Creek,* is an historical novel, there is no distancing between its narrator-protagonist, Philip Ashley and the reader, nor does distancing take place in *Rebecca, The Scapegoat,* or *The Flight of the Falcon.* The sense of expiation is missing here—Mrs. de Winter and Philip Ashley mull over their situations, it appears, endlessly, reliving their pasts over and over again, secretly, internally. Though both Armino Donati and John put their pasts behind them a bit more firmly, both must live with the ongoing awareness that Aldo Donati and Count Jean de Gué represent the wicked forces within all human hearts and they must confront, always, the sense that they, too, could become exploitative, harmful people. Du Maurier underscores the immediacy of these plots by using first-person narration in each book and by adding the element of confession to the extraordinary mix of form, formula, theme and genre she creates.

The protagonists of *Rebecca, My Cousin Rachel, The Scapegoat* and *The Flight of the Falcon* report the most compelling experiences of their lives, often revealing some of their own baser actions and motivations. The reader feels not only keenly interested but also flattered by the sense that it is his ear alone which is singled out for these confessions. The overall effect is one of great force and tension, prime elements in all good fiction, absolutely essential, of course, in the romantic suspense novel, and here, du Maurier amalgamates that tension with uncertainty about those personalities which hide beneath impenetrable masks and with the suspense arising from the *Bildungsroman* protagonists' searches for their true identities.

In popular fiction, two variations of the traditional *Bildungsroman* occur frequently and du Maurier experiments with these varieties just as she does with the traditional pattern in *Jamaica Inn* and *Frenchman's Creek*. As feminist critics have pointed out, the modern gothic novel is a form of the *Bildungsroman*[6] whose youthful protagonists, usually females, are, either consciously or unconsciously, engaged in a quest for advancement as well as for adulthood. They want power, selfhood, love and maturity and much of the time, they tend to perceive these desirables as interchangeable if not synonymous.

In a sense, they feel that they will be forever unworthy if they are not loved by some greatly desirable person, but also, secretly or even unconsciously, they feel themselves to be the equal—if not the superior—of most of the characters surrounding them.[7] This conflicting sense of self-worth (obvious in *Cinderella*) is often painful and almost always results in the protagonists' maintaining a kind of public guise of meekness which hides a fiery, judgmental, or even arrogant personality. Cinderellas, they are not only disguised initially by their lowly positions, but also they actively parade a mask of humility.

The second Mrs. de Winter, the protagonist-narrator of *Rebecca,* is precisely this sort of person and because of the confessional nature of the novel, readers are privy to the seemingly meek, the genuinely humble and the bitingly judgmental elements of her nature from the outset. Though she maintains a quiet, obedient exterior, she denounces thoroughly (and with some good cause) Mrs. Van Hopper, an American of abundant financial means and absolutely no taste, whom she serves as companion. She feels distinctly superior to the Van Hopper world but too inexperienced, uninteresting and plain to be a likely helpmeet of Maxim de Winter. Both attitudes cause her considerable trouble. Ironically, she accepts Mrs. Van Hopper's evaluation of her personality and assumes that to Maxim she is merely a toy, a pet, that she can never truly be his equal. Yet, inwardly, she weeps and rages, for she yearns to be his true companion, to move beyond the shadow of Rebecca and into prominence as the mistress of Manderley, with which she has been entranced since childhood.

Maxim, enigmatic, preoccupied with keeping secret the crime he has committed, withholds a large part of himself from his second wife even though he senses and deplores her unhappiness. In turn, Mrs. de Winter, unaware of Maxim's true thoughts, assumes he is still grieving for Rebecca. Both marriage partners maintain disguises, acting out a "happy" married life, refusing to share, pretending before outsiders and one another.

This Cinderella temporarily acquires both her prince and her castle, but she can genuinely enjoy neither, and when truth does finally prevail between the de Winters, it is too late. The prince, the princess and the marriage survive, but the castle, Manderley, symbol of all the perks of upper-class life, is destroyed. Once again, du Maurier's irony intrudes and the class system prevails. Mrs. de Winter deserves her tainted prince *only if* they are exiled from the social circles to which Maxim was born and to which Mrs. de Winter aspires. Cinderella finds that compromise dominates adulthood and the real world; she acquiesces and endures the consequences of fallen pride. Society has preserved its aura of respectability by protecting Maxim from disclosure of his crime, but nevertheless, it has firmly punished the de Winters. Though this *Bildungsroman* hero has learned her lessons all too well, there is nowhere to use her education.

> We can never go back again, that much is certain. The past is still too close to us. The things we have tried to forget and put behind us would stir again, and that sense of fear, of furtive unrest, struggling at length to blind unreasoning panic—now mercifully stilled, thank God—might in some manner unforseen become a living companion, as it had been before (4).

Instead, the de Winters drift through Europe, maintaining the social façade, marking time until death releases them.

Death will also be the only release for Philip Ashley, one of the very few *male* gothic heroes. Like Mrs. de Winter, Philip seems initially to be a weak, ineffectual person, but he is much quicker than she to exercise the power of money and position once Ambrose Ashley's death places the family fortune under his control. For a time, Philip behaves like an assertive, self-confident adult, the head of his family, an influential person in his neighborhood.

But actually, Philip's assertiveness is a disguise. He is merely imitating his cousin, even reenacting Ambrose's compelling love for Rachel. Philip is simultaneously too judgmental and too vacillating. He waxes and wanes in his perception of Rachel's character, worrying at one moment that her beauty will seduce him from vengeance, for in his last days, Ambrose, ill and possibly demented, has accused Rachel of murdering him. At the next moment, however, Philip, playing the role of self-confident adult, glories in his love for Rachel and presents her with the splendid pearl collar which symbolizes all that the Ashley heritage means in English country society.

Several factors converge to motivate Philip Ashley to irreversible action. Perhaps the most important factor is the pain of vacillation itself; his shifts in mood and attitude are torturous and du Maurier suggests that he hopes to end the pain by taking one irrevocable step. This impulse is strengthened by the fact that Rachel, a true adult, poised, serene, controlled, is really too much for Philip, who seems incapable of maturity. Also, though he has perhaps envied his cousin's position and personality, Philip truly loved Ambrose and remains loyal to his memory; if Rachel killed him, Ambrose must be avenged. The possible need for vengeance is further endorsed by Philip's own fear—will Rachel kill *him*?

But finally—and importantly—a very special kind of social pressure also motivates Philip. If Rachel is actually a deadly, greedy, social climber, she must no longer bear the Ashley name; she must not, with him, head the family. And on that chance, he judges his beloved. The act is truly irrevocable and the social codes that demand that criminals not benefit by their crimes and that socially prominent "good names" must be protected are turned against Rachel very effectively indeed.

Irony again, however, prevails. Philip, a male Cinderella, is left with his castle, his lands, his rank—and nothing else. He can love no other woman; the family line will end with him, for though he has served the social rules by which the Ashleys have always lived, he has not served himself. The most significant of the *Bildungsroman* tests imposed upon Philip Ashley has failed: he still wonders; he still vacillates; he still suffers, and his confession is nothing more than another painful spasm of guilt. Philip has not earned adulthood, nor has he purchased it with Rachel's punishment. Though he has made a costly compromise, he cannot resign himself to live with its consequences and he can hardly bear his constant awareness of it; he remains a child.

In traditional adventure-suspense fiction, the protagonist takes a slightly different view of himself than do gothic heroes such as Philip Ashley and Mrs. de Winter. They do not perceive themselves as better than others and they do not yearn for status. Usually, these characters have seen something of life, have become aware of its stresses and pitfalls and, as protection, have disguised themselves as "small," inconsequential persons. Each must stretch his capacity, admit his own potential, abandon insignificance, *expand* in order to meet and conquer some criminal threat. Doing so will signify emergence from a willfully chosen, prolonged adolescence into full maturity. Generally, they pass their exacting tests and emerge stronger, more confident, no longer hiding their capabilities from the world.

Du Maurier's experiments with this variant of the *Bildungsroman, The Flight of the Falcon* and *The Scapegoat,* allow their protagonists much more promising futures than do her treatments of the traditional *Bildungsroman* or of the modern gothic, even though the events are just as melodramatic, the assessments of human nature just as uncompromising. Furthermore, in these novels, the questions of guilt and evil are expanded considerably, a fact underscored by the use of non-English settings.

Though matters of social class and its privilege remain important in *The Scapegoat* and are echoed by allusions to earlier times in *The Flight of the Falcon,* these novels are allegories and du Maurier uses St. Gilles, the French village dominated by the de Gué family of *The Scapegoat,* and Ruffano, the Italian university city in which *The Flight of the Falcon* is set, as microcosms. In the first novel, she examines the political and economic impact of one man's criminality, selfishness and arrogance. In the second, she explores the effects of a clever, ambitious man's manipulation of oppressive political systems.

Because du Maurier is chiefly a storyteller and not a philosopher, dramatic action dominates theme in these novels; the political implications are not particularly profound and they are certainly not unique. However, these implications intensify the suspense in both books, just as they later intensify her futuristic political study, *Rule Britannia* (1972) and they continue du Maurier's examination of the conflict between personal ambition and one's duty to others which is the subject of such novels as *I'll Never Be Young Again* (1932) and *The Progress of Julius* (1933), novels outside the boundaries of romantic suspense fiction.

Du Maurier complicates the problems of distinguishing between good and evil and of guilt and emphasizes the allegorical nature of *The Flight of the Falcon* and *The Scapegoat* by using Christian symbolism in both. Crucial action in *The Flight of the Falcon* takes place during Easter Week, for instance, and a priest, a character in *The Scapegoat,* states the theme of both books:

> 'There is no end to the evil in ourselves, just as there is no end to the good. It's a matter of choice. We struggle to climb, or we struggle to fall. The thing is to discover which way we're going' (200).

Both novels also depict Satanic and Christlike figures who are very much alike: in *The Scapegoat,* the men are identical in appearance and in *The Flight of the Falcon,* they are putative brothers. Further, the Donati brothers share a kind of *Doppelgänger,* the spirit of Claudio, a long-dead Duke of Ruffano, who is depicted as both tempted and tempter in an old painting, "The Temptation of Christ." These devices help du Maurier move beyond questions of personal complicity and individual destiny around which *Rebecca, My Cousin Rachel, Frenchman's Creek* and *Jamaica Inn* center and focus attention, instead, upon the basic duality of human nature.

As the title of *The Scapegoat* implies, someone must be sacrificed in some way in order to restore order and decency to societies disordered by ambition and the lust for power, and this element, also ironically crucial to *The Flight of the Falcon,* serves not only the Christian imagery but also the crime motif. In crime novels, it is the duty of the detective to discover truth, to establish grounds for punishment of the criminal and thus to restore social order. Both John and Armino must become, reluctantly, detectives of sorts, searching both past and present to identify evil, to uncover a serious transgression and to establish a mode of redeeming the societies in which they find themselves.

That they are able to act redemptively though they are flawed men who simply *behave* in Christlike fashion is the factor which accounts for the rather hopeful resolutions of these two novels and which reflects the ultimately positive view of human nature expressed in most traditional crime fiction. Once the sacrifice has been made and order restored, the effort to live decently, to be "good," can resume. Guilt has been purged and only the decidedly difficult but presumably accomplishable obligation to guard forever against humankind's inherent capacity for evil remains.

Though they are rich in Christian imagery and reflect many Christian concepts, neither *The Flight of the Falcon* nor *The Scapegoat* is, however, a doctrinaire statement of Christian belief. Rather, du Maurier uses these allusions to invoke a very old cultural artifact, the story of Christ (and the even older stories of scapegoats important to other religions), as one of the cultural myths which illuminate the adventures of her heroes. She employs them exactly as she employs the Cinderella motif to embellish and expand her exciting plots, her various experiments with the *Bildungsroman.*

At the opening of *The Fight of the Falcon,* Armino Donati avoids genuine responsibility by working as a tour guide; he is a wanderer following schedules set by others. The impact of World War II, the humiliations and tribulations of the Occupation and certain memories from his youth (he was dominated and sometimes terrorized by his older brother, Aldo) have convinced him that the small life is the safe life, but he is jolted from his security by the murder of an old beggar-woman. Conscience and memory compel him to return to Ruffano, his native city, to solve the mystery surrounding her death.

In Ruffano he discovers his brother, long thought dead, who has become an important figure in the city and its university. Aldo draws Armino into his plans; he seems bent upon controlling the life of both school and town by his charismatic power over much of the student body. To do so, he also invokes the memory of Claudio, Duke of ancient Ruffano, himself a magnetic, potent, violent figure. Despite his impulse to resume a small life in the shadow of his daring brother, Armino becomes alarmed by the ritualism of Aldo's corps of followers and frightened over the intensity of their loyalty and ambition.

Aldo, he comes to believe, is imitating the life of Claudio, "The Falcon," and basely succumbing to the temptations which beset any ruler. When Armino himself is dragooned into impersonating Claudio in a great pageant, his masquerade symbolizes his own temptation. Both brothers, then, in their differing ways, disguise themselves as Claudio, a princely figure. Armino retains some grasp of reality while disguised; Aldo, apparently, does not. The full truth of Aldo's plans is never revealed to the citizens of Ruffano and may be only partially clear to Armino, for Aldo is one of du Maurier's unknowable personalities and here, as in *My Cousin Rachel,* some doubt abides.

But unlike Philip Ashley, Armino has learned from his experiments with power as well as from his brother's mistakes. He plans to take up Aldo's work, to retain its positive elements, avoid corruption, live a life which will demand full use of his capabilities:

> I left my old home. . .and walked up the street to Aldo's house. It was strangely silent.... Yet I did not feel myself alone. Glancing upward, I saw a meteor streak across the heavens and vanish, its golden pathway, for a moment, a brief splendour in the sky (252).

Having tasted both the diminished life of the social dropout and the heady life of the meteroic political manipulator, Aldo strikes a healthy compromise. Though he will abandon life among the cinders and eschew the flames of glory for glory's sake, Armino Donanti intends to kindle a warm glow by serving others.

John, the protagonist of *The Scapegoat,* also suffers temptations. The leader of a life so small and inconsequential that he considers it worthless and is contemplating suicide, John is tricked into masquerading for a time as his double, Count Jean de Gué. While doing so, he discovers the full range of Jean's selfishness, uncovers a particularly cold-blooded crime in the count's past and is tempted to think of de Gue as a completely evil being, one who "struggles to fall."

This temptation is very great, for John values his life as the surrogate count; leaving it would be a genuine sacrifice. He is fond of de Gué's family, loves the count's mistress and living in St. Gilles fulfills his dream of immersing himself in French life. Furthermore, amazingly, John restores the house of de Gué to an order it has not known for years; he heals old wounds, rights old injustices. A reluctant Cinderella, John captures the castle (though his actions are frequently awkward and sometimes enormously puzzling to its inmates). He is tempted to see his achievements as so good that they are worth continuing at any price and he contemplates murdering the count in the name of redemption and goodness.

Ironically, John has achieved all this good by following his double's code of conduct; Jean maintains:

> 'The only motive force in human nature is greed.... The thing to do is to minister to the greed and to give people what they want' (36).

Jean de Gué gave people what they wanted when doing so served his own desires; John gives in order to fulfill their needs. If he murders his counterpart, he will be serving his own desires but denying the family what they really need and want: Jean. Though order seems to have been restored among the de Gué clan, that orderliness is simply pretense unless Jean, the real prince, can sustain it.

This realization couples with John's awareness that he, himself, is almost capable of murder to make him understand that there is more than physical resemblance binding him to Jean. He learns that he and Jean have both good and evil impulses and that neither man can achieve full maturity unless the masquerade ends. The bittersweet conclusion to *The Scapegoat* hints that Jean may rise to John's challenge and suggests firmly that John will put the lessons of his delayed *Bildungsroman* journey to good use. Like Armino Donati, he is a successful apprentice to life: he will "struggle to climb."

An examination of her treatments of the Cinderella story and of her experiments with various forms of the *Bildungsroman,* then, indicate that Daphne du Maurier brings a rich imagination, a sound sense of story line and action, and a great willingness to experiment to her fiction. Though individually the novels considered here—*Jamaica Inn, Frenchman's Creek, Rebecca, My Cousin Rachel, The Flight of the Falcon* and *The Scapegoat*—match Cawelti's definition of formula fiction, together, they demonstrate that any formula—or any literary convention—can be reinvented fruitfully. In the hands of a true storyteller, the old is always new and the "du Maurier Tradition" demands bold inventiveness, intelligence and a special awareness of the roots, artifacts, strengths and weaknesses of the culture from which it springs, toward which it is directed. Du Maurier blends all of these requirements into the heady compounds of the expected and the surprising which are so pleasurable to her readers. In achieving these ends, she surpasses her competitors and her imitators. Others may emulate Daphne du Maurier, but she remains dominant.

Notes

[1]The editions of du Maurier's novels used for this study are listed below, preceded by the original date of book publication; several titles were earlier serialized in magazines. All quotations are cited in the text.
1936 *Jamaica Inn* (Garden City, New York: Doubleday, Doran & Company, Inc., 1937).
1938 *Rebecca* (New York: Doubleday & Company, Inc., crt. 1938).
1941 *Frenchman's Creek* (Garden City, New York: Doubleday, Doran & Company, Inc., 1942).
1951 *My Cousin Rachel* (Chicago: Sears Reader's Club, 1952).
1957 *The Scapegoat* (Garden City, New York: Doubleday & Company, Inc., 1957).
1965 *The Flight of the Falcon* (Garden City, New York: Doubleday & Company, Inc., Book Club Edition, 1965).

[2]Controversy over the originality of the plot of *Rebecca* followed publication of the novel. Du Maurier prevailed in the resulting legal suits.

[3]John G. Cawelti, *Adventure, Mystery and Romance* (Chicago: The University of Chicago Press, 1976), p. 6. Also useful are Cawelti's discussions of Adventure, pp. 39-41; Romance, pp. 41-42; and Mystery, pp. 42-44.

[4]Caesarea Abartis, "The Ugly-Pretty, Dull-Bright, Weak-Strong Girl In the Gothic Mansion," *Journal of Popular Culture,* 13:2 (Fall 1979), 260-261. Abartis also discusses *Rebecca.*

[5]See also Bruno Bettleheim, *The Uses of Enchantment* (New York: Alfred A. Knopf, 1976), pp. 236-277 especially. Bettleheim touches upon even earlier Eastern versions of *Cinderella* and discusses its psychological application. Though critics have not discussed *Cinderella* and *Rebecca,* some have treated other aspects of *Cinderella* and *Jane Eyre.* Useful examples are Jane McDonnell, "Another Orphan's Progress: *Jane Eyre* as *Bildungsroman,*" *Breaking Ground* 2 (Spring 1981), 32-39; Karen E. Rowe, " 'Fairy-Born and Human-bred': Jane Eyre's Education in Romance," in *The Voyage In,* Elizabeth Abel, Marianne Hirsch, and Elizabeth Langland, ed. (Hanover, New Hampshire: University Press of New England, 1983), pp. 72-73; Paula Sulivan, "Fairy Tale Elements in *Jane Eyre,*" *Journal of Popular Culture,* 12:1 (Summer 1981), 61-73.

[6]See especially Ellen Moers, *Literary Women* (Garden City, New York: Doubleday & Company, Inc., 1976), pp. 122-140.

[7]Abartis, 257-263.

Margery Allingham
(Photo courtesy: W. Heinemann Ltd.)

Margery Allingham

1904	Margery Louise Allingham born on 20 May in Ealing, a London suburb, daughter of Herbert John and Emily Hughes Allingham. Her parents were cousins and came from a family of writers and journalists.
1912	First story published in an aunt's paper. Allingham is paid seven and sixpence. A professional at eight.
1912-20	Attended Colchester School and The Perse School, Cambridge
1920+	School of Drama and Speech Training at the Polytechnic in Regent Street, London.
1922	*Dido And Aeneas,* written and produced for her fellow students. She played the lead and made 40 costumes.
1923	Hodder & Stoughton agree to publish *Blackerchief Dick* and she meets Philip Youngman Carter whom she insists must design the book jacket.
1925	*Water in a Sieve,* a play, published by French.
1927	Marries Carter, now editor of *The Tatler.* Moves to a minute flat in Holborn. Income comes from translating silent films into short stories and in writing serials such as "The Society Millgirl and the Eight Wicked Millionaires."
1934	Philip and Margery purchase D'Arcy House, a large country house in Tolleshunt D'Arcy, a village on the Blackwater on the Essex Coast, where they loved to give house parties.
1941	*The Oaken Heart,* a factual description of the impact of the war on Tolleshunt D'Arcy, published.
1943	*Dance of the Years,* a romantic novel, published. In the U.S. it took the title *The Gallantrys.*
1956	*Tiger in the Smoke* released as a film by Rank.
1966	Margery Allingham dies 30 June of cancer.
1969	*Mr. Campion's Farthing,* a Campion novel by Philip Youngman Carter, published.
1970	*Mr. Campion's Falcon,* by Philip Youngman Carter, published.
	Philip Youngman Carter dies.

Margery Allingham

Rex W. Gaskill

> The mystery story and the sonnet have much in common. Each is a literary exercise, artificial in form and highly stylized. Each is governed or should be governed by fairly inelastic rules. Each demands a special skill. And each, in the hands of talented practitioners can be a work of art; can be lighted from within by far more luster than the medium was designed to accommodate. (*Bleak House* is a mystery story. So are *Brighton Rock* and *Wuthering Heights* and *The Turn of the Screw*).

It is with these words that Phyllis McGinley begins "A Report on Criminals at Large" in the *New York Times Book Review,* which is, incidentally, a review of a mystery by Margery Allingham. After a discussion of the work of the mediocre ("...violence takes the place of plot; sadism masquerades as invention. The writing ranges downward from crudeness to illiteracy"), McGinley continues, comparing Allingham with Dorothy Sayers. Allingham is seen as "...a writer willing to take pains with plot, sufficiently talented to write graceful and perceptive prose, sensitive enough to character to make human beings out of victim, criminal and detective alike."[1]

Margery Allingham was accustomed to favorable reviews. "Torquemada," writing in *The Observer* for July 10, 1938, observed, "To Albert Campion has fallen the honour of being the first detective to figure in a story which is also, even when judged by the fixed stars of criticism, a distinguished novel."[2] A reviewer for the *Manchester Guardian* was equally positive: "Miss Allingham's strength lies in her power of characterization, in her striking talent for painting the social background against which she shows her characters, in her skill in the use of words whereby she paints so vividly the scenes she describes."[3]

Over a period of almost forty years, Allingham published twenty-six mystery books, which were either complete novels or collections of short stories. She also wrote a romantic novel, *Gallantrys,* and a war memoir, *The Oaken Heart.* There is fortunately no need to provide the mystery fan with a complete summary of all of Allingham's plots and characters. This has been most competently provided for the Albert Campion novels, which comprise most of the canon, by B.A. Pike in *The Armchair Detective.* In thirteen parts over four years and covering ninety-five printed pages, the Allingham devotee can find a complete chronological compendium.[4]

There are several clear types of detective novels to be found within the Allingham corpus. The earliest works are more adventure stories than anything else: "frankly picaresque" (*Death,* xi) is her own phrase for them. In *The Crime at Black Dudley, Mystery Mile, Look to the Lady,* and *Sweet Danger* there are plenty of thrills and chills, but little of the careful psychological development of character and plot which will mark the later books. Interestingly, the last work, *Cargo of Eagles,* brings us full circle and is in type much like the first, a novel of action.

Beginning with *Police at the Funeral* in 1931, we are given the first of the mysteries which are also careful studies in human interaction. These novels include most of Allingham's best work both before and after World War II, and they provide the secure base for her reputation as a mystery writer who is also a superior craftsperson. Campion changes at this point as well. He begins to drop the inoffensive, P.G. Wodehouse mask of the adventure stories and to emerge as a significant factor in the intellectual life of the story. Again Allingham provides the clue: "The two types of experiences are distinct, and it is perhaps surprising that they should touch the same person" (*Death,* xi).

Allingham also tries variations on the theme of suspense. She gives us several "spy" novels. It is not surprising that we see the first of these, *Traitor's Purse,* appear in 1941, early in the war. She continues to work with the genre, however, as late as 1965 in *The Mind Readers,* which mixes a spy theme with the latest in science fiction technology.

Two of her works are hard to categorize in any of the usual mystery types. These two, *Tiger in the Smoke* and *Hide My Eyes,* are perhaps best put off by themselves and called novels of evil. Evil—the recognition of it and how to deal with it—is certainly the theme of both books. There is very little of the traditional "whodunit." We know who did it and who is about to do it very early in each of these works. The suspense is nonetheless very real. Both are London novels, and the atmosphere of evil which Allingham creates hangs over the old city and is beautifully done in each.

Certainly Campion matures throughout the early novels. Soon he has a companion who is still growing both physically and emotionally. Amanda Fitton is a gawky teenager, interested in mechanics and electricity, when Albert meets her in the romantic Suffolk village of Pontisbright. She is seventeen and a beauty with the flaming Pontisbright red hair. By the end of this work (*Sweet*) she is Lady Amanda, her brother having come into the earldom and she announces her intention to see Albert and us in six years.

It is really only five years later in *Fashion in Shrouds* that she reappears, grown up, sophisticated and employed as an airplane designer. She and Campion go through a mock engagement, which is broken off before the book's end. In *Traitor's Purse,* during the war, they marry. We know of one child, Rupert, whom we meet in *The Beckoning Lady* and who is, by the last novel, a graduate student at Harvard. Amanda appears as late as *The Mind Readers,* an independent, intelligent and mellowing figure.

The detective fiction of Margery Allingham has many strengths. As some of the reviews quoted above suggest, she is a master of descriptive prose. Her settings, which tend to alternate between London and the Suffolk/Essex east coast of England, are always adequate and often beautifully drawn. Also in these works are some of the most consistent and interesting examinations of English social class structure, which form the backdrop against which her characters evolve. Her characters are exceptional. The central three, Albert Campion, Lady Amanda Fitton and Magersfontein Lugg, Campion's ex-convict valet, are, of course, most completely developed. They are all three in their individual ways delightful. Even more rare, however, is the extended development of certain character types better presented in Allingham's works than in those of any other contemporary detective writer.

The first of the classic country descriptions comes in Allingham's third Campion volume, *Look to the Lady:*[5]

> The village of Sanctuary lay in that part of Suffolk which the railway had ignored and the motorists have not yet discovered. Moreover, the steep-sided valley of which it consisted, with the squat Norman church on one eminence and the Tower on the other, did not lie on the direct route anywhere, so that no one turned down the narrow cherry-lined lane unless they had actual business in the village. The place itself was one of those staggering pieces of beauty that made Morland paint in spite of all the noggins of rum in the world.
>
> A little stream ran across the road dividing the two hills, while the cottages, the majority pure Elizabethan, sprawled up each side of the road like sheep asleep in a meadow.... It was a fairy tale village peopled by yokels who, if they did not wear the traditional white smocks so beloved of film producers, at least climbed the rough steps to the church on a Sunday morning in top hats of unquestionable antiquity (38).

Of no less interest are the descriptions of some of the buildings. The pub, The Three Drummers, "stood crazily with its left side a good two feet lower down the northern hill than its right side. It was of brown unrestored oak and yellow plaster, with latticed windows and a red tiled roof" (38). Of the main scene of the action, the country estate known as the Tower at Sanctuary, we are told that "it managed to be beautiful in spite of itself," that it stood in a park with "great clumps of oak and cedar trees," and that it was "a mass of survivals from almost every period of English architecture. . . a great pile of old Saxon stone and Roman brick" (51). It is not only the dwellings of the powerful that attract Miss Allingham's attention. In the same volume she describes the cottage of two of her minor characters as "one of those picturesque, insanitary thatched lath and plaster dwellings which stir admiration and envy in the hearts of all those who do not have to live in them" (135).

That the countryside of the east coast counties was dear to her is clear. She grew up in the rectory at Layer Breton, near Colchester in Essex. Though her youth and early adulthood were spent in London, she and Philip Youngman Carter, her husband and illustrator, early in their marriage, first rented and then bought a large country house in Tolleshunt D'Arcy, a village on the Blackwater on the Essex coast, five miles from Layer Breton.[6] Of this house and the people of the village she wrote lovingly in her non-fiction work *The Oaken Heart.* More important to us, however, was the use she made of her knowledge of this countryside in her many descriptions.

Sweet Danger is one of Allingham's most important early books. Here Albert is introduced to Lady Amanda Fitton, whom he will later marry. Perhaps to mirror the budding love interests (other characters in addition to Albert and Lady Amanda are affected), Allingham offers some of her most beautiful Suffolk descriptions. "The scenery was growing more beautiful and more rural at every mile. . . . Plump little white houses were hidden among great overblown trees" (45). Growing ever more specific, a pattern she frequently follows, she next focuses on one house, ". . . a nearly perfect example of later fifteenth-century architecture. Its wattle-and-daub walls were plastered over and ornamented with fine mouldings. Big diamond-pattern casement windows bulged between rust-red tiles, and the whole rambling place suggested somehow the trim blowsiness of a Spanish galleon" (59). Descriptions of the old rectory and the strange garden of its curious inhabitant are equally evocative. In 1933 all the village is mysterious and lovely.

We return to Pontisbright in 1955 for *The Beckoning Lady.* We are on a different estate which lies "in a hidden valley. . . in a hollow, beside a stream." Albert and Amanda are sitting on a lush hillside while their son Rupert and a fat dog play in the distance. From there they view

> . . . the deep meadows and the fernlands, where the cricket-bat willows look like egret feathers, were tucked about it like a pile of green cushions. At that distance

> it appeared toy-sized and unreal in the very bright light which simplified all the shapes and colours until one could believe that one saw a miniature in a paper-weight. There was the house which was fifteenth century and gabled like the mill, the barn which was thatched and enormous, one of the famous tithe barns of the East Country, a small cottage, a boathouse, even a white dog kennel, very vivid and neat by a yard pump with a hat over it, all scintillating in the dazzling glare. there were white fences and little white gates about, and everywhere a mass of flowers (46).

It is a fitting setting for the party which provides the central focus for the book. Appropriately, *Lady* was, according to her husband, Allingham's favorite book. Certainly it mirrored (without the murder, we assume) the large country house parties she loved to gather at Tolleshunt D'Arcy.

If there is very little difference in the descriptions Allingham gives us of the countryside in the years from 1933 to 1955, there is a vast amount of change in the look of the second major place in which her stories are set. Allingham loved London as she loved the east coast counties. She had been born there, had spent her adolescence and school days there and always maintained a London flat. She knew the city well and she wrote of it with sensitivity and affection.

The first real London description is found in the 1932 novel, *Police at the Funeral.* Not surprisingly it is London seen through the eyes of an old Londoner, a former bobby, now Inspector Stanislaus Oates, lately made one of the Big Five at the Yard.

> London, like all great cities which have been built and rebuilt for upwards of a thousand years, has all sorts of odd corners, little forgotten patches of valuable land which still belong to the public, hidden though they are among great masses of private property.... Immediately his spirits rose considerably, and he set off, penetrating farther into the city until a sudden turning brought him face to face with a narrow arch-way squeezed in between two palatial wholesalers' doorways. The paving stones within the passage were worn narrow strips set crazily together, and on the white-washed wall was a small battered notice half obliterated by dust and further obscured by the shadow, which stated simply: "*To the Tomb*" (11).

At the tomb, of course, Oates will have a chance meeting with Albert Campion, Campion's mysterious client and her even more mysterious cousin (later a victim) and the story will begin. This narrowing of focus, moving always from the general to the specific, is an almost cinematic technique. Though Allingham uses it frequently, it seems always fresh, and in this case, does much to heighten the suspense.

London continues to be an important setting for many of the remaining novels published before World War II. Many of Allingham's characters would echo the sentiments of another London policeman, now retired from the city, who asserts, "London's a rum place. I miss it...in Norwich. London's got the fascination of a girl you never quite get to know" (*Flowers*, 214). *Death of a Ghost* is set in the artists' colony of Little Venice, north of Paddington station. The City is important in *China Governess* and *Flowers for the Judge*. We get a taste of West End life in *Dancers in Mourning* and *Fashion in Shrouds*. London industry is developed as well. *Flowers* takes us inside a publishing house, *Dancers* immerses us in the world of theatre, specifically the musical review, and *Fashion*, not surprisingly, adds *haute couture* to the stage.

It is not until the first wartime novel that we sense a real change in the tone of Allingham's London descriptions. The first hint of change comes in *Traitor's Purse* (1940). Campion and Amanda spend most of the novel in the country combatting treason, but at one point Campion returns to London. "The tall houses looked strangely virginal and unprotected [so]...he could not understand what was missing at first, but when it came to him and he realized the reason for this nudity all the old fighting anger returned to his heart.... London's railings, her secret private little defences, were torn away to feed the big guns" (131).

By 1945 and *Coroner's Pidgin*, the city is in much worse shape. "Many of the familiar landmarks had vanished to leave new squares and avenues of tidied nothingness" (28). The city home of Lord Carados in Carados Square has sustained a direct hit which has destroyed much of it and all of the other adjacent buildings. Lugg, now an air raid warden, keeps pigs in the railing-less park square. London is desolated and Allingham expresses it superbly. There is little traffic and there are no taxis. The restaurants have scarcely any food and no drinkable wine. Yet Campion can still think, "It had spread its ancient charm about him and he knew from the very smell of it that it was still safe, still firmly respectable, still obdurately matter of fact" (2).

After the war, Allingham sets most of the remaining novels at least partly in the metropolis. She pictures brilliantly a city recovering, albeit very slowly, from great devastation. It is a city which is still capable of renewing itself. Even in the 1962 *China Governess*, we can still see a city which has scars. Cockney Chief Detective Inspector Charles Luke, who replaced Oates as Campion's police sidekick, reminisces about the Turk Street neighborhood of East London as it was before four land mines and a sprinkling of incendiaries "renewed" it twenty years before. Its rebuilding had begun, but there still remain many "bald spots...in various stages of reclamation" (1-2). By 1965, however, it is clear that this most unpredictable city in the world has recovered:

> The great city of London was once more her splendid self; mysterious as ever but bursting with new life. In the tightly packed clusters of villages with the ancient names—Hackney, Holborn, Shoreditch, Putney, Paddington, Bow—new towers were rising into the yellow sky; the open places if fewer, were neater, the old houses were painted, the monuments clear. Best news of all, the people were regrown. The same savagely cheerful race, fresh mixed with more new blood than ever in its history, jostled together in costumes inspired by every romantic fashion known to television. While round its knees in a luxuriant crop the educated children shot up like the towers, full of the future (*Mind*, 7).

Allingham's settings, both in developing London and in the changeless countryside of the east coast, provide the realistic field in which her characters are set. The changes of London serve to underscore the commentary on class, which is an important part of her characters' lives. Also, changes help to mark the development of Campion and Amanda, who grow and mature along with the city. At the same time, the changeless quality of Sussex and Essex helps to remind us of certain unchanging values which Allingham tries to represent in her main characters.

Allingham possesses the ability to create believable and interesting characters. One of the central facts about these characters, however, is that they are always clearly set in their proper niches in the English class structure—"against their social background," as the *Guardian* puts it. In this she shares characteristics with Dorothy Sayers. The similarities between Allingham and Sayers have been previously noted—by Phyllis McGinley, by Nancy Joyner in her article on P.D. James in *Ten Women of Mystery*,[7] and by *Murderess Ink,* which lists them both as examples of "the upstairs-downstairs mentality."[8]

Although Sayers and Allingham both portray detectives who are the younger sons of dukes and although they both have a sense of country society, and its stratifications, their approaches are quite different in tone. Sayers' is clearly more romantic. This is most graphically demonstrated in *Busman's Honeymoon.* As Lord Peter's new bride, Lady Peter (Harriet) muses, "...he yet carried about with him that permanent atmosphere of security. He belonged to an ordered society and this was it.... In a village they were all immutably themselves: parson, organist, sweep, duke's son and doctor's daughter, moving like chessmen on their appointed squares.... I have married England."[9] Contrast this with the opinion of Lady Amanda, Campion's intended bride: "Class is like sex or the electric light supply, not worth thinking about as long as yours is all right, but embarrassingly inconvenient if there's anything wrong with it" (*Fashion*, 93).

It is interesting that Allingham and Sayers were neighbors in the country and social friends. Philip Youngman Carter later tells us that

Allingham had read only one of Sayers' books and then quit because she found the two so similar in style and content.[6] One might wonder if a line written in 1934 really expressed her opinion of Lord Peter: "[A] self-important ignoramus with a ridiculous little glass—the sort of thing the detective in a farce might use—crawling about on the floor talking about the texture and pigment as though he knew what the words meant" (*Death*, 123).

Class, or what defines it, is the one topic on which almost any Allingham character is likely to have an opinion. Some of the most delightful of these opinions are those of Magersfontein Lugg, Campion's long-time valet, who is also a former cat burglar, a graduate of one of His Majesty's prisons (he refers to it as his "college"), and a pure Londoner. He feels the obligation, now that he has come up in the world, to guard the "class" of both his employer and himself. Early in 1931, in the second novel in which he appears, we hear him admonishing his employer, " 'You've mixed up with a nice set, 'aven't yer?' he said. 'I've known ticket o' leave men who'd blush to 'ear their names associated with them . . . . It's the class of the thing I object to. No one can call me a snob—not reely—but a gent 'as got to draw 'is line somewhere' " (*Look*, 165).

Lugg changes little as the novels progress. He does discover a "club" (a pub in the mews) where many of the other gentlemen's gentlemen hang out. This simply reinforces his viewpoint about the duties and behaviors of the upper class while making his everyday manner more arch. Alas, Campion will not live up to him. " 'What's the good of me trying to give this place a bit of tone if you don't back me up?' " (*Pig*, 2). Lugg has little doubt about the proper place for a duke's younger son: " 'Why can't you take a quiet couple o' rooms in a good neighbour'ood and play poker while you wait for your titled relative to die? That's what a gentleman would do' " (*Pig*, 4).

Lugg is doomed to disappointment on a number of fronts. Not only is he unable to keep his employer from getting involved in crime "up to the neck," but he is also ultimately disappointed in his hope that Campion will inherit his brother's title and therefore guarantee Lugg's own respectability. It is perhaps as well. As Campion puts it, " 'Even if I become a Duke . . . the chances of you becoming a respectable person are remote—or at any rate I shouldn't count on it' " (*Flowers, 140).* Nevertheless Lugg remains easily captivated by the charms of the aristocracy. When, in *Coroner's Pidgin*, Campion discovers him assisting Lady Carados to dispose of a body, he says, " 'It cast a spell over me; it always does . . . . I can't help it . . . . Ler Hote Mond . . . . That's Pole for the article . . . . I 'ad respeck for 'er Ladyship's manner which was matey, and 'er title which was not' " (*Pidgin*, 140-41).

If Lugg recognizes class when he sees it, so also do the various police officers with whom Campion works. Some, no doubt, might secretly agree with the public statement of Superintendent Yeo to Campion that class is all right in its " 'proper place . . . on the stage,' " adding, " 'I like it better than anywhere on the stage. But when I meet it in my business it gets round my feet' " (*Pidgin*, 70-71). Oates is the first to be frustrated when in *Police at the Funeral* he must face the trials of investigation in an upper-class Cambridge household. He finds it frustrating because he doesn't understand the social codes: " 'It's as bad as a caste system' " (78). He consoles himself with the idea that there are very few murders in England in the upper classes, most of them being committed among " 'navvies, whizz-boys, car thieves, and small tradespeople' " (81).

The police figure most able to hold his own among the upper classes is Charles Luke. Luke is Allingham's last police creation, and he is a lower middle-class cockney wonder. Without being any less a hard-bitten Londoner than he is initially, he appears in one of the most pastoral of the later novels, has his "class" established in the minds of the local gentry by the fact of his residence with Campion and Lady Amanda, receives the commendation from Campion that, " 'He's a very distinguished man in his own line' " (*Lady*, 227), and ends up carrying off Lady Glebe's only daughter.

Luke is clearly unique. Most of the police would certainly echo the comment of Sergeant Picot who finds himself fighting the temptation to like Campion's uncle, Canon Avril, as "he could not believe the old man was genuine, because people of that class never were. Every copper on the beat knew that" (*Tiger*, 11).

However, class in the novels of Margery Allingham is never established by mere money. Both Albert and Lady Amanda are from "good" aristocratic families, although at the time we first meet her, Amanda's brother has yet to establish his claim to the Pontisbright earldom. Neither has an especially large inherited income. We are told early on that Albert works at least in part to eke out the provision made him by his family. Amanda has no family money at the beginning, and even after Hal inherits the title, she chooses to earn her own way in the airplane industry, where she rises from designer and test pilot to director of the company. Yet both are clearly and consistently recognized as being of established social position.

Money, indeed, seems to be more a hindrance than a help in establishing social position. The people with money, from Herr von Faber in *The Crime at Black Dudley* in 1929 to Lord Ludor in the 1965 *Mind Readers*, are most likely to be crooks or unscrupulous business tycoons. In one scene, Lugg is instructed by Branch, once a "classmate" at Borstal prison but now returned to favor with the Gyrth family and installed as butler at Sanctuary, their country estate. Branch explains how he sizes up the class of the guests as he unpacks their suitcases:

> Mr. Lugg whistled, " 'Ard lines on a bloke with ragged pants," he observed.
>
> "Oh, no you don't foller me." Branch was vehement. "Why there's one pair of underpants that's been into this house reg'lar for the last fourteen years. Darned by the Dutchess 'erself, bless 'er! I can tell it anywhere—it's a funny cross-stitch what she learnt in France in the fifties. You see it on all 'er family's washin'. It's as good as a crest." [Asked to comment on some recent arrivals, he adds] "Nice new outfits bought for the occasion .... Not every pair of legs that's covered by Burlington Arcade first kicked up in Berkeley Square, you can take it from me" (*Look*, 65).

Far from establishing class, the mere making of money may well take the recipient out of his proper place. Uncle William "explains" Squire Mercer to Campion as one such person.

> "D'you know what I think about him, Campion? He's the kind of feller who ought to be hanging round sleepin' on people's floors, pickin' up scraps of comfort, lookin' after himself like a London pigeon, but, by means of trick, don't you know, by means of a trick he's made a fortune out of those footlin' songs of his, and it's put the feller out of gear. I've met men like him before, but never one with money" (*Dancers*, 89).

At the *Beckoning Lady* party, the two wealthiest men of the year, Mr. Burt and Mr. Hare, are dismissed as virtual gate-crashers. Campion, who observes them evaluating the place, suggests disparagingly, " 'Some people are always thinking of buying whatever they're looking at' " (*Lady*, 226).

It seems to be a convention of Allingham's works that no person with any real pretensions to class status actually makes large sums of money. Indeed, as one character in *Traitor's Purse* puts it, " 'We come of a class, Mr. Campion, which never acquires money suddenly, except by legacy' " (198). Nevertheless, to suggest that money is inherited and not made is not to suggest that it does not count. In the same work we are allowed to see Campion's thoughts:

> Money? More money? The cash motif cropped up all the time. It frightened Campion. The Tory Englishman never underestimates the

> power of money as a weapon. It is his own, and when he sees it against him he feels betrayed as well as anxious (107).

The money may go, but the class remains. In *More Work for the Undertaker,* the central family is the Palinodes. Although most of their money has been lost through bad investments, they are still treated by everyone in their London neighborhood with deference. Though they live in their former house as virtual charity lodgers, Miss Evadne Palinode can still assert that "the tradespeople call downstairs, the professions come up" (45). And so they do, because class still shows. Lugg is completely caught up in it. He finds himself persuaded to hand round at one of Miss Evadne's parties by her attitude of "You're dirt and can't hardly understand what I'm a-sayin' of, but I 'appens to like you.' " He finds this manner " 'Appealin' especially when you know you could buy 'er at one end of the street and sell 'er at the other. They call it charm' " (192).

The charm clearly works well:

> "Get an eyeful of my old girl," he said. "She's worf it. She's got one stockin' 'arf down, nothin' in her cupboard but an empty sherry bottle. . . . And she's offerin' filth-and-cheese-biscuits to people 'oo've got their minds well on poisonin' to start with. Yet if 'Is Grace and Lady Godiva come in instead of me she wouldn't be surprised, much less took aback. It's what is called poise. Very taking to them what appreciates it" (195).

In Allingham, class is usually recognized quickly and commented upon by another character. Oates is immediately charmed by Belle Lafcadio: "There's something very attractive about the real McCoy when you meet it" (*Death,* 68). On the strength of that recognition, he immediately assures Campion that she is not one of those under suspicion.

Amanda and Campion have their class attested to on many occasions throughout the works. Even as she is severely chastizing some of the employees of Lord Ludor, calling them, among other things, " 'clumsy invertebrates,' " she can still have one of them pay her the compliment, " 'Class, I like to hear it' " (*Mind,* 239). Class excuses rudeness as it establishes position. No one who knows her doubts her word. She provides even Campion with an alibi when needed. It convinces Oates, who says of her, " 'Good class is attractive when it's genuine, isn't it?' " (*Fashion,* 211).

Campion's class is usually apparent. To a lower class detective firm it is the "Grand Manner" (*China,* 82), but to those of his own status it is sympathetic and comfortable. Meg Elginbrodde in *Tiger in the Smoke* is one of these. She sees him as:

> Campion, the amateur, a man who never used his real name and title. In

> appearance a middle-aged Englishman typical of his background and period. She saw him as kindly, unemotional, intelligent and resourceful, all inbred virtues ensuring that his reactions would be as hidebound as a good gun dog's. She knew his kind so well that she was prepared to find almost any hidden peculiarity in him. It was typical of his variety that he should perhaps be very brave, or very erudite, or possibly merely able to judge Chinese prints or grow gardenias (24).

Although it is true that we never do actually learn all of Campion's real name and title, we seem to be almost the only ones who are not in on the secret. From works as early as *Police at the Funeral* right up to *Cargo of Eagles,* there is always at least one character in almost every book who informs us that he/she knows who Campion *really* is. All we learn is that his first name is Rudolf, he is the younger son of a duke, the last name (or title) begins with K and he is very nearly related to the royal family. Perhaps the best guess is that Allingham was having fun with the newly created title, Duke of Kent, which had been recently established for the fourth son of George V. His Royal Highness Prince George Edward Alexander Edmund.

Comforting though his status may be to others, it is not always so helpful to Campion himself. He once wonders if the job he does is really necessary, or whether investigation should be left entirely to the police. Though not given to such introspection as a Lord Peter Wimsey, he does, like Wimsey, find that at times his duties as a detective interfere with his feelings as a gentleman. In *Fashion in Shrouds* he is trapped by "his natural ingrained reluctance to abuse his position as a guest" (132). He remains silent and another murder results.

Though class may have its uses in the city, it is in the country that class distinctions are most clearly observed. Amanda observes that the way to get on in Pontisbright is to know the place. She might have said to know *your* place, for clearly that is the case. Campion finds this to his advantage in *Dancers in Mourning* when the fact that he is so obviously of the right class, that his country place is in Norfolk, that his friends are from the right circles there and that he has the ability to make the right small talk about roses and hunting all so charm the doctor investigating Chloe's death as to influence the coroner's verdict.

Jimmy Sutane, the London actor who owns White Walls, the estate where Campion is staying, does not understand country ways. He doesn't keep up the hospitality to which his house obligates him. For this reason, when a "joke" is played on Jimmy and the local villagers turn up unexpectedly for tea, he is unaware that:

> the company was mixed by a hand that pure ignorance could scarcely have

> directed. The snobbish distinctions which are the whole structure of any country society in England had been deliberately flouted.... The upper stratum came because it had called and been called upon in return and was therefore technically acquainted with the Sutanes; the other had simply been gratified to receive an invitation from a celebrity. Since the one fraternity waited on the other, for the most part, in the way of trade and were therefore well acquainted, it was a particularly unfortunate mixture (42-43).

Linda, Jimmy's wife, is herself a member of an old country family. She recognizes a sympathetic member of her own class in Campion and he in her. This leads to a romance, albeit not a passionate one, which is a part of the conflict in the book.

A related theme in several of Allingham's books is the affectations of the rising middle class. This seems most often to take the form of improving one's accent. Two of the most amusing cases are presented in *Flowers for the Judge.* Mrs. Rosemary Ethel Tripper, resident of the basement flat at Number Twenty-Three Horsecollar Yard, and assistant caretaker of the adjoining office blocks, delivers her evidence in court in "tones of staggering refinement" (81). We later find her speaking in the same affected tones to justify a supper of fish and chips by asserting that some of these places are " 'very high class' " (83). A more serious case is that of Mr. Rigget. An inveterate liar and sneak, he does not await discovery but readily accuses himself in educated accents to whomever will listen:

> "I live with my people. They're very respectable. This is going to break them. They've educated me and made me a better class than they are, and now I've disgraced them." It was all very distressing. Mr. Rigget's excellent accent and obvious misery made him well-nigh unbearable. Mr. Campion realized that he was confronted by a serious modern sociological problem but he decided that it was far too large to tackle, especially at the moment (152-53).

Among the Englishmen who occupy a privileged position in Allingham's world, a strong old boys' network exists. It is widely recognized and commented on, both by those who benefit from its use and by those who do not. The earliest complaint about its existence comes from Stanislaus Oates. When Campion refers to Lord Carados as Johnny, Oates objects. Campion responds, " 'I'm sorry; he was called Johnny at school.' Oates smothered an exclamation of un-police-chief-like nature. 'There you are. "At school." Half the influential people in the country seem to have been at school with him.... You've known of him for a lifetime, therefore he can't be a crook' " (*Pidgin,* 151-52).

Ten years later it is Charles Luke's turn to try to understand the phenomenon. "Luke was uneasy. Mr. Campion's strange world of nods and hints and mysterious understandings among people who trusted each other because they were related or had been to school or served in a ship or a regiment together both bothered and fascinated him" (*Lady,* 172). It is clear by this book, however, that the lower orders are catching on. It is 1955 and in this novel Charles marries the Honorable Prunella Glebe, Baron Glebe's daughter.

The romance between Prune and Charles is marked by opposition from all of Luke's friends. Interestingly, this reluctance is not based on the idea that *he* is not good enough for *her,* but rather the reverse. Campion sees her as a type which is no longer of any use, as someone who is dead while Luke is gloriously alive. It is clear, however, that love is very real on both sides and finally Campion sees the virtue of it. "A vista of years opened before him in which Luke's genius backed by Prune's influence carried the remarkable pair to heights as yet unguessed" (*Lady,* 254). With help, one can rise.

Even Oates finally learns. In the last novel, *Cargo of Eagles,* Campion needs his help. Oates, now retired, is found in Fitzherbert's, a club so staid that "it certainly remained a last stronghold of unregenerate class consciousness and that kind of prejudice which is on the direct route to embalment" (17). Oates is not a member, but another former policeman, now a club servant, sees him comfortably set up in the silver storage room. Albert is embarrassed, but Oates assures him, "Move with the times, my boy. The Old Pals' Act isn't confined to you public-school types above stairs now. You've taught the rest of us the drill' " (18-19).

Being a part of this old boys' network, having the advantage of proper training in the accepted public schools and at Oxbridge, gives to the recipient a habit of command. This stands him in good stead, especially when the person being directed is also used to the system, when he/she accepts the values and status distinctions on which it is built.

The system works well for Geoffrey Levett in *Tiger in the Smoke.* After he is captured by a band of men who have set up as street beggars and musicians, his pockets are searched. The head of the gang, Tiddy Doll, finds a robotyped letter from Lord Beckenham and this immediately suggests that Geoffrey is a person of position. When he asserts that he is also a former army major, his authority is completely established. The men, including Doll, now refer to him as "sir" and want to release him, having first told him all their secrets. He gives them the asurances they seek:

> "I shall forget it." The educated voice carried conviction. Doll accepted the statement as he would have accepted no signature however illustrious. But the performance was not complete. Geoffrey realised they expected a warning from

> him and he prepared to give them one. The absurdity of the situation was not really clear to either of them (106).

Even though, as the story develops, he does not actually get away, the fact of his class and his habit of command are sufficient to secure his ultimate safety.

The China Governess is perhaps Allingham's most extensive discussion of the whole notion of class. In it she seems to posit a notion of inherited breeding. The central character, Timothy Kinnit, has received the proper education. He has been reared in luxury, in ancient homes in London and the country. He finds himself engaged to a beauty who is also an heiress. He also finds, however, that he is not the son of the family. He has been adopted after being left at the Kinnitt country house to which his supposed mother was evacuated during the war. He also finds that the area from which the evacuees came was an East End London slum. This causes him to immediately put his engagement on hold while he goes off in a search for his identity. He is then suspected of murder. Charlie Luke puts the case to Campion, who doubts Kinnitt's guilt:

> "You're a dear chap, Campion," he said, "I like you and I like your approach. It makes me feel I'm riding in a Rolls but sometimes I wonder if you're not a bit too nice.... Here is a boy—not a specially bred one, conditioned over generations to withstand a bit of cosseting like a prize dog—but an ordinary tough boy same like I was,... and he's brought up to believe quite falsely that he's inherited the blessed earth. Money, position, background, servants, prospects....A ruddy great doubt as big as a house crops up. Security vanishes and there's a hole at his feet.... Couldn't that send him bonkers?" (139).

However, the idea of one bred to command is for Allingham exclusively a masculine one. She has Campion's sister, Val Ferris, put the case quite strongly:

> "You're a sensible, reasonable, masculine soul.... [You take] the conventional view and the intelligent path and save yourself no end of bother because your head plus your training is so much stronger than all your emotions put together. You're a civilised masculine product.... [Georgia and I] can't be conventional or take the intelligent path except by a superhuman mental effort. Our feeling is twice as strong as our heads and we haven't been trained for thousands of years. We're feminine, you fool!" (*Fashion*, 140-41).

In contrast to masculine logic, Allingham posits femine feeling.

What it means to be feminine in the world of an Allingham novel is presented in some detail. It is not a picture that is likely to seem attractive to a modern reader, and, I would contend, it is not a picture that is congruent with the realities of either the lives of Albert and Amanda or the lives of

Margery Allingham and Philip Youngman Carter.

There is, according to the theory, an essential difference between men and women in their outlook on the world. Tante Marthe suggests, "The man is the silhouette, the woman is the detail" (*Fashion,* 16). This may cause no raised eyebrows, but the book goes on to develop the idea. We are adjured, " 'Women are terribly shocking to men, my dear. Don't understand them. Like them' " (142). Understanding, you see, is impossible because, as we have been already told, men have cognition, women intuition.

Fashion in Shrouds plays on this theme of feminine weakness. It has as its central characters two very successful women. Valentine Ferris is London's top dress designer and the head of an important fashion house. Georgia Wells (Lady Ramilies) is London's most successful actress. "They were two fine ladies of a fine modern world in which their status had been raised until they stood as equals with their former protectors. Their several responsibilities were far heavier than most men's and their abilities greater." And yet, and yet, "since they had not yet relinquished their feminity, within them, touching the very core and foundation of their strength, was the dreadful primitive weakness of the female of any species" (223-24).

The solution which is posed for this prevailing weakness of feminity is a very traditional one. One should first join that sisterhood (Allingham's term) who "really believe that there is in the mere quality of manhood something magnificent and worthy to be served" (*Flowers,* 136). One will then find oneself "looking after her man as she ought, and so she's going to be happy" *(Tiger,* 183). This is best accomplished, of course, by marriage. Marriage is explained to us in Alan Dell's proposal to Valentine Ferris. She accepts, of course—

> "I love you, Val. Will you marry me and give up to me your independence, the enthusiasm which you give your career, your time and your thought? In return . . . in return, mind you (I consider it an obligation), I should assume full responsibility for you. I would pay your bills to any amount which my income might afford. I would make all decisions which were not directly in your province, although on the other hand I would like to feel that I might discuss everything with you if I wanted to; but only because I wanted to, mind you; not as your right. You would be my care, my mate as in plumber, my possession if you like. If you wanted your own way in everything you'd have to cheat it out of me not demand it. It means the other half of my life to me, but the whole of yours to you. Will you do it?"
>
> "Yes," said Val so quickly that she startled herself. . . . She was a clever woman who would not or could not relinquish her feminity and feminity unpossessed is femininity unprotected from itself, a weakness and not a charm (*Fashion,* 281).

Even Campion and Amanda seem to have entered into the spirit of this kind of relationship. Though we know from our first meeting with her that Amanda is bright, a mechanical genius, and an extrovert, we are still given a picture of her as a traditional wife. "She looked very young and very intelligent, but not, he thought with sudden satisfaction, clever.... His sense of possession was tremendous" (*Purse,* 43). "She would look after him and he must look after the three of them [Rupert having been born]. It was not the only sort of marriage, but it was their sort" (*Tiger,* 193).

Campion and Amanda do not, however, really have a relationship which illustrates the ideal articulated by Alan Dell. In fact, they spend most of the thirty-five years between their first meeting and the action of Allingham's last book apart. Campion maintains his flat on Bottle Street to the last, and Amanda her country home near the Alandel Airplane Works. Amanda's rise in industry continues. She becomes a director as well the top designer. There is at one point some suggestion that she *might* give up her career to join Albert when he goes out to govern a colony. Fortunately, he decides not to go and the choice does not have to be made. In many ways their relationship parallels that of Allingham herself. Again she hardly gave up her work for marriage. Although she and Youngman Carter worked together and did not sustain the physical separations of Amanda and Campion, they just as surely maintained their separate careers.

To Allingham it is class which explains a good deal of the acceptable relationship between men and women. "The degrees of familiarity between the sexes in ordinary social life differ from clique to clique and class to class more than anything else" (*Flowers,* 159). In *Coroner's Pidgin,* Inspectors Yeo and Holly have great difficulty in understanding the relationship between Stavros and Moppet Lewis. They are married but live apart, getting together on occasion. Campion finds this quite understandable. " 'Eminently sensible,' " he calls it, but the inspectors agree with the constable who labels it a " 'loveless marriage' " (72-73).

It is in *Pidgin* that Campion summarizes the view of class privilege assumed by and for Lord Carados in these words:

> It reminded Mr. Campion of an incident of his own youth when the nurse of the small friend who had just pushed him into the Round Pond had turned to his own avenging Nanny and had said in exactly the same tone of startled protest: "But he's a duke."
>
> At the age of four and a quarter, Mr. Campion had taken a poor view of the excuse, and did so now with the added advantage of knowing that ninety-nine per cent of the world agreed with him. All the same he found it interesting to note that the remaining one per cent still existed, and was at large (136).

And some of that one per cent write mystery novels.

Allingham is not the only mystery writer to turn her attention to social class as an issue in her works. No other, however, has developed it as extensively as Allingham did over the course of her work. She is intensely interested in the way social class affects the relationships among people. Not only is the relationship of class to class minutely examined, but we also are presented with an analysis of male and female sex roles and the effect of class on them. If one purpose of a novel is to examine the beliefs of a culture and a time, to hold them up for our scrutiny, then Allingham's work on English social class in the first half of the twentieth century would alone establish her reputation.

In addition to her most famous characters, Allingham develops hundreds of others in her various novels and short stories. Some are quite completely drawn, others are merely suggested. Some are examples of "types" which are developed more uniquely in her work than in that of other writers of the genre. One of the most interesting of these categories is her presentation of the clergy.

Her husband has told us that Allingham was deeply religious. She was not a regular churchgoer, but had developed a personal brand of Christian theology which went beyond the narrow tenets of orthodox faith. Unlike Miss Allingham, all of the clergy in her novels are ordained priests of the established Church of England, regular—we would assume—in their churchgoing habits. Like her, they have developed some rather unique theologies which would seem likely to gain them the reputation for eccentricity at the least.

One of the most regular and one of the earliest is Pembroke, the parson at Sanctuary. He is given hearty commendation as a "very decent old man...who hasn't let the teachings of the spirit blind him to a knowledge of the world" (*Look,* 157).

Other clergy are more interested in social reform. Bathwick, the vicar at Keepsake, is one such "red-hot innovator." "He spoke with passion of the insanitary condition of the thatched cottages and the necessity of bringing culture into the life of the average villager, betraying, I thought, a lack of acquaintance with either the thatched cottage or, of course, the villager in question, who, as every countryman knows, does not exist" (*Pig,* 36). It takes all of Campion's eloquence to convince him that the villagers really only want to be left alone.

One of the most often mentioned of the Allingham clergy is Campion's paternal uncle, the Bishop of Devises. He is mentioned as early as *Police at the Funeral* in 1931 and we are told that he is dead. His death is reiterated in later works, but the war has a reviving effect on him and he shows up quite lively indeed as a character in *Coroner's Pidgin,* 1945. A charming man, dressed in black silk, with a soft voice and "the bluest eyes seen out of Scandinavia" (99), he is, we find, a wine connoisseur, something of a romantic and a good storyteller. To this we add the earlier information that he knew more about dry-fly fishing than any other man and that while at Cambridge he had tied an umbrella to the statue of Henry VIII "disguised as Mrs. Bloomer, then visiting the country" (*Flowers,* 55).

Campion's maternal uncle is somewhat more extensively developed as a character. Canon Avril figures importantly in *Tiger in the Smoke* and in *Mind Readers.* Although his living was once wealthy and is now impoverished, he continues much as he always has, renting out flats in the old rectory. He is calm, contented, loved and protected. He has "exasperated more great churchmen than any other person alive" (*Tiger,* 38). One can easily imagine it. At one point he announces to Mary, his cook, ' "I can't forgive you Mary. I can't forgive sins, dear girl. Whatever next?' " (117). It is hard to imagine any Anglican churchman, even one of very low church persuasion, who wouldn't be frustrated by that. Still he is delightful. It is told of him that:

> the great Dr. Potter...Bishop of London...once heard him deliver a scintillating sermon on an abstruse heresy which but twelve men in England could possibly have appreciated to a congregation of four small shopkeepers and their families, five small boys and a deaf old lady. [When the bishop suggested that no one could follow him] Avril had clasped his arm and chuckled contentedly, "Of course not, my dear fellow. But how wonderful for him if by chance one of them did!" (38).

How wonderful for us that we have him as a character.

Allingham's most unique clergy character, however, is identified to us only as the Revver. He is vicar of Pontisbright and since he is related to the Honorable Prune he may be a Glebe or a Gallantry. Whatever his name, he is a delight. We first hear of his conviction that Minnie Cassands, owner of the title estate in *The Beckoning Lady,* is going to become "religious" because her father, also an artist, painted pictures with "lions and lambs and saints and rather nice interiors" (36).

> He's always warning people not to be religious. The bishop had to warn him to use caution lest by sheer inadvertance he emptied the church. The Revver says you can be as pious as you like privately, but you mustn't think too much about it or you may forget yourself and mention it. [Minnie] said that what he meant, she supposed, was that a Christian gentleman must never run the risk of degenerating into a vulgar Christian. He said that was exactly what he did mean (36).

This is almost topped when he finds Tonker Cassands kneeling in the parish church and asks if he is " 'all right.' " The Revver, who later informs the village that Tonker has got religious mania and is " 'veering to Rome, secretly' " (200), is truly a superlative creation.

The clergy in Allingham's works serve several functions. They are always eccentrics themselves and are usually pushing a cause, although it may be a cause one might not expect an Anglican priest to push. Certainly this is the case with the Revver. It is unusual to have a member of the clergy trying to assist people in not being religious. He does provide wonderful comic relief, however, as do others of her clergy characters. Even Canon Avril is comic at times, both to those in the novels who deal with him and to us. He fills an additional function, though, and that is to serve as an incarnation of good against which the evil around him may be measured.

A second type of character with which Miss Allingham deals is almost unique to her work in this period. This is the gay male. At a time when contemporary mystery writers both English and American were reluctant to admit the existence of homosexual persons, to have six identified over the course of her work is unusual. The portraits are not particularly sympathetic. Allingham shared many of the prejudices and stereotypes of her period, but the characters do exist.

All of the best developed gay male characters are in the early novels. Max Fustian in *Death of a Ghost* in some ways sets the pattern for those who will follow. "They heard his voice, deep, drawling, impossibly affected, from the doorway. 'Lisa, you look deliriously macabre this evening' " (23). His clothing is "exotic and fantastic." He is an esthete: " 'It was a conceit of mine to keep a certain coloured rose in a pewter jar a little to the left of the picture. It formed a group, broke the line and pleased me' " (104). When crossed he becomes petulant, causing another character to say, " 'Don't flounce, Max' " (77). He is also the murderer and villain of the piece, although this is not to be a pattern followed consistently in the other portraits. He is egotistical and self-centered and he comes very close to defeating Campion.

Dancers in Mourning offers us two examples of this character type. The first is Benny Konrad, a dancer/singer and a bicycle enthusiast. His first entrance in the story gives us a picture of him as a golden haired young man in exquisite evening clothes with a face "which was a little too beautiful to be altogether pleasant" (7). Uncle William's comment on his entrance, ' "I hate those fellers' " (9), provides the biased perspective of his age old class. Konrad moves, perhaps imitating Nijinski, "rather too consciously like a young faun" (50). Again Uncle Williams strikes the traditional attitude, remarking, " 'If I was a woman one look at that feller would make me want to cut my throat' " (92). Konrad is argumentative, defensive, paranoid, a trouble-maker and not quite good enough as an actor. In makeup he is quite indecently pretty. He is also one of the murder victims.

His friend and companion in mischief is the other identified gay in this story, although we are assured by Campion that " 'the city's full of them' " (156). Beaut Sigfried is the ballet master and the stereotypical picture of the aging homosexual:

> Beaut Sigfried interviewd them in his beautiful studio. He was a thin, elderly man on whom old affectations hung like faded garlands. His court breeches and silk stockings betrayed aging, sharp-boned legs, and the shoulders beneath his long-skirted velvet coat were bent and weak.... [He had] the face of the traditional, withered spinster, prim, lined and spiteful (248).

He is, in fact, a mass of affectations. Everything he does is a pose, from the position of his hands, the props in his beautiful home, to the mark on the floor where he can stand in order to take the light to best advantage. His voice is high camp and many of his words are italicized. " 'He is an old woman and no mistake,' " Inspector Yeo asserts (252). It is masterful description even as it accepts as truth an unfortunate commonplace.

Fashion in Shrouds gives us Rex, the fashion designer, " 'not quite a lady,' " as Tante Marthe describes him (5). Rex has fits of petulance, little coy exuberances and coy wiggles and giggles. Still, before he says "Beddy-byes" in his last appearance in the book, he has informed Campion that he has served as a Tommy in France during World War I, and consequently Campion has identified him as "a natty, demure little soul, only effeminate insomuch as sex shocked him for its ugliness and interested him because it shocked him" (203). We are never quite sure what this means, but it seems to be intended as a compliment.

Finally among those characters of any prominence we have Ricky Silva in *Coroner's Pidgin,* part of Lord Carados's menage who "existed solely to do the flowers as far as anyone knew" (9). Ricky is plump, babyish and gentle with full, childish lips. He cries easily and one is certain that if we could hear him speak it would be with a lisp. He is also a private in the British army during World War II. Of this fact he suggests:

> "I'm having hell, as I tell you, absolute hell." It dawned on Mr. Campion that he was probably speaking the truth. The life of a man like Ricky Silva as a conscript private in the British Army did not bear consideration (48).

Ricky plays a very minor role in the action of the book and survives the war as far as we know.

The last references in the post-war novels are brief and incidental to the main action. In *Tiger in the Smoke* we have the character of Bill, one of Tiddy Doll's gang, who is effeminate and for whom fear is an excitant. In *The Mind Readers* we have an unnamed minor spy who is variously referred to as "such a dear old lady" (108), "my old queer from the tea shop" (198) and part of "a real old queens' quadrille" (200). Finally in *Cargo of Eagles* we have our first taste of leather. Moo Moo the Dog Faced Boy is the leader of the motor cycle gang and we are assured that he "likes boys mostly" (90).

None of the pictures Allingham presents are likely to cause rejoicing in contemporary gay and lesbian organizations. They are interesting largely because they exist at all at a time and in a genre which usually ignored the issue. They seem less dated, however, when we examine a passage in a P.D. James mystery, *Unnatural Causes.* Ms. James admits to being a fan of Allingham. She is undeniably a modern writer and a good one. Her gay character, Digby Seton, later a second murder victim, sounds familiar:

> He was afraid, too, that I might set up house with a queer. He didn't want his money shared with a pansy boyfriend. Poor Old Maurice! I don't think he'd recognize a queen if he met one. He just had the idea that London and the West End clubs in particular, are full of them.[10]

Allingham creates gay characters which are consistent with the stereotypes that existed in her time. In so doing she demonstrates her facility with stock types, but even here there is a wealth of detail and she succeeds in making some of the most completely developed, such as Benny Knorad and Beaut Siegfried, come alive. She is good enough that they begin to seem more than a convention while at the same time never violating it. Their creation provides additional variety. Allingham is never willing simply to settle for one or two types of people. It is a virtue of her work that all sorts and conditions of humanity can be found within its pages.

Though Allingham is not at her skillful best when creating gay characters, she is always delightful when creating English eccentrics. Create them she does, at least one per novel and usually more. They are often women and usually upper class. On the whole, her lower class eccentrics are not quite as successful, with the possible exception of Rene Roper, the chorus girl turned boarding-housekeeper, but then Rene is a Palinode on one side at least.

One of the most entertaining of her eccentrics, however, is a man. Uncle William is William Farady. He figures importantly in *Police at the*

Funeral and in *Dancers in Mourning.* His death by poisoning at the ripe old age of eighty-two provides a large part of the action for *The Beckoning Lady.* When we first meet him he is "a shortish, tubby individual in a dinner jacket of the 'old gentleman' variety, a man of about fifty-five with a pink face, bright greedy little blue eyes, yellowish-white hair and a mustache worn very much in the military fashion" (*Police,* 45). He is held financially captive by his mother in a great Cambridge mansion. He drinks and quarrels with his relatives. Still he grows on us and when he ends the book by presenting Campion with a mermaid skeleton and announces that he is going to write his memoirs, we are anxious to hear what they will be about.

It is clear that Allingham shares our infatuation. By *Dancers in Mourning, Memoirs of an Old Buffer* has become a huge success and been heralded as the funniest book of the decade. Although Uncle William admits that it is pure invention (his India scenes are from *The Jungle Book*) the book has become the backbone for the immensely successful musical review, *The Buffer.* Uncle William is now wealthy. His mother is dead. Increasingly he is described as a small bear. His white hair now curls into ringlets. He is the perfect old man about town, always ready for a country house weekend. He summarizes his philosophy:

> "Funny thing about those memoirs, Campion. If I'd done the decent thing and kept to the truth no one would have read 'em. As it was, they laughed at me and I made a small fortune. I'm not a chump, you know. I can see how that happened. Better be a clown than a pompous old fool" (*Dancers,* 91).

By the opening of *The Beckoning Lady,* Uncle William is already dead. We find from his obituary that he has written at least three other works which have been presented in the West End. He is described as "Dignity skating on the thinnest of ice with the placid *sangfroid* of the truly courageous. As a man he was generally beloved and a host of friends will miss his shy smile and air of bewildered pleasure at their delightful reception of his sly tall stories" (2). He was near death in any case, but his end has been unnaturally hastened. It is some mark of the affection in which we have held him that when Miss Pinkerton speaks of his death as " 'a happy release—he drank, didn't he?' " (26), we are never again inclined to show her any sympathy—with good cause, as it later turns out.

The clergy in an Allingham novel are eccentrics, but as we have just seen, her creation of eccentrics is not limited to men of the cloth. A separate essay would be needed simply to do justice to such wonders as Aunt Caroline, Belle Lafcadio, Donna Beatrice, Richie Barnabas, the Palinodes, and many others. Consistently, these are people who are important to the plot. To a person, they are presented in a sympathetic light. We come to care about them, even the ones who turn out to be villains. Certainly Allingham upholds the English reputation for loving eccentricity and those who possess it. At the same time she contributes to the lightness of tone which is a characteristic of her work. Even in the novels which are clear-cut struggles of good against evil (*Purse, Tiger, Eyes*) with the fate of civilization hanging in the balance, there is always a healthy portion of comic relief.

Margery Allingham had a facility with language and it never deserted her. She published over a period of forty years, turning out a novel a year in the thirties and maintaining a substantial output until her premature death of cancer at sixty-two.

The settings of Allingham's books can give, even to the reader who has never set foot in England, a glowing word picture of the place. This is especially true of her beloved Suffolk and Essex on England's East coast. So, too, her pictures of London scenes and London life provide a lively and active balance to the stately presentation of picturesque village and country house.

More than any other detective novelist of this century, she was interested in the social background of her characters. She knew and was concerned about class structure and the way in which it motivated people. Within this context she considered such topics as the distinction between class and money, the old boys' network of English society, the role of women, and the relationship between class and sexual customs.

Finally she was a creator of characters. Her main characters are standards of mystery fiction. Her minor characters, her parsons, her eccentrics, even her homosexuals, are always distinctive, different and sharply crafted. We can't call it an accident, for "all these things are ordained, as the old lady said at the Church Congress" (*Look,* 114), and they are "significant, too, as the man said when he heard the last trump" (*Cargo,* 137).

Notes

[1]Phyllis McGinley, "A Report on Criminals at Large," *The New York Times Book Review*, September 7, 1952, p. 26.

[2]"Torquemada," "Campionship and other Standards," *The Observer* (London), July 10, 1938, p. 8.

[3]This is from a quotation from *The Guardian* long used by Heinemann on the fly-leaf of Allingham's books. Grace Cransolm of the Heinemann archives provided the quotation, but could not complete the citation.

[4]The B. A. Pike Series runs in each number of *The Armchair Detective* beginning with Vol. 9, No. 1 (November 1975) through Vol. 12, No. 4 (Fall 1979).

[5]The chronological list of Allingham's mystery/detective fiction is presented below, preceded by the original date of publication. All quotations will be cited in the text, using, where necessary for clarity, the abbreviation given after each entry:

1923 *Blackerchief Dick: A Tale of Mersea Island* (London: Hodder and Stoughton, 1923) (*Dick*).
1928 *The White Cottage Mystery* (London: Jarrolds, 1928) (*Cottage*).
1929 *The Crime at Black Dudley* (Hammondsworth, England: Penguin, 1979) (*Crime*).
1930 *Mystery Mile* (London: Jarrolds, 1930) (*Mile*).
1931 *Look to the Lady* (London: Heinemann, 1966) (*Look*).
1931 *Police at the Funeral* (Hammondsworth: Penguin, 1978) (*Police*).
1933 *Sweet Danger* (Hammondsworth: Penguin, 1978) (*Sweet*).
1934 *Death of a Ghost* (Garden City, New York: Doubleday, 1934) (*Death*).
1936 *Flowers for the Judge* (New York: Manor, 1975) (*Flowers*).
1936 *Six Against the Yard* (London: Sylwyn & Blount, 1936).
"It Didn't Work Out" ("Work")
1937 *Dancers in Mourning* (Garden City, New York: Doubleday, 1937) (*Dancers*).
1937 *Mr. Campion, Criminologist* (Garden City, New York: Doubleday, 1937) (*Criminologist*).
"Borderline Case" ("Borderline")
Case of the Late Pig (*Pig*)
"Case of the Pro and Con" ("Pro")
"Case of the Old Man in the Window" ("Window")
"Case of the Man with the Sack" ("Sack")
"Case of the White Elephant" ("Elephant")
"Case of the Widow" ("Widow")
1938 *Fashon in Shrouds* (New York: Book League, 1938) (*Fashion*).
1939 *Mr. Campion and Others* (Hammondsworth: Penguin, 1950) (*Others*).
"The Window" ("Window")
"The Name on the Wrapper" ("Name")
"The Hat Trick" ("Hat")
"The Question Mark" ("Question")
"The White Elephant" ("Elephant")
"The Frenchman's Gloves" ("Gloves")
"The Longer View" ("View")
"Safe as Houses" ("Safe")
"The Definite Article" ("Article")
"The Meaning of the Act" ("Act")
"A Matter of Form" ("Form")
"The Danger Point" ("Point")
1940 *Black Plumes* (London: Heinemann, 1940) (*Plumes*).
1940 *Traitor's Purse* (New York: Manor, 1975) (*Purse*).
1945 *Coroner's Pidgin* (London: Heinemann, 1965) (*Pidgin*).
1947 *The Casebook of Mr. Campion* (New York: The American Mercury, 1947) (*Casebook*).
"The Crimson Letters" ("Crimson")
"Safe as Houses" ("Safe")
"The Case of the Question Mark" ("Question")
"The Definite Article" ("Article")
"The Magic Hat" ("Hat")
"The Meaning of the Act" ("Act")
"A Matter of Form" ("Form")
1949 *More Work for the Undertaker* (Hammondsworth: Penguin, 1978) (*Work*).
1948 *Deadly Duo* (Garden City, New York: Doubleday, 1949) (*Duo*).
Wanted, Someone Innocent (*Wanted*)
Last Act (*Last*)
1952 *Tiger in the Smoke* (Garden City, New York: Doubleday, 1952) (*Tiger*).
1954 *No love Lost* (Garden City, New York: Doubleday, 1954) (*Lost*)
The Patient at Peacocks Hall (*Hall*)
Safer than Love (*Love*)
1955 *The Beckoning Lady* (London: Heinemann, 1955) (*Lady*)
1958 *Hide My Eyes* (London: Chatto & Windus, 1958) (*Eyes*).
1962 *The China Governess* (Garden City, New York: Doubleday, 1962) (*China*).
1963 *The Mysterious Mr. Campion* (London: Chatto & Windus, 1963) (*Mysterious*).
"The Case of the Late Pig" ("Pig")
Dancers in Mourning (*Dancers*)

Tiger in the Smoke (*Tiger*)
"On Christmas Day in the Morning" ("Christmas")
1965 *The Mind Readers* (London: Chatto & Windus, 1965) (*Mind*).
1965 *Mr. Campion's Lady* (London: Chatto & Windus, 1963) (*C's Lady*).
"Sweet Danger" ("Sweet")
Fashion in Shrouds (Fashion)
Traitor's Purse (*Purse*)
"Word in Season" ("Season")
1968 *Cargo of Eagles* (London: Chatto & Windus, 1968) (*Cargo*)
1969 *The Allingham Case-book* (London: Chatto & Windus, 1969) (*Allingham*)
"Tall Story" ("Tall")
"Three is a Lucky Number" ("Three")
"The Villa Maria Celeste" ("Villa")
"The Psychologist" ("Psychologist")
"Little Miss Know-All" ("Miss")
"One Morning They'll Hang Him" ("Hang")
"The Lieabout" ("Lieabout")
"Face Value" ("Face")
"Evidence in Camera" ("Camera")
"Joke Over" ("Joke")
"The Lying-in-State" ("Lying")
"The Pro and the Con" ("Pro")
"Is There a Doctor in the House?" ("Doctor")
"The Borderline Case" ("Borderline")
"They Never Get Caught" ("Never")
"The Mind's Eye Mystery" ("Eye")
"Mum Knows Best" ("Mum")
"The Snapdragon and the C.I.D." ("Snapdragon")
1973 *The Allingham Minibus* (New York: Manor, 1975) (*Minibus*).
"He Was Asking After You" ("He")
"Publicity" ("Publicity")
"The Perfect Butler" ("Butler")
"The Barbarian" ("Barbarian")
"Mr. Campion's Lucky Day" ("Day")
" 'Tis Not Hereafter" ("Not")
"The Correspondents" ("Correspondents")
"He Preferred Them Sad" ("Sad")
"The Unseen Door" ("Door")
"Bird Thou Never Wert" ("Bird")
"The Same to Us" ("Us")
"The Man with the Sack" ("Sack")
"She Heard it on the Radio" ("Radio")
"A Quarter of a Million" ("Million")
"The Secret" ("Secret")
"The Pioneers" ("Pioneers")
"The Sexton's Wife" ("Wife")
"The Wink" ("Wink")

[6]Biographical information from Philip Youngman Carter, "A Profile of Margery Allingham," preface to *The Allingham Case-Book* (New York: William Morrow, 1969).

[7]Nancy Carol Joyner, "P.D. James," *Ten Women of Mystery* (Bowling Green, Ohio: Bowling Green State University Popular Press, 1981), p. 110.

[8]Dillys Winn, ed., *Murderess Ink* (New York: Workman, 1979), p. 22.

[9]Dorothy Sayers, *Busman's Honeymoon* (1937; rpt. New York: Avon, 1968), p. 82.

[10]P.D. James, *Unnatural Causes* (New York: Popular Library, 1967), p. 82.

Anne Morice

Anne Morice

1918	Felicity Anne Morice Worthington born February 18. Educated Avoncliff School, Francis Holland, Clarence Gate; also in Paris and Munich
1939	Married Alexander Shaw, film director Children: Georgina Mary Premila, Gavin James Patrick, Arabella Marie Rose
1956	First (non-mystery) novel published, *The Happy Exiles*
1956-1970	Living in North Africa, Egypt, Sudan, Liberia, Uganda, Kenya, France and other countries
1970	First mystery novel published, *Death in the Grand Manor*. Written while living in Paris.
1977	Play produced in Oxfordshire, *Dummy Run* (a thriller in two acts)
1982	Seventeenth mystery novel published, *Sleep of Death*

Anne Morice

Martha Alderson and Neysa Chouteau

Anne Morice writes entertaining detective novels that have wit, charm, careful structure and a delightful series character. The stories are quite traditional and quite British. Because they are so traditional and British, one is tempted to liken Morice to Agatha Christie. Because the stories are so funny, one is tempted to liken Morice to Emma Lathen. The most compelling similarity in spirit, however, is to one of the comic strip Katzenjammer Kids gleefully throwing a snowball at a rich man's top hat.

Between 1970 and 1982, Morice has published seventeen mystery novels all of which feature the inquisitive actress Tessa Crichton.[1]

Morice explains her choice of a series character.

> Since numerous members of my family (including my father, sister, two daughters and three nephews) are or were closely connected with the theatre and cinema, in one capacity or another, and I married a film director, this was the background I was most familiar with, and so created Tessa Crichton for the foreground.[2]

Each novel has a small cast of characters including a few continuing characters from Tessa's family. Each takes place in a relatively short period of time (often during a brief vacation or a few days between acting engagements). Each book is confined to a geographical area of a few miles. These constraints effectively unify the plots. As a result of a limited cast, the victims as well as the villains are close associates, sometimes even Tessa's relatives. One might wonder at the kind of personality that attracts so many murderers and murderees. Among the murderers are Tessa's cousin-in-law, an actress friend, a former sweetheart of her adored young second cousin, a friend's husband, her godmother's daughter, the recent fiance of a dear friend's son and a person who describes Tessa as her oldest friend. Among the murder victims are another cousin-in-law, Tessa's housekeeper, her godmother's nanny, another of her second cousin's former boyfriends and numerous acquaintances of varying degrees of friendliness.

The novels are all written in the first person. Tessa Crichton is the narrator. The novels are lively and unself-conscious with none of the ponderousness sometimes associated with first-person stories.

The first-person device allows Tessa to evaluate various social and psychological characteristics in her own charming fashion. Beneath Tessa's sexy and sophisticated veneer lies the honesty of a child. Readers, therefore, feel that any biases expressed or any clues missed are Tessa's fault rather than Anne Morice's. The skill is Morice's, of course, and she engineers the stories to give well-rounded portraits of Tessa and of the other characters. Morice moves the plot along mostly by dialogue. Tessa's editorial comments within the dialogue fairly represent events and frankly assess her own strengths and weaknesses. It is a tribute to Morice's skill that readers accept the fact that Tessa eventually observes all the right incidents and speaks with all the right people.

Tessa is an actress and as such is master of dramatic exaggerations and exit lines. She is upbeat, sometimes caustic, always confident. The early books have too many chapters that end with "had-I-but-known" kinds of lines, but they can be seen as only natural to Tessa's outlook.

Like many other writers, Morice has chosen a territory for her novels. As in Ruth Rendell's novels, the Morice novels depend upon certain limited and partially imagined geography. The focus is London where Tessa and Robin Price, her husband, live. Their place for contemplation, where most of the plots are solved, is Roakes Common, a ficticious village in Oxfordshire where Tessa's cousin Toby Crichton lives an idyllic life. Morice explains that "Roakes is fictional in name only. It's about five miles from here [Hambleden], midway between Henley (alias Storhampton) and Oxford."[3] Roakes Common is described in *Manor.*

> Roakes Common is a hamlet to the north-west of London and some eight hundred feet above sea level, so they tell me. It consists of twenty or thirty houses, two pubs and a combined post office and store, set in a hundred acres of commonland. The Common is divided down the middle by the road which joins Storhampton, in the Thames Valley, with Dedley, twenty miles to the north. (8)

The location of Roakes Common is important since it is close enough for frequent visits from London. It also symbolizes the return to order as Tessa, Robin and Toby gather there at the end of nearly every book to discuss the mysteries.

By the second novel, *Murder in Married Life,* Tessa is married to Robin Price, the Detective Inspector she met in *Manor.* At first they lived in Storhampton, a market town not far from London, but now in a house in Beacon Square in London.

As an actress, Tessa has frequent opportunities to travel. *Murder on French Leave* is set in Paris where Tessa and Robin are vacationing primarily and *Murder in Mimicry* is set in Washington, D.C., where Tessa is appearing in a play at Kennedy Center. Otherwise, novels are set in

England, in or near London, with occasional jaunts to the beach or the country.

Even though Robin is a Detective Inspector, there is very little description of police proceedings and there is a constant shift of police officials as characters from book to book. This lack of police descriptions keeps the focus on Tessa, the amateur sleuth. Except for *Mimicry,* in which Tessa develops a close working relationship with Detective Franklin Meek, Tessa has no police confidant while working on the cases. (Robin provides information and guidance but is always working on an unrelated case.) According to one source, "Miss Morice cheerfully admits that she doesn't know the slightest thing about real-life police procedure and anyway, she doesn't think a crime novel should concentrate on the true stuff."[4] The novels emphasize psychology and logistics with little attention to legality. The lack of attention to realistic police details (the "true stuff") does not detract from the stories. The puzzles are interesting and the clues are fair.

In four of the novels (*Murder by Proxy, Nursery Tea and Poison, Murder in Outline* and *Sleep of Death*) and in the play *Dummy Run*[5] the murderers are not apprehended, three by reason of premature death. In three of the novels, in fact, readers have only Tessa's intuitive judgment (generally reliable) that the cases are solved. The ending of *Outline* is not neatly tied up. Tessa's guesswork about the murderer and the motive is reasonable, but there are several unresolved questions about other aspects of the plot. Is one character a spy? Has another character tinkered with someone's medicine? Will a young thief survive? The ending of *Proxy* is only partially satisfying since the murderer escapes altogether. *Dummy Run* has a similar ending although the murderer does admit guilt before running off. In defense of the ending in *Proxy,* Morice explains she allowed the escape because the murderer was so nasty as to deserve a chance to "get away with it and have a chance to become nice."[6] The same defense must apply to the murderer in *Dummy Run* who is surely a relative of the one in *Proxy.*

There is a great deal of humor in all the Morice books. In the early books, humorous characterizations sometimes seem to be for humor's own sake. Many one-liners are amusing even out of context. An excellent characterization of two neighbors of Toby's includes this description:

> Like many people who had lived together for years, passing their days in close proximity, Peter and Paul invariably spoke as a duet, but rarely in harmony (*Manor,* 38).

Another colorful description is of an elderly character who contrasts vividly with other people at a gathering.

> She looked more bizarre than ever in her dusty, black cape in that throng, all of whom had evidently collected their pastel cashmeres and light blue hair from the dry cleaners that very morning (*Manor*, 133).

In *Death of a Gay Dog*, the third book, Tessa comments that the family felt her uncle's first wife "had died of starvation, for his stinginess was legendary..." (11). The best line, though, is reserved for the second wife who was apparently a good match and who after marriage "acquired an accent of such strangulated gentility as to make her largely unintelligible to her former cronies..." (11).

In the later books, the humor is not as easy to remove from context and, thus, is more natural. Typical is a funny incident in *Hollow Vengeance*, the luke-warm greeting of two female characters:

> Her intention was evidently to embrace Millie, but it was one of those instances of she who kisses and she who turns the cheek and Millie turned hers so fast that the kiss missed its target by inches (34).

In *The Men in Her Death*, Tessa is making a point about crime and criminals and suggests that crime happens "even among the rich. In fact, that's how a lot of them got rich in the first place" (64).

Although Morice's humorous style is enjoyable, sometimes the humor takes over and leaves the sense a little clouded. A series of phrases describing a train ride badly mixes verb forms:

> They begin with the long haul to Dorchester, followed by a wait of at least forty minutes, and ending with the slow, meandering trundle along the branch line to the coast (*Round*, 10).

Some passages are too long to maintain unity. Long strings of clauses making sentences of 69 words (*Men*, 105) and 76 words (*Men*, 106) are rather frequent throughout the books. These weaknesses are disturbing in otherwise well written books.

While humor is perhaps the foremost strength of the Morice mystery novels, another major strength is characterization.

The Continuing Characters

Tessa Crichton Price is the amateur detective who narrates and stars in all of the seventeen Morice novels. Tessa's husband, Detective Inspector Robin Price of the C.I.D., also figures in all of the novels. A third regular is Tessa's cousin, the playwright Toby Crichton. Toby's daughter Ellen is a regular in four of the early novels but makes only cameo appearances after her marriage (which provides the setting for the ninth book *Death of a*

Wedding Guest). Ellen takes an active part in helping Tessa in *Manor* and *Leave*. Robin and Toby largely provide intellectual assistance. They both carry on with their duties and interests quite separately from Tessa's investigating.

Tessa and Toby are industrious, competent adults. At the same time, they are spiritual siblings of Hans and Fritz, the Katzenjammer Kids of comic strip fame. Tessa is nosy. She gives and gets insults on a child-like level with no lasting malice, remaining cheery through verbal and physical assaults. The only thing that really upsets her is to be played for a fool (*Married,* 214). Toby is whiny, has silly fears and misbehaves so far as his social obligations are concerned.

If Tessa and Toby are secret children, Robin is the ideal white knight. Ellen calls him Tessa's swain which describes him well. After Tessa and Robin are married, Robin is frequently Tessa's mentor in a paternal way. Ellen, the perfect child, could also be visualized as a perfect mother-figure—loving, supportive, although with no power to make Tessa and Toby behave properly.

There are a few minor repeating characters who provide familiarity and continuity. Dr. Mackintosh, Toby's family doctor, is a colorful character:

> ...he did possess two characteristics which, to put it mildly, accorded oddly with his profession. He was amazingly indiscreet and he was as confirmed a hypochondriac as Toby himself (*Manor,* 116).

Ellen's brother-in-law, Simon Roxburgh, is introduced in *Wedding* and has a small part in *Round.* Another likable character who has made brief appearances is the lawyer Gerald Pettigrew who was introduced to read the will in *Daughter* and has given Tessa legal advice in succeeding books. Owen, the taxi driver, is also a familiar figure. Tessa's American friend Lorraine Beaseley is a major character in *Mimicry* and again in *Men.*

In order to understand each new novel, it is not necessary to have previous knowledge of the characters which means that the books need not be read in chronological order. Morice rewards her fans with familiar characters, but she does not confuse new readers with esoteric references.

The main continuing characters have distinctive personalities. Descriptions of them from book to book are consistent without being repetitive. They remain interesting throughout the series even though they do not change very much.

Tessa, the Sleuth

Readers first meet Tessa Crichton when she is a young actress (in her very early twenties), single, living in a London flat. She has a reputation of being overly inquisitive and has no compunction about delving deeply into anyone's privacy to satisfy her curiosity. In *Dog,* one of the less reserved characters says to Tessa, "You ask too many questions. You have not been well brought up" (108).

Tessa also has a photographic memory and as a result does not have to delve more than once in the same place. It is handy for Tessa to have a bona fide detective in the house, but Tessa herself is plenty interested in and capable of solving mysteries. Her proclivity for studying crime truly stems from her own inclinations.

First, however, Tessa is an actress. Her stage name is her given name, Theresa Crichton. She is always conscious of her image as an actress and of her box office value. Tessa is a successful actress and she gains experience and popularity in the course of the novels.

In early novels, Tessa mentions that she takes any acting job she has a chance at. She works seriously at each one even as she maintains some objectivity about it. At the beginning of the first novel, *Manor,* Tessa explains her current role and an effect it has on her:

> . . . I am writing this saga in the intervals of rehearsal for a Victorian melodrama and the florid prose is rather infectious. Doubtless, the style will cool down, as the narrative proceeds, particularly if I am fortunate enough to secure a contemporary part in the course of it (*Manor,* 5).

Although Tessa is not acting a contemporary part by the end of the novel, her florid prose and her anxiety have eased.

By the second novel, Tessa has had better fortune.

> Among those whom I had not totally forsaken was an Anglo-American film company, in one of whose productions I had once figured in a modest way, and I believe Robin and I were about equally relieved when they offered me a three-year contract at a far from modest salary (*Married,* 5).

In the same novel, Tessa's self-confidence, at least, is high. Her friend Betty Haverstock explains, "I pretended I had arranged to drive you to Stratford for an audition, and, as you'd probably be kept hanging about for hours, it might suit us to stay the night." Tessa retorts in part, "Stars of my calibre are not kept hanging about for hours" (137).

In the third novel, *Dog,* Tessa has just finished a film. She and Robin take a short vacation since she has a break from work (and since he wants to do some investigating of his own). Her reputation is obviously becoming that of a star.

> In the hurly-burly of the past few days I had almost, though admittedly not quite, forgotten about the premiere of my last film, which had taken place a few days earlier in New York. My agent, ever watchful in these matters, had acquired copies of the local papers which had covered it, and had posted me the clippings. There was quite a batch of them, all long and mostly enthusiastic... (137).

In the fourth novel, *Leave,* Tessa is in Paris to act in a film and also to have a holiday. In the seventh novel, *Kindness,* she is doing live broadcasting. In the tenth novel, Tessa is the second female lead in one of Toby's plays which is scheduled for a month in Washington, D.C., and then for an engagement in New York. By the thirteenth novel, *Outline,* Tessa's career is clearly successful:

> ...she became quite affable, providing me with my first stroke of luck and a fine example of the many blessings which television can bring to contemporary life, for with no help at all she recognized me (112).

Tessa's growing popularity is helpful to her sleuthing as well as to her ego. During a phone call in *Men,* the fifteenth novel, Tessa is being put off until she wisely identifies herself as Theresa Crichton.

> "Excuse me, did you say Theresa Crichton?"
> "That's right."
> "Currently appearing, and all that?" (14).

Tessa explains that she has "gambled on the assumption that he wants to break into the theater and therefore needs all the contacts he can get" (15). The mere mention of her name would not have had the same magic in the earlier books which took place, of course, earlier in her career.

Tessa is clever, intuitive and on occasion sarcastic. Her smooth and clever tactics with strangers are in sharp contrast to her brattish exchanges with her friends. In *Outline* Tessa and her friend Tina Blundell have several conversations with the same tone as in this one:

> "Honestly, Tessa, you make me so furious I can't even remember what I came in here to look for. Have you come to apologize?"
> "Yes, if you like. I never mind apologizing to ostriches. It doesn't carry the same sting."
> "Just because I haven't got your beastly, morbid, suspicious mind!" (102).

Tessa and Tina remain friends and neither seems especially bothered by the insults that fly around. Tessa is in the habit of having heated exchanges with friends. Morice herself has commented that Tessa "annoys me sometimes when she's so cocky and sure of herself."[7]

Tessa tells on herself as cheerfully as she tells on others. In *Sleep,* Tessa admits, "I fancy myself at being able to tell when people are lying, but it's nothing to be proud of. I'm afraid it's mainly because I do it so often myself that I can see it coming from a mile off" (125). While Tessa and Robin are dating, she invites him to dinner. Surely her dilemma is familiar to every host:

> The evening got off to a fine start because Robin was half an hour late which is exactly what I require of all my dinner guests. It is a delicate balance because five minutes' mistiming, either way, can spell disaster. As it was, when the bell rang I was not obliged to go to the front door in my dressing-gown and with my hair uncombed, while still safely on the right side of that depressing stage when the preparations are complete and nothing remains but to sit and wonder whether the guests have forotten they were invited (*Manor,* 184-185).

In *Death of a Heavenly Twin* Tessa is an unwilling guest in a mansion belonging to someone she knows only by name. She naturally wants to make a good impression. Her slight paranoia surfaces when she first meets Sarah Benson-Jones.

> She was wearing a maroon Thai silk tunic and trousers which did plenty for a figure that could have gotten by without any assistance at all. As it happened, I also possessed a Thai silk tunic and trousers which I was rather proud of but there and then rejected the idea of sporting them around at Eglington Hall. As I have often tried to explain to Robin, it is precisely in anticipation of such emergencies that I am driven to carting about forty tons of luggage along every time I spend a night away from home (15).

Tessa's personality traits, then, include abrasiveness along with cleverness and cheerfulness. The effect is that Tessa is real. Morice seems almost to have no control over Tessa (and, of course, that means she has very skillful control). Tessa's haughtiness, impulsiveness and frankness seem child-like but not childish, an effect which helps readers excuse and tolerate those characteristics as part of an overall delightful personality.

Robin, the Inspector

Tessa Crichton meets Robin Price in the first novel *Manor.* He is a 30-year-old sergeant with the Dedley C.I.D. By the next book, Tessa and Robin are married. He is promoted quickly to Detective Inspector and moved to Scotland Yard. On his and Tessa's fifth wedding anniversary, Robin is promoted to Chief Detective Inspector (*Mimicry,* 7). In *Sleep* Tessa reminds one of the other characters that Robin is "a real detective...not an amateur like me...." (30).

Robin not only gives Tessa advice about her sleuthing but also comes to her rescue in the nick of time to save her life in the first three books. The pattern of Robin-to-the-rescue is broken after three books until the eleventh book, *Scared to Death,* in which Robin captures the murderer after Tessa explains whom he should chase. In the fifteenth novel, *Men,* Morice again gives Robin the honor of showing up in time to rescue Tessa from the clutches of a mad murderer. Robin receives much deserved admiration from Tessa who never feels inadequate but is always grateful for help.

In some of the books, Robin's official connections and professionally trained observational skills make the difference in solving the crime. In *Leave,* the real reason Robin suggests he and Tessa vacation in Paris is that he wants to study some details of an international case. In *Dog,* Robin obtains special knowledge about a financial swindle which fully explains the motive. In *Kindness,* Robin lets Tessa know enough nonconfidential police details to keep her own analysis progressing. Robin reports, "I'd asked the local branch to keep me informed as a personal favor and they did" (48). Usually Tessa's mysteries are not under Robin's jurisdiction which has the effect that his interest in her puzzles is not official, although his advisory capacity is valuable.

Generally, Robin Price's status is simply that of Tessa Crichton's husband. At a wedding reception, to Tessa's chagrin, they are announced as Mr. and Mrs. Crichton (*Wedding,* 73). A movie magazine makes comic, condensed references to Tessa and Robin as "Cinemactress Crichton" and "Husband Price" (*Dog,* 138).

Tessa and Robin have different outlooks philosophically. Tessa explains her surprise at being attracted to a person so different from herself.

> "You have to commit yourself, you know," he told me very seriously, as we slowed down for Storhampton bridge. "At least, if you're like me, you've got to plump for one side or the other. It's no use hiding your head and hoping all the nasty crooks will go away. And it's no good whining about them when you get hurt, and adopting bits of their morality when it suits you. You have to be for or against, and, smug as it may sound to you, I'm against. This is the only job I know which gives me the chance to do something about it."
>
> I watched his profile as he manoeuvred us through the town traffic and marvelled that anyone so beautiful could be such a prig, paying a passing tribute to Nature on the side. It was one of her subtler tricks to have me fall, like a dead sparrow from a tree, for a man whose philosophy of life was so alien to my own (*Manor,* 145).

In *Wedding,* when Tessa and Robin have been married about four years, Tessa explains to Robin why she would not care to tell him her latest theories. She says, "Because I know you, my darling, and you could not love me, dear, so much, loved you not law and order more" (173). Tessa's respect for law and order is reserved for moments when law fits her purpose of orderliness, but she knows Robin's is more absolute.

Tessa and Robin share serious dedication to their vocations. Tessa perceives Robin's suggestion of a short vacation to Sussex as more than a grand gesture. She says, "Some wives, I dare say, would take such proposals, out of the blue, with a grain of salt. Speaking as the wife of a C.I.D. detective, I took it with a spadeful" (*Dog*, 5). As it happens, Robin does have ulterior motives and a Sussex vacation is business, pleasure and near catastrophe.

In the beginning of *Hollow,* Tessa takes a phone call in the kitchen to avoid disturbing Robin's television program. She reports her plans and Robin "...raised his eyebrows, warned me to take a rug...and went back to his American police serial" (7). Even relaxing, Robin is thinking of law and order.

Robin and Tessa's relationship is that of friendly antagonists. Quarrels seem to be fairly common, but they do not seem to have much emotional fallout. Robin sometimes belittles Tessa's intuitive conclusions. Tessa sometimes belittles Robin's trust in the system and in his ostensibly infallible colleagues. Robin sometimes plays devil's advocate. As he explains in *Nursery,* "I always hate it when your theories fall apart. Frustration doesn't become you. I hoped that by needling you a bit I'd inspire you to find the explanation" (120).

Robin is concerned for Tessa's welfare and sometimes discourages her sleuthing because he knows the danger that can result. A typical conversation as Tessa begins to get involved in a mystery is this one from *Wedding:*

> "I shall be working on the fringes and my suspect won't even guess what I'm up to. There, does that satisfy you?"
> "Not remotely, but I suppose I know when I'm beaten. All I ask is..."
> "That I mind how I go and try to stay out of trouble?"
> "Why do I bother?" he asked (174).

Tessa can rarely keep those promises, of course, since she is determined to solve murders and inevitably must confront dangerous people. It is to Robin's credit that he participates in Tessa's victorious feelings in the end.

Robin and Tessa are a perfect match. They are mutually proud of each other. Tessa is understanding about Robin's demanding job and Robin adapts to Tessa's sporadic engagements. They do seem to understand each other. In the heat of excitement over a new acting part, Tessa exclaims her enthusiasm, and *Outline* ends this way:

> "Oh, but this is wonderful! I can't believe it! I've never been more happy or terrified in my whole life. Now perhaps we'll be able to afford a second car? One thing I know for certain, though: I'm going to make a success of this, if it's the last thing I ever do. From now on, I shall devote myself exclusively to work, heart and soul and twenty-four hours a day. I'll never again get mixed up in other people's lives or their deaths either; and this time I do mean it. Are you listening, Robin?"
>
> But he was already half asleep. He had heard it all before (188).

Toby, the Eccentric

If Tessa is unfortunate in many of her relationships, she is indeed fortunate to have as her cousin the playwright Toby Crichton. Toby is Tessa's playmate. He is always ready to fall in with Tessa's schemes, he writes plays for her and he lives in a "let's pretend" world. He is also satisfyingly imperfect.

Tessa says of Toby that, "the fact is that despite his tiresome prejudices and quarrelsome disposition, Toby had a unique place in my affections" (*Manor,* 5). The descriptions of Toby include many negative characteristics. He is a hypochondriac, an acrophobiac, vain and easily bored. He dislikes telephones, correspondence, horses and dinner engagements.

> Toby was a playwright by profession and a recluse by inclination and could only rarely be enticed out of his country retreat... (*Married,* 39).

Morice uses Toby as a vehicle of comment on modern society. Toby is eccentric but lovable. He is distrustful of modern conveniences and modern people in a way that most readers can identify with in certain measure. Somehow each of Toby's many faults makes him more endearing. When Toby refuses to fly from New York City to Washington, D.C., Tessa observes that "practicalities...had never been known to influence Toby, whose distrust of mechanical transport functioned in direct ratio to their speed and efficiency" (*Mimicry,* 8).

Toby is Tessa's confidant. Since she spends many weekends at Toby's home in Roakes Common, Tessa has access to Toby's analysis during almost every case. Often Toby's greatest value is in listening as Tessa reviews the events and speculates upon solutions. Dialogue is crucial to Tessa's thought processes and Toby is excellent at providing the second voice. Sometimes Robin joins in and a three-way discussion moves the plot along. Largely, though, Tessa and Toby weigh the evidence and possibilities. In *Mimicry* Tessa admits that "In the end, rather to my annoyance, it was Toby who broke down the defences..." (156).

Toby is a witty combination of opposing points of view. He lives in a country village and is apparently well off. He drives a Mercedes but a very old one. Toby dislikes social events and seems to make a point of misremembering names; yet, as a successful playwright, he is dependent upon certain social skills.

Toby is a master of self-deceit. He has had two unsuccessful marriages and claims to shun any association with women, now believing that they can only ruin his life. Nevertheless, after complaining bitterly about the designs of a new female neighbor, Toby jumps at a chance to help her with a minor problem (*Daughter*, 24).

If they did not deal with grown-up matters, many of Toby's actions could be those of Penrod or Tom Sawyer. He deceives himself in his attention to household matters and in his creative efforts. He shoves all his bills into a drawer waiting for final notices—or hoping they will rot. Although a successful playwright, Toby's "annual output averages about half a play and a couple of television scripts" (*Outline,* 29). He is insecure and suffers from frequent bouts of writer's block, the solution to which he seems to think is to pretend to write:

> . . . Toby said that since he had wasted a whole morning and the best part of an afternoon he must drag himself off and do some work. He then went directly to his room to lie down for an hour or two (*Manor,* 113).

Tessa knows to look for more than the obvious in Toby. She knows his contradictions. Her comment is this:

> That was the trouble with Toby. Much of what he said sprang from the observation of a highly individual mind, but at other times he was inspired solely by sour grapes, or the uncomplicated desire to take the opposite view from everyone else (*Manor,* 75).

Toby himself admits that "The workings of my mind are sometimes a little too subtle even for me to follow" (*Married,* 39).

Toby fills an important role in Tessa's life. He is like Tessa in many ways: he is involved in theater; he has a child-eye view of his friends and of society; he has a colorful sense of humor. Robin is loving and serious and helps Tessa by his professional expertise and his support. Toby, though, sees the puzzles from a less rational point of view. He is emotional and inconsistent and these traits are useful because they help Tessa think of new possibilities.

Ellen, the Perfect Cousin

In Ellen Crichton, Morice presents a contrast to the flip Tessa, the serious Robin and the eccentric Toby. Ellen is Toby Crichton's daughter and a tribute to Toby's gentler nature. Ellen is a bright child in *Manor*, a clever teenager in *Leave* and a beautiful bride in *Wedding*.

Tessa obviously adores Ellen. None of the sarcastic comments or reservations Tessa showers on her other friends, relatives and acquaintances are even sprinkled on Ellen. Tessa's unwavering praise of Ellen shows a very positive side of Tessa, balancing her usually acerbic personality with that of a doting older relative. Tessa describes Ellen in glowingly unqualified terms:

> She had grown even more stunning than when I had last seen her, which is saying a lot.... She was about the most capable and poised young female of my acquaintance, with an innate serenity which had a most heartening effect on everyone around her (*Manor*, 10).

Tessa's appreciation of Ellen's fine qualities is reasonable and not based only on physical beauty or manners. In a special tribute, Tessa says that, "had I been asked to choose between Ellen and the tomb as guardian of my secrets, the decision would not have been lightly taken" (*Manor*, 220). In this way Ellen is similar to Tessa, but at times, even at a much younger age, she is a bit more level-headed.

Several of the plots are built around Ellen's activities, for she shares the dubious family distinction of having murderers and murderees as friends and relatives. In one or the other category are Ellen's natural mother, stepmother, two former boyfriends and her dog. Ellen's dog is the first victim of malice in *Manor*. Ellen goes to Paris with Robin and Tessa to escape a domestic science course in *Leave*. She is kidnapped but helps to bring about a satisfactory conclusion through clever actions and some help from a new friend. The setting for *Wedding* is Ellen's wedding. In *Manor* and *Leave* Ellen holds the key to the solutions of the murders and she handles her information competently and maturely. It is ironic that in *Wedding*, even though Ellen is the focus of the event, her actions contribute very little to the plot.

After Ellen's marriage, she does not get involved in Tessa's sleuthing. She is mentioned occasionally and provides bits of information sometimes. It is unfortunate that Ellen virtually disappears from the novels after she marries Jeremy Roxburgh. Perhaps Ellen is not, after all, following Tessa's example of picking friends who run afoul of the law. Or, perhaps Ellen has outgrown the fascination with mystery leaving Robin to provide Tessa and Toby with a parent-like calming influence.

Except for Ellen, who grows up and more or less out of the books, the continuing characters change very little. Toby does not seem to change at all and Robin and Tessa change only in that their careers advance. Morice gives the impression that she is not the least bit interested in expanding from the classical amateur detective form or from the characters she first introduced. After all, there are many top hats awaiting snowballs.

The Social Scene

Morice's social comments are witty and vivid. She describes new characters with what the reader feels is stingingly accurate detail. Morice has Tessa say of the twins, Sarah and Julie Benson-Jones in *Twin*, "You could tell they were related, but they were no more identicial than the fifth carbon copy is to the original page of typing" (17).

Tessa's world is varied enough to present many tempting targets. In fact, her targets are sometimes national or international. One of the main characters in *Nursery* has spent the last several years in Canada. Tessa uses her sociological perceptiveness to peg him:

> I daresay that most people who spend long periods abroad end by falling into one of two categories. They either work overtime at acquiring local color, becoming more papal than the pope, or else cling with such tenacity to their native characteristics that they end up as caricatures of the original. Perhaps for Englishmen the second course is more usual... (18).

Mimicry is set in Washington, D.C., and appropriately contains Britishers' appraisals of American customs. An especially enjoyable observation of American morality appears in Tessa's description of her friend Lorraine Beaseley.

> She had already been married four times, for, in addition to being pure gold, she was extremely moral and would not have contemplated entering into an informal relationship with someone she was deeply in love with, if he were free to marry her. I think this may be true of many Americans, men as well as women, and sometimes gives rise to misunderstandings abroad (30).

Most Americans would be surprised to hear that a high divorce rate is attributable to high morality. The conclusion is fair, though. Tessa correctly perceives that morality dictated by legality (since cohabitation is illegal) can lead to impracticality (hasty marriages result in frequent divorces). Tessa's social comments are amusing largely because they ring so true.

Both the Americans and the British are ridiculed in another passage from *Mimicry*. Tessa has been warned repeatedly about the rampant violence in American cities. She has some skepticism about the graphic warnings admitting that, "I've noticed dozens of people walking about and none of them looks in the least apprehensive" (43). She has found a little bar where she and Toby can meet and where even Toby feels he is safe. It is dark and hidden, though, which leads to Tessa's observation.

> . . . like so many establishments of its kind, it was not only inaccessibly situated but so dark inside that the customer was temporarily blinded and liable to collide with the mock font, filled with plastic flowers, which had been placed immediately inside the entrance. It is an odd perversity, for in general there is nothing in the service or merchandise on offer to be shamefaced about and must, I believe, reflect some deep rooted national prejudice, paralleled to some extent by certain rich people nearer home who buy the priciest car on the market, while insisting that it should be in the most hideous colour the manufacturer can devise, perhaps with the sub-conscious idea of indulging themselves to the hilt without incurring the envy of the less fortunate (43-44).

Tessa manages to criticize custom and snobbishness in the same comment.

Through Tessa, Morice comments on idiosyncrasies of the British railway system. In *Round* Tessa explains her journey to the Rotunda Theater in Dearehaven.

> All rail journeys to Dearehaven are divided into three unequal parts. They begin with the long haul to Dorchester, followed by a wait of at least forty minutes, and ending with the slow, meandering trundle along the branch line to the coast. The last part is made even more uncomfortable by every seat being so positioned that the passenger has to sit with his back to the engine. This is not my favourite way of viewing the countryside, but I was sustained through my first experience of it by the reflection that what goes back must come forward and that, in the nature of things, we should all be facing the right way round on the return journey. However, this proved not to be the case and I was driven to the conclusion that the inhabitants of that part of Dorset, who differ from the rest of mankind in a number of ways, actually prefer to travel backwards and that British Rail are therefore compelled to go to a vast amount of time and trouble to shunt things around at each terminal, which could presumably also account for the forty minute wait (10).

Morice also makes a witty observation about the airline industry. Tessa reads an airline advertisement and notices the surprising emphasis:

> For some mysterious reason, they had chosen to promote their image not, as one might expect, with undertakings to fly from place to place in reasonable time and all engines turning over, but with proud boasts of *haute cuisine* they dish up on the journey. One got the impression that they considered it almost worth the trouble of crossing the Atlantic in order to sample the menu. . . (*Dog*, 139-140).

The observation is not original but is well stated and reminds readers of how far afield advertising can go from the real purpose of a product.

Sexual morality, snobbery and the transportation industry are targets of Tessa's biting wit. Her conclusions come from observation at close range which makes them meaningful and enjoyable.

A recurring theme in Morice's novels is that change, while inevitable, should come about gracefully. When change is made with force and without consideration, it invites disastrous consequences—such as murder. One of the sins most likely to raise high passions in Tessa's part of England is to attempt to mar the countryside or to take land from one of the landed gentry. In *Manor, Twin, Vengeance* and *Proxy*, a good part of the story springs from attempts to change the countryside. In *Nursery* the peculiarities of English inheritance laws figure heavily. In *Dog*, skirmishing arises over a cottage on a country estate. In *Vengeance* Mrs. Trelawney moves onto the Pettits Farm and begins tearing down hedges and old barns, putting up "concrete concentration camps for pigs and battery hens" (12) in their place. The story springs from her attempts to cut down a 200-year-old oak tree. When the tree is hacked, Tessa remarks that the tree will recover. Millie tells her, "But it isn't only the tree, Tessa, it's what it represents. It's sort of like a permanent threat. None of the things we've always taken for granted seem to be safe any more"(30). Physical changes in the countryside were attempted precipitously and murder resulted.

Morice's concern with the countryside sometimes seems to imply that among the upper classes, the only good money is old money. Possessors of new money do such obnoxious things as to "build some hideous monstrosity and completely ruin our view..." (*Manor*, 42). Perhaps almost as bad, the nouveau riche are unappealing in social situations. In *Dog*, Christabel Blake castigates the Harper Barringtons:

> "I can't really do with them, myself. They're culture climbers. Always asking my advice about what pictures to buy. 'Buy any damn bloody thing that gives you pleasure to look at,' I tell them. They don't go for that; they're vulgarians" (18).

When Tessa is at dinner at the vulgarians', she notes that Mrs. Harper Barrington "was valiantly harping away on the absurdity of owning four cars when she would have been perfectly happy to travel by bus..." (50).

The newly rich are traditional and perhaps overworked targets. The most established members of society do not escape unscathed, however. One elderly upper-class woman is described as follows:

> "A bit snooty, you know. Only to be expected, really. It takes more than two world wars and a social revolution to get it in their head that they're no longer the top dog" (*Manor*, 40).

The Hargraves of *Nursery* are wealthy and presumed to be happy. In the course of the novel, though, it is revealed that Rupert Hargrave, the late husband of Tessa's "chief godmother" Serena (5) was cruel, selfish and hot-tempered as is his twin brother Pelham. The flaws in Rupert's character planted the seeds of destruction that have now grown.

Harry Purveyance of *Proxy* is a traitor to his class because he proposes to despoil his ancestral acres. Of course, he had been on a downhill slide for some time.

> [Harry] had degenerated, through laziness and self-indulgence, into a somewhat fond and foolish, unmistakably overweight and uxorious middle-aged man, a landowner bereft of his land and a scholar with no higher ambition than to gratify every passing whim (31).

Harry's misuse of his resources caused enough anxiety to lead to violence. He is socially irresponsible and Morice is critical of him for that.

The working class are not excepted from social criticism. In *Men* Morice draws a devastating portrait of Mrs. Cox, the cleaning woman:

> As I had noticed on a previous occasion, Mrs. Cox's tight-lipped and subservient manner was a very thin veneer and, once tapped, the flow of sanctimonious prejudice soon came bubbling up (133).

Morice makes it clear that Mrs. Cox is not unique. When Tessa asks if Lorraine recognized anyone at the inquest, Mrs. Cox is labeled as one of the "drab looking women of her sort, taking in a thrill or two on their way home from the supermarket" (115). Mrs. Cox's "sort" are not frequent targets of Morice's satire, but they are not excused when their weaknesses are obvious.

The young come in for their share of ridicule in the Morice novels. Young people have significant roles in nearly half the books. Aside from the near-perfect Ellen, the teens tend to be lumpy, overweight and carelessly dressed:

> Emily Carrington, at this time, was a stout, somewhat pasty and inclined to be surly sixteen-year-old, who had every prospect of being beautiful as soon as she fined down and started preferring men to banana cake (*Vengence*, 9).

The problem teenagers include Jonathan of *Leave,* Millie (Emily) of *Hollow,* Primrose Hargrave of *Nursery,* Hattie McGrath of *Outline* and Mary Purveyance of *Proxy.* Many flaunt the symbols of their age. Anabel Harper Barrington of *Dog* has braces. Millie is a vegetarian. Digby Roche of *Daughter* is a folk singer with a motley mustache and hair worked up into a red-gold haystack. The young are generally treated quite kindly overall, however. For example, Millie and Jonathan rally to become the quiet decent and likable people they are trying to grow into.

Morice's social comments are serious but are projected humorously Many social comments are pertinent to the upper class—new land development, inheritance, art theft. Other comments are based on problems that are classless—prejudice, jealousy, blackmail, revenge. Most of Morice's social observations are delivered from Tessa's adult side. While witty, they are realistic. There is also room, however, for more child-like observations in which social commentary is considerably more wacky. In the summing-up scene in *Men,* wealthy Lorraine and Toby are greatly comforted when assured that the poor are murdered just as frequently as the rich (188).

The Victims and the Crimes

In *Scared* Tessa says, "If I were to moralize, I should probably say now that people mainly get into trouble through their own weaknesses" (185).

This is true of many of Tessa's victims. Most of them are arrogant, dishonest and selfish. In *Manor,* victim Bronwen Cronford has established herself as a thoroughly strange and unpleasant person. In *Married,* Julian Brown is a collector of dirty secrets. Sebastian, in *Married,* is a snoop and a petty thief. In *Dog,* Maddox Brand may be a child molester and is certainly a bully. In *Leave,* Leila Baker is an annoying intruder of privacy. In *Kindness,* Mike Parsons is unveiled as so unappealing that one is practically forced to cheer his death. In *Mimicry,* Hugo Dunstan is a parasite and a mean-spirited practical joker. In *Proxy,* Anne is a whiner, a Cassandra and worse.

This pattern does not hold true for every victim, however. Victim Betsy Craig of *Daughter* is someone Tessa is quite fond of, as is Christabel Blake of *Dog.* Camilla Mortimer in *Scared* was a friend of Tessa's. Melanie Jones in *Round* is an interesting young person, although most of the other characters do not think so. In all of these cases, the likable victims are not the first victims and they are unexpected victims. The only foreshadowing of Betsy Craig's murder, for example, is in the title of the book because she *is* the dutiful daughter. In *Twin,* victim Sarah Benson-Jones is the most attractive of the new characters, except perhaps for the person falsely accused of the murder. Sarah is the first victim and again the title implies that she, as the heavenly twin, will be a victim. Morice does not create a maudlin atmosphere for the unlikely (by being likable) victims but handles the deaths as matter-of-factly as the other crimes. These cases, though, cause Tessa to work even harder in puzzling out how these likable people could have had weaknesses so strong as to cause their untimely deaths.

Generally, Tessa has not been terribly fond of any person who turns out to be the perpetrator of the crime. She says to Robin in *Married,* "I could never be friends with a murderer; not real friends..." (224). Of course, for the story to work, all the characters have to have an equal chance of being guilty and so Morice does not have Tessa voice clear preferences until after the solution. Only once does Morice not quite play fair with her readers by having a very minor character be the villain (*Men*). Tessa has been neither fond of nor critical of that murderer since she has had hardly any contact with the person. In other cases the murderers are quite busily involved with Tessa but are never real friends.

In *Kindness,* Tessa voices compassion for a person who had to use her limited resources for evil because she had not developed the resources to cope with her problems:

> "...I believe she might have been quite a brainy type if she'd had a proper education. I expect there must be thousands of women like her, don't you? All their latent intelligence turning to cunning, simply because they've never had a proper outlet for it or a chance to develop it constructively" (151).

This person was not an unlikable person. Tessa had, in fact, befriended her. But she was not a strong or positive person, certainly not a real friend.

As befits the English upper class, the favorite murder weapon is poison. Poison is used in seven of the novels. A blunt instrument is the next most popular weapon. The murder methods are all conventional and are not nearly so important as clues to solving the crimes as other factors such as motive and opportunity.

The key to the crimes is in the characters' weaknesses, as Tessa says on several occasions. The victims have weaknesses that cause them to be perceived as threats by the murderers. The murderers have character flaws that cause them to be easily threatened. Tessa's observations and intuitions help her sort out all of these important factors.

The Anne Morice novels follow the British tradition of gentle murders, quiet settings and good humor. An amateur detective, Tessa Crichton, brings her professional knowledge of the theater and theatrics to bear in interesting ways upon the solution of crimes. The books are lighthearted and written basically to entertain, although social comments are made through underlying themes.

Morice's greatest strengths are her excellent characterizations, her humor and the tight plot structure. Her weaknesses are the sometimes windy prose that sacrifices clarity for cuteness and an occasional weak conclusion that leaves some loose ends dangling.

Morice's first-person technique works very well. The dialogue moves swiftly enough so that readers can keep track of the speakers. Tessa is perceptive, though not infallible. Tessa's career as an actress allows her enough flexibility to be in the right places at the right—or perhaps the wrong—times.

Tessa is indomitable as Morice readers expect her to continue to be. Tessa says of a colleague,

> "...like many actors, he was extremely observant," I said, modestly lowering my eyes.
>
> As this brought no response from the audience, I went on... (*Wedding*, 191).

Tessa should have many more opportunities to use her actor's skill to observe people involved with murders and to hurl her well-aimed verbal snowballs at their complacently poised, symbolic top hats.

Notes

[1]The editions of Anne Morice's novels used for this study are listed below, preceded by the original date of publication. All quotations will be cited in the text using, where necessary for clarity, the abbreviation given after each entry.

1970 *Death in the Grand Manor* (London: Macmillan, 1970). (*Manor*)
1971 *Murder in Married Life* (London: Macmillan, 1971). (*Married*)
1971 *Death of a Gay Dog* (London: Macmillan, 1971). (*Dog*)
1972 *Murder on French Leave* (London: Macmillan, 1972). (*Leave*) [author's copy of publisher's reading proofs was used for this paper]
1973 *Death and the Dutiful Daughter* (New York: St. Martin's Press, 1973). (*Daughter*)
1974 *Death of a Heavenly Twin* (New York: St. Martin's Press, 1974). (*Twin*)
1974 *Killing with Kindness* (New York: St. Martin's Press, 1974). (*Kindness*)
1975 *Nursery Tea and Poison* (New York: St. Martin's Press, 1975). (*Nursery*).
1976 *Death of a Wedding Guest* (New York: St. Martin's Press, 1976). (*Wedding*)
1977 *Murder in Mimicry* (New York: St. Martin's Press, 1977). (*Mimicry*)
1978 *Scared to Death* (New York: St. Martin's Press, 1978). (*Scared*)
1978 *Murder by Proxy* (New York: St. Martin's Press, 1978). (*Proxy*)
1979 *Murder in Outline* (New York: St. Martin's Press, 1979). (*Outline*)
1980 *Death in the Round* (New York: St. Martin's Press, 1980). (*Round*)
1981 *The Men In Her Death* (New York: St. Martin's Press, 1981). (*Men.*)
1982 *Hollow Vengeance* (New York: St. Martin's Press, 1982). (*Hollow*)
1982 *Sleep of Death* (London: Macmillan, 1982). (*Sleep*)

[2]*Twentieth-Century Crime and Mystery Writers*, ed. John M. Reilly (New York: St. Martin's Press, 1980), p. 1092.

Morice's husband is Alexander Shaw who has been a film director.

The article "Starring Tessa Crichton" in *Murderess Ink*, ed. Dilys Winn (New York: Workman, 1979) states that Morice's "father was a playwright, her sister is an actress, her eldest daughter worked at Royal Court, her brother-in-law is a theatrical producer and her two nephews, Edward and James Fox, have had successful stage careers" (p. 290).

[3]Personal correspondence with Anne Morice, November 1981.

[4]"Starring Tessa Crichton," p. 291.

[5]The play *Dummy Run* is an unpublished "thriller in two acts." It was professionally produced in Henley-on-Thames in 1977 by Philos Productions. Christopher Cazenove played the lead in that production.

[6]Interview with Anne Morice conducted by Martha Alderson and Neysa Chouteau, May 29, 1982, in Hambleden, England.

[7]"Starring Tess Crichton," p. 290.

Dorothy Uhnak
(Photo courtesy: Jerry Bauer)

Dorothy Uhnak

1930	Born April 24, Bronx, New York
1950	Marries Tony Uhnak
1953	Joins the New York Police Department
1954	Receives Exceptional Merit Citation, NYPD
1955	Receives Outstanding Police Duty Medal, NYPD
1956	Daughter Tracy born
1964	Publishes *Policewoman: A Young Woman's Initiation into the Realities of Justice*
1967	Leaves the New York Police Department
1968	Receives B.S. in Criminal Justice, John Jay College of Criminal Justice, CUNY
1968	*The Bait* receives the Best First Novel Award from the Mystery Writers of America
1981	*False Witness,* her sixth novel, published

Dorothy Uhnak

George N. Dove

Any assessment of the work of Dorothy Uhnak in the early 1980s is necessarily tentative and exploratory, for two reasons. In the first place, she is still relatively young as an author and should have the bulk of her production ahead of her. Moreover, she is an experimental writer who has tried new approaches with each undertaking and has thus far refrained from settling upon a tight formula. She is not a series writer: with the exception of the three Christie Opara stories (which have been substantially overshadowed by later successes), Uhnak's books represent discrete approaches to the craft of popular fiction, with the result that, in order to get a clear view of what she has accomplished to this point, we must review the special nature of each undertaking before attempting a summary of her work as a whole.

Policewoman (1964)[1]

This non-fiction book can not be classed strictly as autobiography because, as Uhnak explains in the introduction, she draws upon the experiences of her fellow policemen as well as her own, although for the sake of continuity she tells the story as if she were the policewoman primarily involved. The seeds of much of her fiction are to be found in *Policewoman,* not because she has borrowed from the stories themselves for the narrative content of her later books, but because *Policewoman* reveals a deep insight into the workings of the police subculture. The shaping of many of Uhnak's own attitudes is revealed, generally in her sympathy for persons in trouble with the law who are more victims than villains and specifically in her disquieting associations with the world of television (184-90), which are reflected in the atmosphere of artificiality in

False Witness.

The Christie Opara Trilogy (1968-70)

The Bait (1968), Uhnak's first attempt at book-length fiction, introduces Christie Opara, a second-grade detective assigned to the New York District Attorney's Special Investigations Squad. Christie has been a policewoman for four years and the widow of a murdered policeman for five years; as the only female on a squad of sixteen men, she is faced with the double challenge of proving to herself that she can overcome her own personal tragedy and at the same time measure up to the demands of a male-dominated profession whose compulsions are embodied in the person of Casey Reardon, the commander of the squad and one of the most overbearing and capable superior officers in police fiction. The plot of *The Bait* centers upon the efforts of the District Attorney's Squad to capture the degenerate sex-murderer Murray Rogoff, an undertaking in which Christie's performance is so creditable that at the beginning of *The Witness* (1969) she has been promoted to detective first-grade.

The atmosphere of *The Witness* is heavy with the violence and threatened violence of the racial conflicts and youth-activism of the late 1960s; the tensions in the story are generated in the context of the participation of Casey Reardon's daughter in a demonstration, with the result that she becomes a witness to murder, and also in the involvement of the black activist Eddie Champion. Christie Opara again distinguishes herself, first by rescuing Barbara Reardon from entanglement in the murder case and then by devising a solution that will exonerate a policeman accused of shooting one of the youth-activists during the demonstration.

The conclusion of *The Ledger* (1970) makes it evident that Uhnak did not intend to continue the Opara saga beyond these three stories. The squad headed by Casey Reardon is about to be broken up, with Reardon standing a good chance of becoming District Attorney. More important to Christie's involvement, however, is the suggestion that she and Reardon may become lovers, leaving open a question that a further book would have to answer. The mystery in this story centers around the location of an incriminating ledger in which the head of a drug syndicate has recorded his transactions, and the solution produces a stratagem that is Uhnak's most original suspense ending to date.

The Christie Opara trilogy belongs in the class of the police procedural, a kind of mystery in which the work of investigation and solution is carried on not by gifted amateurs or private investigators but by regular police detectives. Characteristically, in the procedural tale, the job of detection is performed by a police team; in keeping with the traditions of popular fiction, there is usually a "main character" who bears the burden of narrative interest (as Christie does in these stories), but he or she works with other members of the team with the result that solution of the mystery is the outcome of a cooperative effort. The term "procedural" derives from the methodology employed in detection: questioning of suspects and witnesses, use of informants, reliance on the police laboratory and other aspects of forensic science, in contrast to the ratiocination of the transcendent super-sleuth of the classic tale and the dramatic pursuit of the private detective. Procedural stories are typically rich in their reflections of the police subculture and the workings of the police mind, including the tendency of policemen to cover up each other's derelictions, the complicated one-upmanship involved in the system of favors and revenge, and such pervasive fetishes as status and territoriality. Another quality of the police procedural, especially strong in the Opara stories, is the portrayal of the police detective as a member of a family, with the result that home involvements may be featured secondarily only to the business of detection.

The police world is still a man's world and a strong element of interest in the Opara stories is created by Christie's efforts to make her way in a strongly male-dominated profession, asking no favors and expecting no concessions because she is a woman. She succeeds, not because of her sex or in spite of it, but because of her personal integrity and courage. Reardon at one point confesses that he is used to talking only to the "guys" and keeps forgetting that Christie is a "girl": "I'm a second-grade detective," she replies, "and I got second grade on the basis of my *ability* as a *cop*" (*The Bait,* 49).

Uhnak's refusal to settle upon a narrative formula is evident in the suspense techniques employed in the Opara trilogy. Although the three stories are pieces of the same cloth, the structural patterns vary to a noticeable degree. *The Bait,* for example, is the typical "inverted" mystery, in which the reader is not only permitted to witness one of the series of murders but is given an extensive account of the murderer's background, including the accident that caused him to become a psychotic pervert. As a result, the suspense in the novel is directed not to the identification of a perpetrator but to the efforts of the police to trap him; at the same time, while the author develops our sympathy for the efforts of the police and for the society that must be protected against a moral degenerate, she preserves for us an element of pity toward a villain who is himself also a victim. The development of suspense in the concluding chapters of *The Bait* is an example of Uhnak at her best as a mystery writer; with the police trap set and the murderer moving toward the baited apartment for another kill, the point of view shifts from one to another of the participants, policemen and murderer, bringing the tensions of the story to a well-timed climax at the resolution.

There are two murder-mysteries in *The Witness,* one handled with the "inverted" approach and the other with the traditional method: the reader is permitted to witness the killing of the young undercover policeman Rafe Wheeler, but the circumstances surrounding the shooting of the idealist-activist Billy Everett (including the involvement of Casey Reardon's daughter, who witnessed the murder) are not revealed until near the end of the story. *The Witness* is remarkably free of cliffhangers and other facile tricks, with the suspense naturally produced by development of the related mysteries.

The structure of *The Ledger* is that of the conventional mystery, with the dynamics of suspense evolving directly from the efforts of the police to locate the missing ledger and particularly from the efforts of Christie Opara to locate and identify the missing child of the chief witness, Elena Vargas. In this story Uhnak develops an addiction to the cliffhanger technique, building up to a high tension in one narrative strand, then dropping the subject and returning to it a half dozen or so pages later. She does one thing, however, that is most unusual in the police procedural, a device she was to develop more fully in *The Investigation:* Christie Opara, pulled off the case, continues the search on her own and eventually comes up with the missing piece necessary to the solution.

The most impressive accomplishment of this trilogy is the development in depth of Christie Opara, whose complex and often paradoxical personality makes her hard to classify. James Sandoe wrote her off as "nitwitted,"[2] apparently missing those other elements that contradict the image of the scatterbrained female. Uhnak's method of characterization of Christie is that of the multiple view, with the result that the reader gets a series of impressions of her as seen by herself, by her author and by the people in the stories.

The other series characters—particularly the policemen with whom Christie works—tend to remain two-dimensional throughout. Casey Reardon, the Assistant District Attorney and commander of the squad, is the conventional hard, aggressive superior officer who can not make up his mind whether he would rather fire Christie Opara for her misjudgments, or admire her for her bright ingenuity, or make love to her. Stoner Martin, second in command and the only black member of the squad, is consistently noble and competent. Marty Ginsburg, the Jewish detective, is the constant comedian, always ready with the quick gag.

Law and Order (1973)

Law and Order, Uhnak's most ambitious fictional undertaking to date (and her biggest best-seller), is not a mystery. It is a police story that follows the careers of three generations of the O'Malley family, all of whom are uniformed policemen, not detectives. The story opens with the murder of the father, Brian O'Malley, a tough sadist who collects "tribute" from the defenseless merchants in his precinct (14, 18), who classifies minority persons as "niggers" and "kikes" (11) and who is killed by a black prostitute he is attempting to rape. Most of the narrative is given over to the career of his son Brian, who works his way to a high-level administrative post and who believes that operating within the System and using the weapons of the police subculture are the only means by which necessary reforms in the New York Police Department can be accomplished. The third generation is represented by the grandson, Patrick, a Vietnam veteran who is not convinced that the corruption within the Department can ever be cleaned up without outside interventions.

The leading role in *Law and Order* does not belong to any individual, not even to the O'Malleys collectively, but to the New York Police Department. The thrust of the story is with the Police System, including not only the officially recognized structure based on law, regulations and hierarchies, but a complex of folkways that find expression in an amalgam of influence and intimidation, graft and coverup, favors and revenge.

Consequently, the suspense in *Law and Order* is generated by the dynamics of the System, which not only supplies most of the motivations of the people in the story but serves as a test of their own qualities, as they operate within the System and react to it.

The impulsive forces of the System are influence and intimidation. Young Brian O'Malley experiences the weight of influence based on rank when he arrests a peeping tom who turns out to be the brother of a Police Department captain; when the captain rescues his brother at the station house, he assures Brian that he now "has a friend" and "won't be forgotten" (214). Intimidation is a weapon that can be wielded by any hand that holds an advantage, but it is especially effective when supported by status and influence. When Brian O'Malley, now a Deputy Chief Inspector, decides that it is time to crush two corrupt officials in the Department, he presents each of them with overwhelming documentation of his infractions and forces a resignation without so much as an argument (496,498).

The grid of favors and revenge is the cohesive force that holds the System together. Among policemen, favors become the medium of exchange and debts incurred are never forgotten until they are repaid. The only time Brian O'Malley is really staggered during his one-man campaign to force the crooks out of the Department is the occasion on which an old cop who knew his father tells Brian the whole story of how the elder Brian was murdered and how his friends concealed the scandal to protect the good name of the O'Malleys. As repayment, Brian is expected to "back off" from his cleanup (477). The criminal world also participates in the recognition of favors. When young Patrolman Brian O'Malley catches Angelo Di Santini fornicating with an under-age female and refuses to arrest him, the hood says, "I won't forget this," (249) and he does not: later, Di Santini violates the code of the street, tipping Brian off to the location of a pair of murderers whose arrest affords Brian considerable credit (298-9). Vengeance in police dealings with criminals is just as automatic. When Timmy Mulcahey rapes Kit O'Malley, Brian does not arrest him, partly because he wants to spare his little sister the shame of a court trial but chiefly because he knows a better way: he frames Mulcahey for a jewelry-store robbery and gets him sent up for fifteen years (334-7).

The protective shell of the System is the coverup, designed for mutual protection and usually represented as being done "for the good name of the Department." Police ingenuity in the coverup is almost unlimited, as when the murder of the elder Brian O'Malley by the prostitute is transformed into heroic death in a shoot-out during a liquor-store robbery (38). The tendency to cover for other policemen is essentially reflexive: after Brian O'Malley has finally broken a ring of corruption within the Department, he presents his son Patrick with a complete exoneration of Patrick's five days' absence from duty without leave, prompting the young patrolman to remark, "In a way, that's how it starts. . . ." (512).

Suspense in *Law and Order* reaches its climax in the story of the cleanup of the corruption in the Department, engineered chiefly by Brian O'Malley, who works not through official channels but through the only way he knows, by threats, blackmail, "fighting immorality with immorality" (511). If there is a "message," it seems to be implicit in the idea that police reform must come from within, using the familiar methods of the System, otherwise there is no real regeneration, only "showcase" operation and continued coverup.

The Investigation (1977)

Uhnak returned to the format of the straight police procedural mystery for *The Investigation,* but in this novel she for the first time employed the first-person narrator. The story is told by Detective Second-Grade Joe Peters, attached to the Queens County District Attorney's Investigating Squad, who participates in the investigation of the murder of the two small Keeler boys. The use of the main-character point of view is particularly appropriate to the novel because it gives the reader an opportunity for insight into the motivations of Peters as he becomes progressively involved emotionally with the chief suspect, Kitty Keeler, mother of the murdered children, and also because it is a vehicle for Peters' reactions to the political plotting and counter-plotting within the police department.

Although *The Investigation* is a murder-mystery, the major suspense elements come to be centered less and less around the question of who killed the Keeler boys and more and more around the true nature of their mother. Kitty Keeler becomes the obvious suspect early in the story, but the question of her guilt is soon transformed from the mechanical puzzle of motive-means-opportunity into the problem of who and what the *real* Kitty Keeler is. In the development of this personality (her most enigmatic until *False Witness*), Uhnak employs the same device she had used with the portrayal of Christie Opara, multiple and contradictory views by other people in the story. To her sitter, Mrs. Silverberg, Kitty is a wonderful person, "a loving girl," "beautiful not just on the outside" (85), but to one of the investigating policemen "this bitch is iron" (105) and to the wife of one of Kitty's men friends she is a remorseless whore (124). The paradox of Kitty Keeler comes through even more strongly, however, in the varying perceptions of Joe Peters, who sees her early in the story as vulnerable beneath her toughness, as "another Kitty, another facet we hadn't seen" (121). Joe becomes emotionally involved with her, makes love to her, but toward the end of the novel he confesses that "Kitty Keeler was as much of a puzzle to me as she had ever been" (302). Ultimately, the solution of the murder merges into the solution of the real nature of Kitty Keeler.

Uhnak repeats a device she had employed in *The Ledger,* that of permitting her policeman-protagonist to go ahead with the investigation of a case on his own initiative, a stratagem that is habitual in the private investigator story but almost never occurs in the police procedural. Three-fourths of the way through the story, the mystery is apparently solved to the satisfaction of everybody except Joe Peters, who, partly because of his personal involvement with Kitty Keeler and partly because of his own nagging curiosity about the real nature of the situation, now goes it alone in the manner of Raymond Chandler's Philip Marlowe or Ross Macdonald's Lew Archer until he has cleared up the residual mystery. Usually, fictional policemen don't do that; their professionalism prevents their becoming emotionally involved in a case and their heavy case loads will not permit their extending a single investigation beyond its normal limits.

False Witness (1981)

False Witness is a mystery but not a police story; as in the Christie Opara trilogy and *The Investigation,* Uhnak attaches her protagonists to the district attorney's office, but in this novel they are lawyers: Lynn Jacobi (the narrator), Assistant District Attorney and Bureau Chief of the Violent Sex Crimes Division and her assistants Bobby Jones and Lucy Capella. The suspense techniques are those of the standard mystery, with hints and foreshadowings, suggestions and summaries. Uhnak's handling of the mechanics of suspense achieves a new technical maturity in this novel, to the extent that many readers may feel a distinct jolt at her employment late in the story of the expedient of intentional misdirection, which would be more appropriate in a Golden Age puzzle-story than a novel of the emotional intensity of *False Witness.*

The atmosphere of *False Witness* is heavy with intense hostility (chiefly racist and sexist) and a sense of artificiality. Most of the hostility is generated in the rape and mutilation of Sanderalee Dawson, a black television personality who has espoused the cause of the Palestine Liberation Organization and it becomes especially intense with the emergence of a Jewish surgeon as the chief suspect. The feeling of artificiality, essentially a metaphor of city life in twentieth century America, manifests itself most obviously in the tinsel world of television, ranging all the way from the publicity-consciousness of the police working on the case to the unreal perceptions of the television executives, the "glamorous people," one of whom actually asks if it will be necessary to cancel Sanderalee Dawson's show the night after she is attacked and mutilated (23). More pervasive, if less obvious, is the omnipresent sense of gamesmanship practiced by almost everybody in the story: "Games. Games," says Lynn Jacobi to herself during a confrontation with a black activist, "More of life's little games" (114) and during another one with a belligerent television newswoman, "We're behaving as though we've been in the middle of an ongoing game" (88).

The narrator of *False Witness* is Uhnak's most complex character creation to date. Lynn Jacobi, with her trendy speech and her bright scorn, is an aggressive feminist who believes that "God does occasionally watch over her own" (183) and who keeps her essential self isolated from those closest to her. Even her love-making with Bobby Jones is "separate and sealed off from our own persons. Games. We play games" (44). Lynn is proud of her toughness and her reputation for going for the jugular and she purposely "dresses like a Nazi" to discourage molestors on the E train, a costume so effective that she has trouble getting a taxi until she softens her appearance (222). The hard exterior is not impenetrable, though. She informs the Chief of Detectives that she played with her last doll at the age of eight or nine, after which she recognized that a trap was being set for her (8), but she has spotted a six-foot stuffed giraffe in a store and plans to slip in secretly and buy it, maybe as a gift for her fortieth birthday (57). She and Bobby Jones, according to her account, never say "I love you," but when she feels that Bobby has deceived her she wonders what you can say to someone who has betrayed you "when you still love him" (44,221). The same kind of ambivalence seeps through her militant objectivity in the form of a curious ethnic consciousness that modifies her perceptions of Anglo-Saxon middle America. She seems unable to forget Bobby Jones' Nebraska origins: he looks at her with "his honest, open midwestern face" (17); she thinks of him growing up in Lincoln, "doing all those things Gentile kids in the Midwest did" (41) and, to her, Bobby even has "clear midwestern eyes" (163). Lynn perceives in the glamorous, pushy Gloria Nichols much the same kind of image: "the pretty little Miss America media-lady" (232), "so *American*, without the slightest hint of any ethnics lurking in the background" (88).

We should not leave *False Witness* without some comment on the ferocity of the crime that opens the story. The attack on Sanderalee Dawson is one of the most violent in crime fiction: although Sanderalee is not killed, she has been raped, her hand is hacked off with a meat cleaver, the bones in her face are fractured and she has bitten off her lower lip during the struggle. It seems proper to raise the question whether so much blood and brutality are necessary to the story, or whether this initial shock is merely a cheap substitute for legitimate suspense. One thing that can be said immediately in Uhnak's behalf is that, having established the air of violence in her opening chapters she does not try to top it with more and greater horror. *False Witness,* in this respect, invites comparison with Lawrence Sanders' *The Third Deadly Sin,* which was published during the same season and which is built around a series of almost incredibly bloody murders, decidedly surpassing the violence of *False Witness* in both quantity and intensity. The real justification for the violence in this novel and her others, however, is that Uhnak is dealing with the world of crime and law enforcement, where violence becomes part of the reality that can not be ignored or glossed over.

As a matter of fact, the one quality of Uhnak's writing that has consistently caught the attention of critics and reviewers is her faithful portrayal of the reality of the police world, based upon her own experiences as a policewoman. Almost invariably, any review of her most recent book, any feature story about her in the press, or any critical comment in a serious study of her mystery fiction, will remark on her fourteen years of experience in the New York Police Department, her winning the Outstanding Police Duty Medal and her completion of a degree at the John Jay College of Criminal Justice.[3] In preparation for the writing of *Law and Order,* in which the frame of experience transcends her personal knowledge, Uhnak spent a year in research, studying the backgrounds of the immigrants who came to New York City during the past century, the ethnic groups in the city and the general social-political-economic history of the period covered in the novel.[4]

Direct personal acquaintance with the realities of police work can have strong advantages for a writer in the crime-and-mystery genre, and such is certainly the case with Dorothy Uhnak. Her knowledge of the methods of investigation supplies a sense of plausibility to such situations as the preparation of the apartment for trapping the psychotic killer in *The Bait* (166-7), carried out with all the meticulous attention to detail of a scientific experiment and the assumption of "good guy-bad-guy" roles by the police in *The Investigation* (77), designed to implant a false sense of security in a suspect. Even more impressive, though, is her knowledge of the whole complex of police attitudes and value-systems. *Law and Order* is especially rich in insights into the police subculture: young patrolman Aaron Levine has completed two years at City College, but he is cautious about even mentioning his education in the presence of his street-wise sergeant (12); young Brian O'Malley is disgusted after being assailed by a crazy prostitute at the station house, but he knows he must accept the fact that the older cops staged the scene as an initiation rite (183-4). The same kind of authenticity is strong in *The Investigation* when Joe Peters comes up for promotion as a result of favors performed for the right people: he says all the right things and looks blank at the right times and he makes detective third-grade (57).

Immersion in reality does, at the same time, present a considerable number of problems to the writer of police fiction, the most obvious being that real-life police work is dull and unexciting, and the police detective lives in a world far removed from the neat rationality of the classic formal-problem tale of detection and the spectacular involvements of the private-eye story. As a result, any novelist who attempts to portray police detection as it really is, with much of the work of investigation done on the phone and most of the rest of it carried out in endless questioning of witnesses and suspects, would produce a novel that almost nobody would want to read.[5] There are, as the work of a great many exciting writers has demonstrated, ways of handling the problem. One solution is to build into the stories an over-riding theme or constellation of themes that will at once tolerate both the sense of police reality and the drama of basic human dilemmas, a resolution that conceivably represents Dorothy Uhnak's greatest strength as a novelist.

The most obvious of these thematic patterns in Uhnak, from the Christie Opara stories through *False Witness,* has been the image of home and family as safeguard against alienation from society. Undoubtedly, part of her commentary on the direction of civilized living in the twentieth century lies in the shift of emphasis from the security of strong family cohesiveness in the Opara trilogy and *Law and Order* to the disruption of family in *The Investigation* and to estrangement and isolation in *False Witness.*

One of the atmospheric conventions of the police procedural is the image of home and family as the Great Good Place, at once the antidote against the frustrations of police life and the symbol of the community a policeman is sworn to protect. Christie Opara lives with her mother-in-law Nora, who shares the trauma of Christie's widowhood and understands her far better than her police colleagues could, and her five-year-old son Mickey. In these stories, returning home or receiving word from home serves as insurance against the dangers and anxieties of the job, most pointedly in *The Ledger* when Christie, suffering from a bad cold and the tensions generated by her confrontation with Elena Vargas, takes time out to talk with Mickey on the phone and is reassured (42-3). A threat to the security of the family is perceived as a greater danger than is a menace to one's own safety: Christie is completely courageous in her face-off with the crime-boss Enzo Giardino (134-7), but she experiences real fear when Giardino makes a veiled threat against Mickey (137-8).

The theme of family solidarity has a broader base in *Law and Order,* with a strong sense of loyalty binding the various units of the O'Malley clan, the response to any crisis being a family conference composed of senior uncles and brothers, to the accompaniment of plenty of the best whiskey and resulting in a decision binding upon every O'Malley involved (118-20). The sense of responsibility within the family unit is automatic, as it is with Margaret O'Malley when she knows she must be strong for the sake of the children after her husband is killed (52-3) and as it is with her son Brian when he beats his brother Kevin for involvement in a theft (150-8). Reliance on the family in times of emergency is instinctive: at the time Brian O'Malley recognizes the seriousness of the corruption in the New York Police Department and needs a job done in absolute secrecy and without explanation, he calls upon Kevin (484-6). Blood ties bridge the gap between generations of O'Malleys, as when Brian seeks a way to heal the breach between himself and his disillusioned son Patrick: "What the hell, you're my son, right?" (511).

The disruption of home and family makes its appearance in *The Investigation.* Joe Peters is estranged from his frigid wife, who has moved to Florida and wants him to give up his police job in New York and join her. Jen Peters diagnoses the danger to Joe as a result of the failure of their marriage: "Stuck with a cold frigid wife, which of course would drive any hot-blooded normal male into the arms of other women . . ." (118). She is right: assigned to play the "good guy" role in the investigation of the murder of the Keeler boys, Joe finds himself drawn into an emotional involvement with Kitty Keeler that seriously impairs his professional objectivity. A comparison with the same situation in *Law and Order* will illustrate the thematic shift: Brian O'Malley is also driven by an unresponsive wife into the arms of other women, but his solidarity with mother, brother and son is unimpaired. Joe Peters has no such family unit to fall back on; his son and daughter have moved away from New York and are out of touch with him.

The sense of alienation, coincidental with the breakup of family units, reaches a much higher level of intensity in *False Witness.* The narrator Lynn Jacobi is divorced, both her parents were killed in an accident and she has no contact with her surviving brother. Her only off-hour friends are a pair of homosexuals next door, in whose apartment she watches "bootleg movies" on a Sunday afternoon (86). Even her love-relationship with Bobby Jones, as we mentioned earlier, is conditioned by the atmosphere of isolation and artificiality. Bobby is another individual wihtout ties: after Vietnam made it impossible to "cope with the innocence of Lincoln, Nebraska," and after divorce had ended an unsatisfactory marriage, Bobby moved to New York, where he eventually became Lynn Jacobi's assistant and her lover (42-3). The third member of the team, Lucy Capella, is a "dropout nun" and is thus in a sense also divorced, but unlike Lynn Jacobi and Bobby Jones, she enjoys membership in a family of sorts, her "friends from the old lapsed-priests-and-nuns commune," who take care of her dogs and cats while Lucy is on extended duty and look after Lucy herself when she is released from the hospital (184.) It is no accident that Lucy, with the security of her "family," is also the most stable and dependable of the three. Lynn jokingly calls her "my Lucy-look-at-the-sunny-side" (225), but she is tearfully conscious of Lucy's serene faith while her own life has gone desperately awry (223).

Uhnak does not point any explicit moral in the progression from strong family cohesion to alienation and isolation, but absence of the family unit in the stories inevitably parallels estrangement from the general community.

The other recurrent theme in Uhnak is the juxtaposition of the phony and the genuine, a device that manifests itself with special effectiveness in the development of Patrick O'Malley, the third generation policeman in *Law and Order*. The most important outgrowth of Patrick's Vietnam experience has been his friendship with Dudley Kenyon, a black fellow medical corpsman whose attitude toward human relationships is always honest, if elemental and even primitive. Two weeks before their tour ends, Kenyon is killed and Patrick O'Malley's first obligation when he returns to New York is to pay his respects at Kenyon's wake. He is uneasy among the black mourners, but the one quality of the members of Kenyon's family that comes home to him is their unabashed sincerity (377-86). An understanding of the emotional honesty of this scene is necessary for the appreciation of the one a little later, in which Patrick has a date with Eileen O'Flaherty, the airline stewardess who flew back from Vietnam with him. Eileen explains that she and her fellow stewardesses "date only Viet vets" and she tries to have sex with him, telling him, "I want to make you feel alive. Don't let them [the unarmed, helpless civilians] get in your way." Patrick walks out on her (409-15).

The polarity of the genuine and the phony comes through with special strength in another scene in *Law and Order,* in which a group of policemen, most of them Vietnam veterans, are enrolled in a humanities seminar at John Marshall College of Criminal Justice. The course is supposed to be unstructured, taking whatever turn the interests and concerns of the participants seem to demand, but the very existence of a reading list is a signal to the street-wise, war-experienced cops that a structure is already implied and that they are being conned. Throughout the episode, the flat certainties of the policemen are contrasted with the lack of purpose and definition of the humanist and the psychologist who are team-teaching the course (421-6).

The same kind of polarity dominates the political theme of *The Investigation*. Joe Peters' superior, Captain Tim Neary, wants to be police commissioner, a post he can have only if the incumbent district attorney is defeated in the upcoming mayoralty primary. Joe consequently becomes involved in the plotting and counter-plotting of departmental politics, which goes on throughout the investigation of the murder of the Keeler boys, but he takes the politicking in stride, considering it something of a sham in comparison with the realities of his own imperiled marriage and his commitment to determining the guilt or innocence of Kitty Keeler (29, 197-8).

The theme of the genuine versus the phony in *False Witness* is merged with the general atmosphere of artificiality, and it is realized especially in the guileful efforts of the television people. It reaches its climax in the scene in which Bobby Jones, certain that he has found Sanderalee Dawson's attacker, sets up a confrontation between the two, the whole episode carefully stage-managed by the newswoman Gloria Nichols. As the confrontation develops, Gloria calmly dramatizes the scene for the benefit of the television audience, ordering the cameras to close in on the surprised anguish of the suspect and the mutilated face of Sanderalee Dawson, as if from a prepared script. The scenario is ruined for Bobby, however, when geniune emotions intervene: he is shot by Sanderalee Dawson and dies on the way to the hospital (237-40).

Commentators on Uhnak's narrative technique almost invariably praise her solid professionalism and her faithful portrayals of the police world. They are almost unanimous, though, in their criticism of her prose style, especially in regard to her addiction to cliches, her over-emphasis of the obvious and her tendency to make three adjectives do the work of one. More than one reviewer has taken exception to her handling of characters and scenes as being more appropriate to the slick facility of television writing than to serious fiction.[6]

Uhnak's maturity as a writer becomes increasingly evident in her ability to create plausible characters. With the exception of Christie herself, the series people in the Opara trilogy are stereotypes: Casey Reardon is the consistent bully who browbeats his subordinates and assaults his equals and superiors; Marty Ginsburg is invariably the Jewish comedian; Stoner Martin is uniformly noble; Nora Opara is always patient and understanding. In *Law and Order*, however, the characters begin to develop a new dimensionality that becomes apparent when we compare the complexity of Aaron Levine, the Jewish policeman in that novel, with the superficiality of Marty Ginsburg in the Opara stories: Levine not only has depth and complexity as a character but undergoes fundamental changes as the story progresses.

At the same time, Uhnak has from the first declined to stereotype her criminals as monsters. The perpetrator in each of the Opara stories is as much victim as villain: Murray Rogoff in *The Bait* suffered a head injury that was responsible for his becoming a psychopath; the mother of Eddie Champion in *The Witness* tried to kill him when he was three years old, with the result that he was so covered with scars that the other children called him "Frankenstein"; Elena Vargas, in *The Ledger*, experienced a need to belong that was eventually satisfied only by her involvement in the world of crime. The theme of the villain-as-victim comes through most strongly in *The Investigation*, in the complexity of paradoxes that surround the person of Kitty Keeler. Uhnak abandoned this design in *False*

Witness, where no extenuations are offered in the murderer's defense.

Uhnak's worst habit as a mystery writer is her tendency to concoct situations that are specious to the point of contrivance, the most obvious example being the intentional misdirection in *False Witness,* where the reader is led to believe that Mrs. Cohen's curse, "Damn you for all time, you have destroyed my family" (203), is directed at Lynn Jacobi. The impression is reinforced twice, once in Lynn's ill-advised public reply (219) and again in her account of the incident to Lucy Capella (226). It is not until the Epilogue, when the point of view is away from Lynn Jacobi, that we learn the identity of the object of the curse, who also turns out to be the culprit (247-8). This kind of auctorial sleight-of-hand was conventional with the writers of the puzzle-stories of an earlier generation, but it is strikingly out of place in the harsh atmosphere of *False Witness.*

Much of the contrived quality arises out of a tendency to squeeze too much juice out of a potentially dramatic situation. In *The Ledger,* for example, Christie Opara blunders into the hands of the syndicate boss Enzo Giardino, who sends his hood Tonio LoMarco off with her with instructions to "take care of her" (177), but Christie tricks LoMarco and sends him to the hospital for stitches in his head (178-9). All of which is handled with a reasonable degree of plausibility, but when, on the next page, the sinister Giardino calls the tough Casey Reardon to threaten to have Christie arrested for assault and battery (180-1), the reader may feel that the writer is laying it on a bit thick. The same inclination to staginess is manifest in the scene in *The Investigation,* in which Joe Peters calls upon the dying Alfredo Veronne, whose career in organized crime has been submerged under the memory of his philanthropies to the extent that the priests and well-wishers who surround his death-bed are preparing him for near-sainthood. Joe whispers a devastating threat into the ear of the aged gangster, who points a finger at Joe, cries "Jesus Christ," and dies. "He saw God," a relative screams. "He called out the Savior's name with his last breath!" (333), whereupon the sensitive reader may wish the author had left well enough alone.

Dorothy Uhnak is a sufficiently inventive writer, though she does show a tendency to re-cycle her fictional situations. A favorite circumstance is this one: in an election year, the district attorney plans to resign and make a try for higher office; in order to insure the election of a designated successor, he appoints a favored assistant to the post of acting district attorney, who will then enjoy the advantage of incumbency in his/her campaign for election as permanent DA. This situation appears first at the conclusion of *The Ledger,* where Casey Reardon is in line to make the attempt (216). It provides the setting for the political theme of

The Investigation, in which Joe Peters is drawn into the conspiracy to upset the DA's plans to establish his hand-picked sitting incumbent (69). It appears again in *False Witness,* in which Lynn Jacobi is being groomed to succession as interim district attorney, with a good prospect for election (30,47). The situation has been repeated to the extent that it has become a standard of the Uhnak plot. Character types also tend to recurrence, like the beautiful lonely woman drawn into criminal involvements (Elena Vargas in *The Ledger,* Kitty Keeler in *The Investigation*), and the bold, brash television newswoman: Karen Day of *Law and Order* is revived in the person of Gloria Nichols of *False Witness,* an evocation of Karen Day after tutoring by a barracuda.

Another trademark of Uhnak's stories is the open-ended conclusion. The basic mystery is always solved, but a big question is left unanswered. Earlier we called attention to the ending of *The Ledger* (which concludes the Christie Opara trilogy), in which there is a suggestion that Christie and Casey Reardon may be entering a physical love-relationship. As Reardon leaves Christie at the hotel while he goes off to clear up some unfinished business, he asks if she will wait in his room for his return. "Ya never know, Mr. Reardon," is Christie's reply. "Guess you'll just have to wait and see" and the story ends (224). The absence of finality is even more strongly felt at the end of *Law and Order,* where the lasting effectiveness of Brian O'Malley's cleanup of the NYPD is still in question, along with the possibility of Brian's reconciliation with his son Patrick, who remains unconvinced that his father's way is best but is willing to suspend judgment (512). *The Investigation* ends with a resolution of the problem of Kitty Keeler's guilt, but the reader is never told whether Kitty took Joe's advice to accept the district attorney's deal for a lesser charge or whether Joe and his wife Jen are finally reconciled: Joe leaves for Florida, determined that those two decisions are in the hands of Kitty and Jen (344). Lynn Jacobi of *False Witness* flies down to the Bahamas after the ordeal of the Sanderalee Dawson case, her career possibly ruined and herself the object of a lawsuit, though she is now in possession of evidence that will clear her (243-5). This time, however, Uhnak varies her technique a little with a complete resolution of the mystery in an epilogue, a scene not witnessed by Lynn Jacobi and hence outside the stream of the narrative (247-8). The suggestion left with the reader is that, although mysteries may be solved and criminals brought to justice, there is no such thing as attainment of ultimate finality.

Most writers of popular fiction, when they achieve one big success, tend to capitalize upon it by either extending the triumph into a series or repeating the successful formula in subsequent stories. Dorothy Uhnak has purposely refused to do either, in spite of the fact that two of her books have become impressive best-sellers. The Christie Opara trilogy could have been continued through a series of ten or twenty stories, but she chose to terminate it after *The Ledger* and to undertake a history that covered more than three decades and encompassed the totality of a big city police department. When she returned to the police procedural format, she introduced a theme of passionate involvement and moral relativism that overshadowed the conventional framework of mystery and detection. *The Investigation* could easily have been extended into a series, but once again Uhnak refused to capitalize on success, choosing instead to produce, in *False Witness,* a harsh tale of human entanglement that almost becomes a study of pathological emotions.

Undoubtedly, one reason for her varied approach is that her interest is not primarily detection or mystery, but people, who must be considered as human beings apart from the crimes they commit or those committed against them. In an interview several years ago, Uhnak explained how, when she was a policewoman, she would go home and write a story about every person she arrested: "My writing was a way for me to come to terms with my working experience."[7] Which may explain why she has refused to fall into a mold: people are, after all, hard to categorize and impossible to stylize.

Notes

[1]The following is a chronological list of Uhnak's books, including the editions cited in this study:

Policewoman (New York: Simon and Schuster, 1964)
The Bait (New York: Simon and Schuster, 1968)
The Witness (New York: Simon and Schuster, 1969)
The Ledger (New York: Simon and Schuster, 1970)
Law and Order (New York: Simon and Schuster, 1973)
The Investigation (New York: Simon and Schuster, 1977)
False Witness, Book Club Edition (New York: Simon and Schuster, 1981)

[2]Review of *The Ledger, The Armchair Detective,* 13 (Fall 1980), 292.

[3]See, for example, Carol Cleveland, "Dorothy Uhnak," in *Twentieth Century Crime and Mystery Writers,* ed. John M. Reilly (New York: St. Martin's Press, 1980), pp. 1403-4; Chris Steinbrunner and Otto Penzler, "Dorothy Uhnak," in *Encyclopedia of Mystery and Detection* (New York: McGraw-Hill, 1976), p. 395; Marion Meade, "Madame Sleuth Confesses," *McCall's,* July 1971, p. 43; Raymond O. Sokolov, "Seven Who Do the Whodunits," *Newsweek,* 22 March 1971, p. 103.

[4]Dorothy Uhnak, "Visualizing Fiction on Paper," in *The Writer's Handbook,* ed. A.S. Burach (Boston: The Writer, 1976), p. 80.

[5]Good discussions of the problem of "reality" in the police procedural may be found in Hillary Waugh, "The Police Procedural," in *The Mystery Story,* ed. John Ball (Del Mar: University of California-San Diego, 1976), pp. 163-187; Lillian O'Donnell, "Routines and Rules for the Police Procedural," *The Writer,* 91, No. 1 (January 1978), 17-19; and Collin Wilcox, "Writing and Selling the Police Procedural Novel," *The Writer,* 89, No. 1 (January 1976), 20-2, 46.

[6]For example: Carol Cleveland, "Dorothy Uhnak," p. 1403; Christopher Lehmann-Haupt, rev. of *Law and Order, New York Times,* 4 May 1973, p. 35; Webster Schott, rev. of *Law and Order, New York Times Book Review,* 27 May 1973; p. 6; Barbara Gelb, rev. of *The Investigation, New York Times Book Review,* 21 August 1977, pp. 14-15; and Margo Jefferson, rev. of *The Investigation, Newsweek,* 22 August 1977, pp. 70 D-F.

[7]Raymond O. Sokolov, "Seven Who Do The Whodunits," p. 103.

Lillian O'Donnell

Lillian O'Donnell

1920	Lillian Udvardy born March 15 in Trieste, Italy, to Dr. Zoltan D. and Maria (Busutti) Udvardy
	Attended first grade at Notre Dame de Sion in Trieste, then Sacred Heart Academy in New York
1939	Attended American Academy of Dramatic Arts, New York City
1941	Appeared in Broadway production of *Pal Joey*
1943	Became first woman stage manager for production of *Private Lives* starring Ruth Chatterton and Ralph Forbes
1941-1954	Directed *Rosemarie, The Merry Widow* for Schubert Organization, New York City. Appeared on live television in *Danger, Suspense, Westinghouse Theater, Philco Playhouse, Robert Montgomery Show.* Appeared on Broadway and on tour with Ruth Chatterton, Elizabeth Berguer, Paul Lukas, Jane Cowl, Diana Barrymore
1954	Married J. Leonard O'Donnell
1960	First mystery novel published, *Death on the Grass* (Tennis, one of O'Donnell's special interests, provides the setting.)
1972	First Norah Mulcahaney mystery novel published, *The Phone Calls* (Novel used as basis for French movie, *The Night Caller,* starring Jean Paul Belmondo)
1977	First Mici Anhalt mystery novel published, *Aftershock*
1980	Third Mici Anhalt mystery published (currently under option for television), *Wicked Designs*
1981	Twentieth mystery novel published, *The Children's Zoo* (seventh Norah Mulcahaney novel)

Lillian O'Donnell

Neysa Chouteau and Martha Alderson

Lillian O'Donnell's first mystery novel, *Death on the Grass,* was published in 1960. Her twentieth mystery, *The Children's Zoo,* was published in 1981.[1] The books fall rather naturally into three groups: the ten books she wrote before she developed a series protagonist, the seven books that feature Norah Mulcahaney of the New York Police Department and the three books that feature Mici Anhalt of the New York State Crime Compensation Board.

O'Donnell has employed a variety of forms and generally has worked fairly closely within the conventions of the form. That she works within conventional frameworks is appropriate to her greatest strength, that of storyteller. Almost all of O'Donnell's works are fast-paced and suspenseful.

In spite of her adherence to conventional format and pace, however, there have been two major changes in O'Donnell's novels. One major change has been in her treatment of women. O'Donnell could be classified as a "woman's writer" in two senses. Most of her earlier works carry a strong romantic thread which is presumed to appeal especially to women readers. With the introduction of Norah Mulcahaney, the books move into women's issues, although O'Donnell states that she was not conscious of such a trend.[2]

The other major change is in the author's purpose. Her early books are simply entertainment. Beginning with the first Norah Mulcahaney book, a sense of involved moral concern replaces the abstract morality of the traditional mystery story. By *The Children's Zoo* (1981), the sense of moral outrage is so strong that the reader is left with a sense of unease rather than with the simple satisfation of having completed a fast-paced story.

The Pre-Norah Mulcahaney Books

O'Donnell's previous careers include those of actress, dancer and the first woman stage manager in the history of the New York theater. Some of the biographies given in the novels also state, "after marriage, she turned to writing novels." From this information, it is easy to imagine an intelligent, energetic woman who has given up a career for marriage restlessly seeking an outlet for her talent. Writing mystery novels could have presented a highly appropriate stay-at-home occupation because it allowed her to employ the devices she had learned in the theater, such as mutually accepted conventions and carefully constructed plot, setting and pace. In her early books, it almost seems as though O'Donnell began by focusing on the devices that make a mystery story work. Then, as she gained mastery over the devices, she developed fuller characterizations and settings, although it took several novels for the characters to move away from the somewhat stock characters one might expect to be sent out from central casting.

Romance is front and center in all of the pre-Noah Mulcahaney books, although not all of the romances are of the happy-ending variety. Women are the main characters in most of the books, but all of the sleuths are men.

Six of O'Donnell's first eight books are in the classical mode, using such devices as a limited number of suspects, a trap for the murderer and a gathering of the suspects in which the detective reveals the murderer. For example, in *Death on the Grass* (1960), suspects are limited to people who could have been in the players' area at Forest Hills. In *Death Blanks the Screen* (1961), only a person who was on the set for the television show could have been the murderer. Generally, the clues are provided fairly, but an exception is *Babes in the Woods* (1965) in which facts provided in the courtroom scene were not available to the reader earlier (although the groundwork was well laid).

While working within the classical framework, O'Donnell did not always develop the vivid character, plot twist, or mood that can make a book memorable, but she soon maintained a fast pace that makes the books very readable. In the third book *Death Schuss* (1963), the story starts fast and, toward the end, breaks into almost as many twists as the Seven Turns of the Devil's Whip ski run in the story. The snowbound castle setting, with the bilingual ski fete which triggers the climax also adds considerable flavor to the story.

O'Donnell's fourth book *Murder Under the Sun* (1964) is even more readable. The characters, with the exception of Juan Ortiz, the villain, are still out of central casting, but they are more fully drawn and the several romantic threads are more complex and realistic. O'Donnell used another exotic setting, Puerto Rico, and did a nice job of evoking a sense of place through people, as when Juan Ortiz feels pride as he drives down Avenida Ponce de Leon and thinks the men of the New York Police Academy should see it and "they'd change their minds about his country" (39).

Later, Peggy Hoyt is bemused by the stiff smile of the veterinarian's receptionist until she learns the reason.

> In an unguarded moment, the girl smiled, whole-heartedly, lips parted, before she undulated out. And Peggy winced. No wonder she hid those teeth: they were the blackened stunted teeth of poverty (71).

By touches such as these, O'Donnell brought forth the human dimension of the contrast between luxurious tourist facilities and local poverty.

A first clue to O'Donnell's moral stance also appeared in *Sun*.

> But the hint of a sneer irritated Peggy. She admired what the Puerto Ricans had done, were doing. She had come to the island expecting indolence and stupidity, prepared to excuse it on the grounds of climate and lack of education; but found instead vitality and ambition, in fact—"Operation Bootstrap" (24).

O'Donnell's later work is permeated with respect for the working class and indignation at those who would denigrate or exploit them.

In O'Donnell's first five books, she relied heavily on love and glamour to enhance the plots. In four of the books, the heroines are breathless young virgins who manage to find Mr. Right while Mr. Right is either helping solve the crime or actually solving it. Three of the heroines are actresses and one is a tennis champion. The romances are enhanced by being set in Puerto Rico, the theater, Forest Hills, or the snowy wonderland of *Schuss*.

In her sixth book, *Babes in the Woods* (1965), O'Donnell made great strides in both mood and characterization. In *Babes*, Florence Hopwood is a beautiful woman and a mediocre dancer. Her greatest asset, her beauty, will soon fade. She marries Wallace Avery because she thinks he is a well-to-do-business man. He isn't. Up to this point, Florence seems not unkind and willing to work hard. She is mercenary and manipulative, using sex to get what she wants, but she is also willing to give for what she gets. As death begins to strike her four stepchildren, young attorney Jason Cluet gets involved. We then begin to see Florence Avery through his eyes. Through Jason's eyes, Florence becomes more exotic, more complex, perhaps capable of murder.

For the first time in ODonnell's works, there is no glamour in place, occupation, or circumstance. Unremitting ordinariness becomes oppressive or even sinister. As the setting moves to Wally's cheap summer cottage, even the police chief finds the location unnerving:

> But as he stepped inside the tunnel of trees he was not prepared for the sudden darkness, nor for the utter desolation (99).

In *Babes,* O'Donnell used characters from a fairy tale, children and a hated stepmother. She nicely added a tantalizing ambiguity to their roles and further enhanced the story with a grubby pedestrian background that carries its own horror.

The fairy tale element is even more specific in O'Donnell's sixth book, *The Sleeping Beauty Murders* (1967). The setting and most of the characters are quite realistic. The opening situation, as a beautiful young girl is awakened from a coma by a single-minded suitor, is so compelling that one hardly notices there has been no murder. O'Donnell based the story on the Sleeping Beauty legend and did an outstanding job in first setting the mood of the fairy tale. The action then unfolds as a natural consequence of the fact that all of the characters are in thrall to the legend and the mood is successfully sustained to the conclusion.

By 1967, O'Donnell had become quite adept at the romantic mystery (*Schuss, Sun, Player*). She also had moved into richer, more complex stories with *Babes* and *Sleeping,* which combined fairy tale elements with a realistic setting. In her next three books, she moved in three new directions.

The Tachi Tree (1968) is a classic Gothic in which Lydia Lyall, a sheltered impoverished orphan, goes to a distant place to meet a sexy man who may be a hero or a villain. *Dive into Darkness* (1971) is a suspense-chase story as Rosemary Remsen tries to deliver secret papers to her husband who mysteriously moves ahead of her from Mexico City to Cuernavaca to Taxco to Acapulco. Both of these novels are well written and fast-paced, but neither has a surprising twist or other distinctive touch. *The Tachi Tree* does have one disconcerting lapse that indicates carelessness on the part of either the author or her editor. Lydia makes a classic trap-the-murderer statement, "It doesn't matter, does it, as long as Phil thinks so?" (186). The only problem is that Phil is dead.

The Face of the Crime (1968) is a police procedural. The police procedural was not a completely new form for O'Donnell as she had blended a romance with the procedural in *Death of a Player* (1964). *Face,* however, did mark a significant new direction for O'Donnell. Both women in the story, actress Mary Hudgin (or Marietta Shaw), the victim, and Medical Examiner Diane Quain are clearly portrayed as competent and committed professionals. *Face* is also an unusual story. The most interesting character, the one who dominates the story, is the victim, Marietta Shaw. The officer on the case is half in love with her, so the novel is somewhat evocative of Vera Caspary's *Laura. Face* is significantly different, however, because Marietta Shaw is irrevocably dead.

Hillary Waugh has pointed out that the police procedural can become the equivalent of a daytime serial in its use of continuing characters whom the audience comes to know.[3] The two pre-Norah Mulcahaney police procedurals introduce a number of characters who will become familiar in the Norah books.

In *Player,* O'Donnell used one of her favorite main characters, the innocent young actress who happens to be in the wrong place at the wrong time. The male lead is Jim Felix. Felix is more realistically and fully drawn than any of O'Donnell's previous detectives. Later, Felix appears in all the Norah Mulcahaney books as Norah's boss.

Two of the minor characters of *Player* who will appear again and again are the gloomy detective Roy Brennan and the crusty eccentric Chief Medical Examiner, Dr. Asa Osterman. Also appearing is darkly handsome Detective Joseph Capretto who is established as quite a ladies' man. Joe appears again in *Face* in a more extended and sympathetic role as young David Link's knowledgeable and unflappable superior. In fact, he is appealing enough to eventually become Norah's husband.

Jim Felix also returns in *Face*, although he does not play the main role. The featured police officer is David Link, a rookie.

The character of Norah Mulcahaney apparently evolved rather naturally from these two earlier novels. In discussing the police procedural, O'Donnell described the process as follows:

> In my own instance, I started with a pro—Lieutenant James Felix of Homicide North. Jim Felix had men and women under him and above him. They began to take shape. I began to know them and like them. Each one in turn had his or her book, but "the lieut" remained throughout in major or minor capacity as required. I chose the detective to fit the crime. My novel, *The Face of the Crime,* dealt with the murder of a movie star trying for a comeback. My detective was a recent recruit, young, impressional, and half in love with the actress. When I became personally incensed over the epidemic of obscene telephone calls to lonely, frightened women, I decided that the story begged for the empathy of a woman to investigate and Norah Mulcahaney appeared.[4]

The Norah Mulcahaney Books

If Norah was created in part as a result of personal indignation, she was also created in part as a result of personal admiration. O'Donnell was riding in a police car with two policewomen during the first blackout in New York City. O'Donnell writes of her reaction as the women carried out their duties:

> I was impressed, and at the same time I was shocked to realize that if these two officers had been men I would have taken their efficiency and composure for granted.[5]

A remark made by one of the officers led directly to Norah:

> That set me straight. They thought of themselves as officers: gender didn't enter into it. At that moment, I made the decision to use a policewoman as heroine in a story—sometime.[5]

Thus Norah Mulcahaney was born as a result of two real-life situations: an epidemic of obscene phone calls and the first New York blackout.

Norah's cases continued to follow the headlines closely, or even to anticipate them: housewives' prostitution rings in *Don't Wear Your Wedding Ring* (1973), rape in *Dial 577 R-A-P-E* (1974), black market babies in *The Baby Merchants* (1975), crimes against the elderly in *Leisure Dying* (1976), job discrimination against women in *No Business Being a Cop* (1978), and juvenile crime in *The Children's Zoo* (1981). They also anticipated or closely followed many developments in the New York Police Department. Norah joined Homicide in 1972. In real life, women didn't make it until 1978.[6] The special unit for senior citizens in *Leisure* and the one for combatting rape in *Dial* are closely related to real ones (*Dial* v-vi, 183).

George Dove has identified five conventions of the police procedural: the hostile public, interservice hostility, the overworked force, the police officer with family problems and the young cop.[7] O'Donnell has used all of these conventions, usually emphasizing one convention over others in a particular book.

In *The Phone Calls* (1972) Norah is very much the young cop, as David Link had been in *Face*. When the story begins, Norah is 28 years old and she has been on the force a year. She is impetuous and outspoken.

> Norah watched and listened, diffident at this first meeting with superiors.... (104)

> She started for the door, but she just couldn't let go without one more try.
> "Lieutenant?"
> "What is it, Norah?"
> "Well, sir, everything you said is perfectly logical and rational...."
> "Thank you."
> Joe raised his eyes to the ceiling and groaned.
> "That's what's the matter with it."
> Oh, no! Joe thought. O, no! He wondered if there were any way to stop her (105-106).

She also fails to follow procedure in a few instances. As a result of being careless with a suspect she trusts, she loses her gun. She learns rapidly, however, that police officers work as a team (a basic characteristic of the police procedural):

> Norah called the lieutenant right away. She'd learned by now that playing a lone hand was for amateurs and fools (21).

By the end of the book, she is promoted to detective. When she thanks Felix, he responds,

> "As long as you realize you have a lot to learn."
> "Oh, I do, Lieutenant."
> "On the other hand, you'll have plenty of teachers; we've never had a woman on the squad before." Then Felix grinned broadly. "I don't suppose I have to worry about you being squelched, though" (253).

Norah does not stay a young cop, of course. By the sixth Norah Mulcahaney book, *No Business,* Norah is a veteran:

> Tall as a fashion model, but far from gaunt, Norah Mulcahaney Capretto was thirty-five and at her peak—in energy, confidence, skill, and looks (7).

Although O'Donnell uses all of the conventions of the police procedural, she relies most heavily on the convention of the cop with family problems. Every Norah Mulcahaney book has a family problem subplot. Family problems revolve primarily around Norah's relationship with her father Patrick Mulcahaney, with Joe and to a lesser extent with Joe's mother Signora Emilia Capretto.

Pat Mulcahaney is one of the honest working people whom O'Donnell admires. She describes both Pat and Norah:

> Pat Mulcahaney understood his daughter well because she was like him: strong, self-reliant, to the point of stubbornness sometimes (*Phone,* 21).

In *Phone* the family problem lies in Pat Mulcahaney's efforts to get Norah married. In attempting to set up a romance for Norah, Pat actually puts her life in danger because he has been set up by a psychotic murderer who wants to use Norah as a pipeline to police operations.

In *Wedding* family problems do not bear upon the mystery, but they sustain a separate story line. The problem is that Joe Capretto and Norah have started dating. This does not please Joe's mother.

> Lately Signora Emilia Capretto had taken to dropping dark hints about the selfishness of career women, their lack of interest in homemaking, their fickleness and restlessness. Women in police work had come in for particularly tart comment (16).

Patrick Mulcahaney is just as reluctant for Norah to date Joe.

> "Now that sergeant is a nice enough feller, getting on in years, of course, but. . . ."
>
> "Oh, Dad." Norah laughed.
>
> "But he's spoiling your chances."
>
> "That's not so. Dad, why don't you like Joe?"
>
> "I've got nothing against the sergeant."
>
> "Why do you keep calling him. . . ."
>
> "Except that he's a ladies' man" (151).

It is true, of course, that Joe is getting on in years and that he is a ladies' man. Joe is 38 years old and he has been firmly established as a Latin lover from his first appearance in *Player*. As the story ends, however, Joe makes it clear that he intends to continue seeing Norah.

In *Dial* the family problem again is separate from the story line. Joe proposes and Norah accepts. She has, however, to come to understand that the Joe of old—a playboy who would never settle down, according to Patrick Mulcahaney (20)—is not the Joe who wants her to meet his family and who suddenly tries for promotion in order to have more to offer her. An old flame who turns up in hot pursuit of Joe makes Norah question Joe's motives and commitment. Her own difficulty in communicating her feelings deepens the problem.

In *Merchants* family problems are much more complex. In fact, one critic complained that in this novel the domestic story takes precedence over the mystery story to the detriment of pace.[8] Actually, the domestic story is very much a part of the mystery story. The plot is also unusually complex in that Joe's case is a fully developed story, Norah's case is a fully developed story and the two cases intertwine with each other and with the family problems.

The family problem stems from Norah and Joe's attempts to become parents. Norah endures parental pressure, guilt as a devout Roman Catholic who has been on the pill and ambivalence about her commitment to parenthood. She decides, without consulting Joe, to adopt. This decision leads her to the gray market for babies.

Pat Mulcahaney meddles again, finding a boy who is available for adoption. Joe and Norah take the plunge. Almost immediately, they are threatened by a phone call. "Tell the lieutenant the adoption won't stand up. Tell him if he wants to keep the kid, he should lay off" (57). Pat has been set up again. Before the final unhappy resolution, severe strains develop between Joe and Norah. Norah's inability to share her feelings and ideas contributes to the domestic problem. Signora Emilia's character is developed more fully as she shows affection for Norah and exhibits shrewd thinking in realizing why Norah gave up the child. By the end of *Merchants,* Norah and Pat are much the same, but the new Joe is more firmly established as a good family man and Signora Emilia has shown new depth.

Family problems also constitute an important subplot in *Leisure.* Norah is now a sergeant. Joe is head of Fourth Homicide and Norah works for him. As the story develops, Norah's career goes very well, but she inadvertently endangers Joe's career. He is forced to step down temporarily as head of Fourth Homicide. Norah then works secretly to restore Joe's command. Joe is crushed because of her sercrecy and moves out. The story ends with Norah and Joe considerably more sophisticated about the rewards and problems of a two-career family when the careers are more nearly equal. Signora Emilia has emerged yet more clearly as a shrewd, salty and funny lady.

In *No Business,* Joe goes to Italy with his mother, leaving Norah to figure much more strongly as hero. The nature of the family problem also changes sharply as befits the much more sophisticated Norah. Norah suddenly finds herself strongly attracted to the man she is working with, Captain Sebastian Honn. When Norah eventually suspects Honn of murder, the sexual tension is broken. Still, a Norah who could even consider an affair is a much more complex person than the old-fashioned Irish-Catholic virgin of the first novels.

Zoo, pubished in 1981, also examines some family problems. It relies far more heavily, however, on the police procedural convention of public hostility. O'Donnell also used this convention in *Leisure* when bad publicity over five unexplained deaths forced Joe to give up command of his homicide unit temporarily. In *Zoo,* the hostility is more direct. Norah endures a hostile crowd, a police station picket line against her "brutality," a barrage of unfavorable publicity, and a petition calling for her removal from the force.

All the police procedural themes are present in the Norah Mulcahaney books to a certain extent. The convention of the over-worked force is used in several books. In *Leisure* Norah's long hours compared to Joe's relative inactivity put a strain on their relationship that wasn't there before. In *Merchants* Norah sees the long irregular hours as a real problem in planning for a career and motherhood.

O'Donnell shows the overworked force convention as presenting more of a problem for a policewoman than for a policeman. The words of a doctor who had been engaged to a policewoman illustrate this:

> But a doctor, who has an unpredictable schedule himself, to be married to a woman who works the crazy hours you people take for granted . . . . It's just not

> feasible. I want a wife I can count on, who'll be home when I get home. I want her there and waiting (*No Business*, 35).

Another convention of the police procedural is interservice rivalry. Cops usually resent other cops when they feel the other cops are invading their territory. Rivalry and hostilty are directed at outsiders, while there are strong loyalties within the group. Because Norah is a woman, however, some male cops feel that she is invading their territory, or forsaking her own territory, even when they are on the same team. In *Wedding* Norah runs into three different sets of problems because she is a woman. From Officer Barnstable, she draws flat hostility:

> "I didn't know who you were, *Miss*."
> That was a deliberate insult! (14)

From David Link she encounters overprotectiveness. He goes to the lieutenant to have Norah withdrawn from a particularly gruesome murder case.

> "We try to look after you, Norah, all of us. You're like a kid sister to us."
>
> "That's nice. Really nice, David. Except that I'm a Detective Third Grade—same as you." She let it sink in. "So don't pick my cases for me anymore. Okay?"
>
> "Okay, Kid ... uh, Norah" (39).

To Assistant District Attorney Dan Comer, her sex represents opportunity:

> Breaking the ring with the help of a woman detective would mean points with Women's Lib (117).

This unfortunate but realistic picture has not changed much five years later. In *No Business* Norah once again meets an officer who tries to spare her from viewing a grisly scene. Norah, of course, will not be stopped:

> He didn't like the answer and, Norah suddenly realized, he didn't like her either. It pulled her up for a moment. Policewomen had not gained the acceptance in the department that women thought they had. Discrimination was still practiced subtly and not so subtly. However, Norah felt she personally had established her own credentials as a detective and, particularly since she'd made sergeant, rarely ran into resistance anymore. When she did, as now, she ignored it; she'd learned it was the best way (9).

Sexual discrimination is not just a problem for Norah. It also affects Joe in *Leisure*:

> "Oh, some of the men have been making cracks. It doesn't mean anything."
> "What kind of cracks?"
> He shrugged."Do I resent your appointment? How do I feel about getting all that publicity? Who gives the orders at home? Like that. Most of it is good natured."
> "Most of it?" (72).

Norah comes to realize that she too is guilty of discrimination. Her relationships with her sister officers broaden and deepen with each novel. In *Phone* the only other woman officer mentioned is May Cuddahay who had been on the force for years without being promoted. In *Wedding* Norah feels both professional and personal jealousy for Marianne Beck, the police officer who is selected to pose as a prostitute in the case Norah is on. By *Dial,* however, Norah reaches a much deeper relationship with some of her sister officers. She reluctantly accepts the assignment with the newly formed Rape Analysis and Investigation squad:

> The Rape Analysis and Investigation squad was composed entirely of women and headed by a woman—would they resent her? Would she be able to work with them? To be relegated to a squad whose principal function appeared to be follow-up interviews of rape victims, backtracking the work of other officers at that, seemed almost a demotion. That was pure snobbishness; Norah knew it and tried to suppress it, but it persisted (61).

The feeling is not easy for Norah to shed.

> Once again Norah was impressed that Lieutenant Wilburn was up on everything that was happening, yet if it had been Lieutenant Felix, she would have taken it for granted. She continued to underrate Lee Wilburn for no other reason than that she was a woman, and Norah of all people shouldn't be doing that (93).

Norah does, of course, develop respect for her sister officers. In *Leisure,* when Norah is allowed to choose officers for her newly created senior citizens squad, Dolly Dollinger is one of the officers she chooses. Dolly also becomes a friend, someone Norah thinks of calling upon when she is lonely (178).

By *No Business,* women officers have become as multidimensional as men. Like the men, they are good, bad, or indifferent officers. Katie Chave didn't like her job. Pilar Nieves was a competent and enthusiastic officer who loved the challenge and variety of her work. (In another instance of author or editor carelessness, Norah states that Pilar had worked for her on the Senior Citizen squad. There is no mention of Pilar in *Leisure.*) Audrey Ochs was sensible, slow but reliable.

These women are victims of a killer who seems to be conducting a vendetta against women police officers, perhaps stemming from the class action suit that women officers had won against the police department. Norah, who "had never been an active women's libber" (71), becomes a leader in trying to protect both the rights and lives of sister officers. To complete the range of characterizations of the policewomen in *No Business,* two of the policewomen are crooked.

A fascinating aspect of the first six Norah novels is that Norah is living in real time. In the first Norah book, published in 1972, she is 28 years old. In *No Business,* published seven years later, she is 35 years old. If the true time pattern is continued in future books (and may there be many more!), O'Donnell may do all women a great service by showing that a woman in her fifties and sixties can be competent, courageous and interesting.

Women are well characterized in the Norah Mulcahaney books, including both women police officers and women criminals. The women who triggered the first Norah book *Phone,* however, were victims. *Dial* and *Leisure* also focus on women victims. It is, therefore, perhaps to be expected that among the most sympathetic characters are victims such as plucky Arabella Bloom of *Phone* and Gabriella Constante, the innocent rape victim who courageously rebuilds her life in *Dial.*

O'Donnell's concern for the elderly is as great as her concern for women. In *Leisure,* Horace Pruitt and Cordelia Youngbeck stand out as particularly warm portraits of intelligent, proud, self-reliant old people.

In counterpoint, teenagers appear in several books as villains and as symbols of decay in our society.

> "I don't know what bothers me more," Norah admitted, blue-gray eyes flashing. "I don't know whether it's that the victims are so old or that the criminals are so young."
>
> Joe sighed. "Both."
>
> "Children not only don't have respect for their elders, they're contemptuous of them. They choose them for victims because they're easy; they can't fight back. Which means that besides being criminals, the children are also cowards. And what does that say about us?" (*Leisure,* 20).

Teenagers are also portrayed negatively in the three Mici Anhalt books which appeared between *No Business* and *Zoo*. O'Donnell's dismay over what our children say about us is the subject matter for *Zoo*. The guard at the children's zoo in Central Park is killed when he interrupts three teenagers who are slaughtering the animals. Norah's niece Toni is violated by five girls using a coke bottle. The guard's death and her niece's violation are the triggering events which lead Norah to track down three teenaged boys who torture, steal and kill. O'Donnell's concerns about teenagers and by extension, our world, are expressed in several ways. How does crime affect the victim? As Joe's sister Lena tells Norah when it appears that the girls who attacked Toni may not be punished, Lena is concerned for what this unfairness will do to Toni:

> "I mean, we've brought her up, Jake and I, to understand right and wrong. To expect punishment for doing wrong. We've brought her up to respect others—their persons, their property, their feelings. Okay. What is this going to do to her moral sense? How is it going to influence the rest of her life?" (154).

O'Donnell also expresses a sense of helplessness. The boys' crimes cannot simply be blamed on the people who raised them.

> No matter how hard she tried, Norah could find nothing to excuse the boys, no extenuating circumstances. Peter Tomasiello had above-average intelligence and came from good, hard-working parents. Rex, perhaps neglected by his parents and overdisciplined by his grandfather, had certainly not lacked for love; his grandmother had showered it on him (193).

If teenaged crime cannot be blamed on parents, what then?

> Was this his idea of how the pros (criminals) did it? And where did he get it from? Books, movies, TV? Who was responsible for him and other youthful criminals? What dreadful contaminant in our society was producing these morally deformed children? (205).

O'Donnell may not have an answer to why it seems that "an atavistic strain had been spawned in this generation" (193), but she has a strong sense of what must be done. Regardless of the age of the criminal, crime should not go unpunished—

> ...the juvenile-justice system in trying to protect the child had given him license (137).

In New York, juveniles can now be tried as adults for certain violent crimes. The chilling news item that serves as an afterword to *Zoo* makes it clear, however, that the legal change alone is not enough. The headline reads, "For most violent teens, crime pays."

In *Zoo*, O'Donnell is still a story-teller. The pace is fast. Norah faces danger and personal crises. For the first time, however, there is no romantic story line. Further, the sense of despair over decay in our society is not limited to children. David Link, the idealistic young cop of *Face*, and Norah's trusted friend in the early books, has become corrupt. Small wonder, then, that O'Donnell ends the story like a preacher calling us to action. One wonders: Will the next Norah Mulcahaney book pull back to a more conventional story line, or move even more overtly into exhortation?

The Mici Anhalt Books

With *Aftershock*, published in 1977, O'Donnell introduced a new series character, Mici Anhalt. In turning to Mici, O'Donnell also turned to another set of mystery story conventions, those of the hard-boiled superhero who works outside the law enforcement system.

Mici is an investigator for the New York City office of the Crime Victims Compensation Bureau. Like her male counterparts, Mici is tough, but she has a heart of gold. Unlike most of the males, Mici's heart of gold does not beat beneath a gruff, hard-bitten exterior. She is beautiful and her golden heart is almost as obvious as her red-gold hair. Mici is active and risk-taking in the private-eye tradition. She is nearly run down by a car and nearly shot by the murderer in *Aftershock*. In *Falling Star* (1979), Mici is nearly raped and is threatened by the murderer. In *Wicked Designs* (1980), she is kidnapped. She is guilty of "breaking and entering" into a yacht. She also is nearly run down by a car—again. (Several careless repetitions and errors mar the Mici Anhalt books and *Zoo*.)

Mici (pronounced "Mitzi"), the subject of three novels to date, is a sophisticated woman. One gets the impression that O'Donnell turned to Mici Anhalt for a chance to write about a more sophisticated and romantic hero than the popular but matter-of-fact and faithfully married Norah Mulcahaney. Lovely Mici always turns men's heads. All of the novels include romantic interludes, some of which are satisfying if brief for Mici.

There are differences, however, in the way O'Donnell handles Mici as a romantic hero from the way she handles Norah. Norah meets Joe in the first book of the Norah Mulcahaney series. By the third book, they are engaged. Three books and two years may not seem like a speedy courtship in modern terms, but there is never really any question in the reader's mind that the match was meant to be.

In three books, Mici Anhalt has had three semi-serious romances but none that promises to be lasting. Thus, if a character's sex appeal ends when he or she settles down in a marriage, Mici Anhalt remains the ideal romantic hero. Mici's sex life is unresolved or is only temporarily resolved. This allows her a sort of feminine macho quality—ever open to a new encounter, never tied down.

O'Donnell's return to romance as a subplot, however, does not include a return to the lightness of some of the pre-Norah Mulcahaney novels. Mici can sparkle, but she is not a cute young thing such as Sally Pepper of *Screen* or Maggie Wellyn of *Player*. She never sports a comically woebegone face.

Mici has a more exotic background than Norah. She came to the New York City office of the Crime Victims Compensation Board after two years of dancing professionally; three years in Washington, D.C., with Robert Kennedy's staff; and, most recently, eight years at the Vera Institute of Justice. With Mici, O'Donnell also returns to more glamorous surroundings. Her suspects include an opera singer and a senator in *Aftershock;* a gubernatorial candidate, the son of a Mafia boss, and a gypsy in *Designs.* In *Falling* actors and actresses provide glitter and spice, particularly the first victim, Julia Schuyler, alcoholic daughter of a great star, who seems to be patterned after Diana Barrymore, John Barrymore's daughter.

In the Norah Mulcahaney novels, O'Donnell focuses an unusual amount of attention on the victims. With the Mici Anhalt series, the focus falls even more on victims because dealing with victims of crime is Mici's job. The stories are no longer concerned solely with tracking down the guilty; there is also a strong focus on protecting the innocent. In the afterword to *Aftershock,* O'Donnell states, "In the past, concern for justice for the criminal has led us to forget the victim. It's time to remember" (224).

Thus, in addition to the murder mystery and the subplot of Mici's love life, Mici's victim-clients provide another subplot as Mici tries to determine whether they are or aren't entitled to payment under the Crime Victims Compensation program. In *Aftershock,* a tennis pro is shot and paralyzed by a gang of teenagers on a subway and a retarded old man is beaten by a gunman in a holdup. In *Falling,* a witness to a crime is blinded. In *Designs,* a shopping-bag lady is set afire by three boys; a girl is raped and her forearms are cut off.

If the stories seem almost too gruesome to be realistic, unfortunately they probably are not. O'Donnell's source material seems to be the newspaper. The case of the girl whose forearms were cut off made headlines in 1977.

With Mici, as with Norah, fiction anticipates reality. When the first Mici book was written, little was being done for crime victims. Now, over half the states have victim assistance laws.

With O'Donnell's knack for topicality, Mici Anhalt fans might wonder about what will happen in the next book on two levels. First, what will happen with her love life? There is a possibility of a continuing romance with Tony Rygel (*Designs*), but their relationship promises to be stormy. Another possible attachment is with her supervisor Adam Dowd, whose alcoholic wife conveniently dies between books. There are no obvious sparks between them as between Dorothy Uhnak's Christy Opara and Casey Reardon, but the roles are similar. Second, will whatever is part of Mici's life in the next book be part of our lives the year after?

While O'Donnell's works break very conveniently into the three categories discussed here, there are certain threads that carry through all the books.

As befitting O'Donnell's prior careers, actors, actresses, and dancers figure strongly in most of the early books. They do not disappear in the Norah Mulcahaney books. In addition to references to Jim Felix's actress wife Maggie (originally from *Player*), theatrical people are important characters in *Leisure* and *Wedding*. The Mici Anhalt books return even more to the theatrical world. An opera singer is an important character in *Aftershock*. Mici's dancing skills save her life in the same book. *Falling* is built around theatrical people.

A great respect for working people is shown throughout O'Donnell's novels, from the receptionist in *Sun* through the Tomasiellos of *Zoo*.

While O'Donnell's works have always been essentially serious, she has also used touches of humor. The light touch of appealing humorous characters who appeared in earlier books, such as young Terrance Moore (*Grass*) and Miss Sarah Pepperidge (*Screen*), or humorous situations, such as Jim Felix's bemused encounters with famous actress Sybilla Lord (*Player*), remain in many of the Norah Mulcahaney and Mici Anhalt books. In *Wedding* the scene in which the virginal Norah has to catch a couple in the sex act is amusingly drawn. The scene with Signora Emilia, Joe, and Joe's date in *Leisure* is quite funny. In *No Business* there is an unusual, wonderfully humorous episode when a stakeout with Norah at the center backfires. There are also some humorous episodes in the Mici Anhalt books, such as Mici's attempt to host a dinner party while a drunken stranger is asleep on her couch (*Aftershock*). The humorous touches, however, are far more vital to the Norah Mulcahaney books because they soften Norah, keeping her from being too stuffy, too priggish. (A touch of humor might have helped alleviate the sense of dismay that permeates *Zoo*.)

O'Donnell's early female romantic protagonists seem to be quite the conventional helpless young things. Although they are bright and courageous, the crimes are solved by men and they are rescued from precarious situations by men. At this stage of her writing career, O'Donnell does not seem to be a feminist. Yet, even in the earliest book, sexual discrimination is touched upon:

> Did he care whether she won or lost? Dora wondered. Probably not. Men dismissed women's achievements lightly (*Grass*, 11).

In *Sleeping*, Elsa Meisen is a formidable woman. In *Dive*, Rosemary Remsen realizes that her husband did not want her to grow to be his equal.

In *Face,* Medical Examiner Diane Quain outthinks David Link several times and victim Marietta Shaw is protrayed as a fighter who asked no quarter. By the end of *Tachi,* Lydia Lyall is the rescuer rather than the rescued. The feminism of Norah and Mici is, then, the evolution of a point of view rather than a new outlook. Respect for women has always been a part of O'Donnell's work.

Careless touches in O'Donnell's last four books suggest that perhaps she has become too much at ease with her craft. As mentioned earlier, Mici is nearly run down by a car in the first Mici Anhalt book, *Aftershock,* and this device is repeated in the third book, *Designs.* In *Aftershock* a poodle is named Pinocchio; in *Designs* a poodle is named Pinocchio. In *Falling* Mici is 33 years old on page 17 and 34 years old on page 146. As Jane Bakerman has noted, in *Zoo* the description of the eye injury on page 2 is uncharacteristically awkward as the author speaks of "fluid material necessary to the eye's function" without ever identifying it.[9] Also, *Zoo* states that when Joe married he set himself to studying (8). Actually, he started studying before he proposed.

These lapses should not obscure the fact that over the years O'Donnell consistently has been willing to experiment, change and grow. From a wobbly beginning, she became quite adept at the light romantic suspense story. She then went on to new forms. She introduced Mici Anhalt after her most successful Norah Mulcahaney book.

Topicality has been a hallmark of O'Donnell's books. They, therefore, reflect a great deal of change. Sally Pepper of *Screen,* whose maiden aunt worries so about proprieties, is a world away from Mici Anhalt who is "neither a virgin nor promiscuous" (*Falling,* 107). Peggy Hoyt's unquestioning assumption that she will have to give up acting when she gets maried (*Sun*) contrasts sharply with Pilar Nieve's refusal to give up her work for her fiance (*No Business*). Yet the women are not that different from one another. They are all attempting to function as fully as they can within the context of their time and background. O'Donnell has always had respect for women. What has changed is that she has become a champion of women.

Becoming a champion of women is one great change in O'Donnell's work. Another great change is that she has moved from entertainer to preacher. Her first books were concerned only with giving the reader a pleasant few hours. Her latest books are deeply concerned with the state of the world.

All good preachers are also entertainers, of course, and O'Donnell is still an entertainer. While O'Donnell's purpose seems to have changed, certain aspects have remained constant: reliance on a theatrical background; the use of humor; respect for older people, working people and women; the periodic use of new forms; and, above all, the ability to tell a cracking good story.

Notes

[1]The editions of O'Donnell's works used for this study are listed below, preceded by the original date of publication. All quotations will be cited in the text using, where necessary for clarity, the abbreviation given after each entry.

1960 *Death on the Grass* (New York: Arcadia House, 1960). (*Grass*)
1961 *Death Blanks the Screen* (New York: Arcadia House, 1961). (*Screen*)
1963 *Death Schuss* (New York and London: Abelard Schuman, 1963). (*Schuss*)
1964 *Murder under the Sun* (New York and London: Abelard Schuman, 1964). (*Sun*)
1964 *Death of a Player* (New York and London: Abelard Schuman, 1964). (*Player*)
1965 *Babes in the Woods* (New York and London: Abelard Schuman, 1965). (*Babes*)
1967 *The Sleeping Beauty Murders* (New York and London: Abelard Schuman, 1967). (*Sleeping*)
1968 *The Face of the Crime* (New York and London: Abelard Schuman, 1968). (*Face*)
1968 *The Tachi Tree* (New York and London: Abelard Schuman, 1968). (*Tachi*)
1971 *Dive into Darkness* (New York: Abelard Schuman, 1971). (*Dive*)
1972 *The Phone Calls* (New York: Putnam, 1972). (*Phone*)
1973 *Don't Wear Your Wedding Ring* (New York: Putnam, 1973). (*Wedding*)
1974 *Dial 577-R-A-P-E* (New York: Putnam, 1974). (*Dial*)
1975 *The Baby Merchants* (New York: Putnam, 1975). (*Merchants*)
1976 *Leisure Dying* (New York: Putnam, 1976). (*Leisure*)
1977 *Aftershock* (New York: Putnam, 1977). (*Aftershock*)
1979 *No Business Being a Cop* (New York: Putnam, 1979). (*No Business*)
1979 *Falling Star* (New York: Putnam, 1979). (*Falling*)
1980 *Wicked Designs* (New York: Putnam, 1980). (*Designs*)
1981 *The Children's Zoo* (New York: Putnam, 1981). (*Zoo*)

[2]Lillian O'Donnell, "Norah Mulcahaney: New York's Finest," in *Murderess Ink*, ed. Dilys Winn (New York: Workman, 1979), p. 120.

[3]Hillary Waugh, "The Police Procedural," in *The Mystery Story*, ed. John Ball (San Diego: University Extension University of California), pp. 163-187.

[4]Lillian O'Donnell, "Routines and Rules for the Police Procedural," *The Writer*, February, 1978, pp. 19, 46.

[5]O'Donnell, "Norah Mulcahaney: New York's Finest," p. 119.

[6]O'Donnell, p. 120.

[7]George N. Dove, "Realism, Routine, Stubbornness and System," *The Armchair Detective*, 10 (April 1977), pp. 133, 137.

[8]Newgate Callendar, rev. of *The Baby Merchants*, by Lillian O'Donnell, *The New York Times Book Review*, 5 October, 1975, p. 47.

[9]Jane S. Bakerman, rev. of *The Children's Zoo* by Lillian O'Donnell, *The Mystery Fancier*, (6:(6:2) (March/April, 1982), pp. 39-40.

Craig Rice

1908	Born Georgiana Anne Randolph Craig in Chicago, 5 June, daughter of painter Harry (Bosco) Craig and Mary Randolph, daughter of a wealthy Chicago physician.
1914-1926	Lived with father's sister, Mrs. Elton Rice, in Fort Atkinson, Wisconsin, on a ranch in Okanagan County, Washington, and in San Diego. Privately educated by her Poe-loving uncle and a Jesuit missionary.
1926-1930	Tried poetry, novels and music in Chicago, while earning a living in journalism.
1931-1938	Chicago radio writer and producer. During the Chicago years she married three times and had three children.
1939	*Eight Faces at Three* published under name Craig Rice by Simon and Schuster, after rejection by twelve other publishers. For the next decade she will produce one to four mysteries a year, under three pen names, *Craig Rice, Michael Venning* and *Daphne Sanders.*
1941	*Trial By Fury*. Listed (with *Home, Sweet Homicide*) in Haycraft-Queen Mystery Bookcase. Moved to Santa Monica with fourth husband Lawrence Lipton. Wrote movie scripts, including *Home Sweet Homicide* (1946) and *The Underworld Story* (1950), from her short story "The Whipped.")
1949	*Innocent Bystander,* last novel for eight years, published. Committed to Camarillo State Hospital for chronic alcoholism.
1957	Died August 29, age 49, in Los Angeles. *Knocked for a Loop* published posthumously.

Craig Rice

Peggy Moran

By any ordinary concept of parenting, Craig Rice[1] was an orphan—a poignant fact of life she later alchemized into literary gold. Decades before runaway mothers became an almanac statistic and short weeks after the 1908 birth of Georgiana Anne, Mrs. Mary Randolph Craig parked her infant daughter with her husband's mother and rejoined husband Bosco abroad. The parents did put in an appearance for several years between Georgiana's third and sixth birthdays; they then departed, more or less permanently, for Europe and, later, the Orient. Harry Moscheim (Bosco) Craig was a painter whose imaginative talents extended to business; he dealt variously—and sometimes precariously—in tea, tin and iron. (The Tuesday brothers of *The Right Murder* pursued similar, if rougher, careers.) Bosco forsook Oriental ventures in 1941 and visited Craig—now a celebrity author with children of her own—shortly before his death.[1] In 1946, when her daughter made the cover of *Time Magazine* (the first mystery writer to be so recognized) Mrs. (Craig) Randolph (then living in Chicago) was quoted as saying that she and "George" were on very good terms, that she admired the novels and (though she hadn't seen her daughter for twenty-five years) that she probably wouldn't have time to visit her before leaving for Europe.[2]

Still, there are degrees and varieties of orphanings: Craig Rice was never an orphanage inmate like her characters Police Detective Art Smith (*Innocent Bystander*), detective-despite-himself Bingo Riggs (*The Sunday Pigeon Murders, The Thursday Turkey Murders*) and companion-cum-spy Sarah White (*Jethro Hammer*), among others. Her abandonment was positively benign compared to those of Jethro Hammer (*Jethro Hammer*), and Jay Otto (*The Big Midget Murders*). Like Dick Dayton (*Eight Faces at Three*), Jeffrey Bruno (*Murder Through the Looking Glass*), Frank Faulkner (*The Man Who Slept All Day*) and Elizabeth and Kenneth Fairfaxx (*The Fourth Postman*)—all of them very nice people—she was reared by a loving aunt and uncle, the Eldon Rices.

Her selective education, conducted in a cross-country series of homes by Poe-quoting Uncle Eldon and a classic-loving Jesuit priest, is reflected in at least one eerie scene per novel (surprising, but curiously complementary to the hardboiled pace and patter) and in the Junius-Plautus dialogue which delightfully enlivens *Trial By Fury*. As if to claim her heredity, Rice's pen name is doubly patronymic—Craig for the peripatetic father, Rice for the uncle who gave her home, heart and a love of mysteries.

At eighteen Rice was off to Chicago to what the *Time* article labeled "...a decade of failure and booze."[3] Here she worked as a journalist (background for series character Jake Justus) and a radio writer and producer (setting of *The Corpse Steps Out*). In a 1944 *Writer* article, Rice describes the "method" she used to create her first mystery, *Eight Faces at Three*. It seems she had an idea for the first chapter which she believed was as baffling as anything yet contrived. Hastily she wrote it down and then quit cold—too baffled herself to continue. It *was* baffling. Eighteen months later, when she finally, apprehensively, typed the heading "Chapter Two," she still hadn't figured out who had stabbed Holly Inglehart's great aunt or why all the clocks had stopped at three; she simply plunged in, creating and solving clues as she went along.[4] The baffling first chapter became a Rice trademark: *Corpse, Having Wonderful Crime, The Lucky Stiff, Fourth, Slept, Class,* and *Jethro* all open, as does *Eight* into the befuddled consciousness of the chief suspect or the murderer.

Eight sold less than 5,000 copies, but six years and fifteen novels later, Rice was regularly approaching half a million paperback sales. Her popularity was unexpected and vehement: *Time* believed it was a toss-up whether she or Agatha Christie would win the first Gertrude for million-copy sales of a single paperback.[5] She was now writing movie scripts as well as churning out novels and also ghost writing for Gypsy Rose Lee and George Sanders. Proceeds from this prodigous output went into supporting her children and, soon, their children, a brother, past and present husbands and her aunt, Mrs. Rice. After 1949, there was an eight year hiatus, filled with health and addiction problems, until 1957, a year of two publications and her too-early death at 49.

E.T. Guymon, Jr., in his essay on Rice for *Murderess, Inc.*, describes her fifth wedding, which took place in his library at her request. Rice reveled in the attendant publicity, autographed copies of her latest book for the guests and ordered a cake whose base consisted of small ivory skulls.[6] Love of publicity (and the sheer fun of it) once led her to accept the invitation of Harry Reutlinger, editor of the *Chicago Herald American*, to serve as special consultant on the spectacular William Heirens child-murder case, which was being solved and tried in an unprecedented blitz of newsprint. Rice swept in from Santa Monica, imperiously deductive, demanding interviews and predicting her feminine intuition would soon crack the case. The Hearst papers illustrated her "thrilling, analytical stories" with cartoons—Rice, plump and popeyed, looking for clues in the newspaper morgue; Rice, crouched over the bathtub where Susanne Degnan's body had been dissected. Within days, she announced her dramatic conclusion—one diametrically opposed by every paper in town, including her employer, by the public and ultimately by the jury. Heirens (little more than a child himself) was innocent—the kind of boy you'd trust your teenaged daughter with.[7]

This response probably owes less to sociology than to a kind of prelapsarian optimism, a denial of inherent evil, or, simply, the umbrella maternalism which colored Rice's life and work, making the characters, regardless of age, sophistication, virtues, or crimes, mostly Penrods and Pollyannas, adrift in a milieu dominated by maltshops and friendly saloons. Here in Oz with rye chasers, foul deeds falter in the glow of *gemütlichkeit*. Sentiment, leavened with wit, insouciance and breakneck pace: these are the appeals of Rice's unmistakable style, most brilliantly in evidence in the eleven John J. Malone-Jake and Helene Justus mysteries for which she is best remembered.

The Malone-Justus books made Rice a celebrity, (President Roosevelt wrote her a fan letter) and established her as a writer of funny, fast-paced detective farce—with an overpowering aroma of alcohol. The plot of *Eight* involves motherless twins reared by a tyrannical and wealthy great aunt. Their blacksheep father, who has been paid to give them up and stay out of their lives, has reappeared with proof that the boy twin, Glen, is not actually related to the Inglehart family but a substitute child acquired when Holly's infant brother died suddenly. Proud, family-besotted Aunt Alex (who has greatly favored Glen) now plans to disinherit him. Luckily for Glen, Holly appears the more likely disinheritee, for she has just married the unacceptable Dick Dayton, bandleader. Glen has carefully plotted the murder scene to implicate Holly, but because, related or not, she *feels* like a sister, he has skewed the evidence to suggest insanity.

Jake Justus, who is Dayton's manager, believes strongly in Holly's innocence from the outset and calls in John J. Malone, his famous criminal-lawyer friend. Helene Brand, the beautiful heiress who lives next door, insists on joining in and the three are bonded, closer and a lot more fun, than a megrim of Seagram's.

Helene specializes in bemusing the local constabulary, carrying out escape plans (they spring Holly from the cops down a laundry chute) and careening wildly around the icy streets of Chicago clad in mink and ice-blue satin pajamas. Jake's brawn and impulsive temper extricate Helene from such unpleasantries as being held as a material witness; he also contributes his connections, garnered from police-reporting days, with Chicago's shady underside. Malone, compromised seriously by the escape of his client, must now solve the case instead of merely guaranteeing Holly's acquital with an infallible Malone-style (that is, rather more Las Vegas than law library) courtroom performance.

The exposure scene takes place, conventionally enough, in the Inglehart library, with all parties assembled. Glen flees along the frigid lakefront, slips and despite the heroic efforts of Jake, falls to his death. Malone ties up all loose ends, poetically, if not entirely legally.

The general format of the Malone-Justus (and most of the other Rice books) is established here. About half of the novels open with the "baffling" chapter; all conclude with the weary, reeling Malone orchestrating the revelations, usually in two sections, the first strictly for the police. The setting is vividly Chicago, an amalgam of the milieus of Helene (North Suburb-Lake Shore Drive) and Jake (newspaper, radio and later, nightclub) and Malone (Washington Street office-City Hall bar). Rickett's, Ricardo's, Henrici's, the Chez Paree, the Dome at the Sherman Hotel. The Christmas crowds on State Street and Marshall Field's clock. The El and the Ambassador.

Newspaperman Tom Burrows says of Jackson, Wisconsin: "...A little town like this is all currents and cross-currents. Everybody is related to everybody else, or entangled with everybody else through birth, church, or business affiliations, hatred, love affairs, or debts (*Trial By Fury*, 47). Substitute "social" for "church" and you have Rice's Chicago. Malone, in *Knocked for a Loop* (123-4), reflects on the oft-expressed notion that if you stand on the corner of State and Madison Streets long enough, everyone you know in the world will come by; he feels that if he stays in this case long enough, everyone he knows in the world is going to be connected with someone else connected with it. The Inglehart, Brand, Venning estates march contiguously along the lakefront; the Lacy-Fairfaxx mansions share addresses and lives. Lake Shore Drive houses the best families as well as Max Hook, gangster boss—and they are hardly unknown to each other. The elegant, gossip-mongering Mrs. Ogletree (*The Wrong Murder*) sells racy tidbits to Hook to pay her gambling debts. Both Lily Bordreaux and the lovely Jane Estapoole (*Loop*) are fascinated with Frank McGinnis, a Hook hood who wears a suit dangerously close to the color purple.

But these ties between wealth and crime generally omit the necessary police cravat. Only in *The Lucky Stiff* is a murder frame, conviction and even repression of the confession which would clear the innocent possible because of the kind of political-criminal outreach so prevalent in Chandler and Hammett. The highest political official seen to patronize Joe the

Angel's City Hall Bar is the janitor (this may be a political comment in itself). Except in *Stiff* (where he is not consulted until after the fact), and *Fury* (where he is out of his territory), Malone is able to juggle Chicago justice with lighthearted impunity—and a surprising amount of justice.

As for the detecting team, there is not a professional among them (some would argue that Malone is not even a professional attorney, as his much-vaunted courtroom style is never once seen in court), though Malone does collect a fee (sometimes against his will) or win a reward in compensation.

The trio's initial involvement in the case is always personal. Jake is Dick Dayton's manager (*Eight*), Nelle Brown's press agent (*Corpse*), Mona McClane's challenger (*Wrong* and *Right*), and Jay Otto's employer (*Midget*). Even if Malone is hired to solve a problem (*My Kingdom for a Hearse*) or mount a defense (*Postman*), Helene and Jake will turn up; Helene's family is sure to share portfolios with the client. Sometimes, as in *Right*, Jake and Helene are at odds; each is involved to prove a point, rendering their respective stakes in the case more matters of healing personal relationships than achieving justice—though the two *do* coincide.

Although Malone excels at precise placement of the disparate pieces, both Helene and Jake are sharp of wit and eye—and luckily, too, for feelings sometimes impair Malone's perceptions (love for Anna Marie [*Stiff*], awe at Jane Estapoole's poised perfection [*Loop*]). Legwork is also shared, each of the three questions suspects, milks contacts and investigates the contents of courthouse files, cemeteries and other peoples' apartments. The conjunction of these efforts, is, however, a far cry from clockwork; there is a deal of dashing off in independent directions, and the case and their personal lives frequently collide. A principal function of the plot is to interrupt Jake and Helene at making love (*Eight*), getting married (*Corpse*), going on a honeymoon (*Wrong*), patching up a honeymoon dispute (*Right*) and Helene's discovering which business crisis is disturbing Jake this time (*Midget, Stiff, Hearse*). Malone's concentration is continually punctured by threats of eviction, the loss of credit at Joe the Angel's Bar, and lack of cab fare.

Despite the high level of hilarity, there *are* risks to life and the pursuit in freedom. One or more of the team is endangered (sometimes seriously) during the conduct of each case. Malone is knocked out, tied up and locked into an abandoned basement (*Postman*) and bombed and nearly incinerated (*Fury*); Helene, exquisite and intrepid, without ruffling a hair on her furs, dives into dangers in *Midget, Wonderful* and *Hearse*. Jake alternately deduces discerningly and bumbles. Under the influence of booze, chicken pox, or sheer stubborn pride, he moves bodies about (three times in *Corpse* alone), removes evidence (the fatal gun in *Wrong*, the hammer in *Postman*), becomes the intended victim of a lynch mob (*Fury*) and is hauled onto Homocide Chief Von Flanagan's carpet with predictable regularity—as suspect, witness, or consultant.

Some thirty-nine murders occur in these nineteen works (an average of 2.27 in the Malone books, 2.50 in Bingo-Handsome territory, two in the atypicals and one in the Melville Fair tomes). Of the murderees, close to half can be called the deserving dead, for they're a rotten lot: Paul March and John St. John (*Corpse*), Joshua Gumbril and sister Fleurette Sanders (*Wrong*), all the Tuesdays (*Right*), Jay Otto and Mildred Goldsmith (*Midget*), Jesse Conway and Warden Garity (*Stiff*), McGurn and Sgt. O'Mara (*Bystander*), plus three or four gangsters who will never be missed. Coming close, or at least little mourned, are Aunt Alex and Holly's father, Miller (*Eight*), Rufus Carrington (*Glass*), and Senator Peveley (*Fury*). The only truly innocent victims are Amby (*Bystander*), Jethro Hammer (*Jethro*), Frank Faulkner (*Slept*), Cora Belle Fromm (*Fury*), and (on the whole), Ellen McGowan (*Fury*), plus three quite anonymous postmen (*Postman*).

In the killer department, the men outnumber the women about three to one. Two of the six women killers are Ellens: socialite Ellen Ogletree (*Wrong*) and backstreet Ellen Haven (*Bystander*); both kill for money. The peerless Jane Estapoole (*Loop*) kills by accident (and Malone will win her acquittal). Mona McClane has bet Jake her nightclub, the Casino (*Wrong*), which he believes might occupy him in a manner a rich wife could be proud of, that she can get away with murder. Ellen Ogletree, who is present, takes this opportunity to murder a blackmailer in the manner Mona has proposed. Malone is extremely annoyed at being dragged into an investigation based on a bet, and the trio is generally reluctant to nail Mona, an internationally famous sportswoman of awesome capabilities and great charm. When a teen-age marriage is found to link Mona with the deceased, Helene is crushed; the commonplace motive is unworthy of Mona. And, of course, the murder Mona does commit—in the following book, *Right*—is of the imposter Gerald Tuesday, who has abused his wife (Mona's dear friend) and the killing constitutes (for a change) genuine self-defense. *Wrong* and *Right* are rather a showcase for the character of Mona McClane, gallant and gay in the face of false incrimination, protector of the innocent and generous in defeat—or is it victory? In any case, she hands Jake the deed to the Casino at the conclusion of *Right*.

Gay Lacy (*Postman*) covets the boy millionaire next door, and slum-bred Rosalie Gay (*Glass*) kills for profit. The two Ellens, Gay, and Rosalie are all killed at the exposure scene, when they run. Gay Lacy and Ellen Ogletree are members of Helene's set and their unrelieved detestability is well established. Less successful as villains are Rosalie Gay (*Glass*) and Ellen Haven (*Bystander*), the low-life Loreleis. Rosalie, who has killed Rufus Carrington in pure greed, contemplates giving it all up and fleeing with the neighbor she has elaborately framed (she has just realized what a sweet person he is). Ellen Haven, seen only through the eyes of the two men who love her, is more convincing; her secret smile indicates that she enjoys killing—the only such villain in all the books. Thus, in all cases, the deserts are just.

Four of the sixteen male killers are motivated by love. Of these, Mr. Cherington (*Home Sweet Homicide*), who kills the kidnaper-murderers of his daughter, dies of a stroke. Malone improvises an on-the-spot insanity plea for the other three: the lovable Tootz (*Corpse*) whom everybody believes to be harmlessly dotty in any case and who has only killed the deserving dead; Allswell McJackson, the gentle giant (*Midget*), who has rid the world of the evil Jay Otto and his cohorts; Huntleigh, the Lacy's butler (*Postman*), who has secretly supported his employers for years and kills the Lacy daughter Gay to prevent Malone's exposing her as the postmen murderess.

Almost all of the remaining men kill for greed and are themselves killed running from disclosure; several are already in prison. The hypocritical, blackmailing Alvin Goudge, who has betrayed the entire town of Jackson, Wisconsin (*Fury*), will get a well-attended trial.

Among the more reprehensible killers are Gerald Tuesday (*Right*), who kills Michael Venning, forces Venning's wife to live with him in the Orient for twenty years (!), then, about to inherit the Venning millions, kills his own two brothers who wish to share in the proceeds. Dennis Morrison *(Having Wonderful Crime)* kills two wives in one night but is foiled by the surgeon father of wife number one, who decapitates the corpses and exchanges the heads, then buries the head of rich wife number two to prevent Dennis from profiting.

Some of Malone's more provocative comments about murderers and their victims occur in the morally ambivalent *Wrong* and *Right*. (In *Right*, Helene is the houseguest of Mona McClane while she is engaged in discovering whom her hostess has murdered.) Everyone has the makings of a good murderer in him—and is probably entitled to it, says Malone (*Wrong*, 97). Everyone alive also deserves, at some time in his life, to *be murdered;* a few people he knows deserve murdering at regular intervals (*Wrong*, 98), for example, Joshua Gumbril, whom it's about time somebody killed (*Wrong*, 41). Murder becomes justified when the existence of another person becomes sufficiently obnoxious to warrant the risks in removing him. (*Wrong,* 97). People defend themselves against many things other than death; hence murder is always a form of self-defense (*Right,* 242). In a later book, when Helene says there's never any excuse for murder, Malone answers quietly "Isn't there?" (*Fury,* 61).

As for the general wrongdoing, Malone finds it pretty prevalent: if there were such a thing as ethics, people wouldn't need lawyers (*Eight,* 41). Of Max Hook, gambler czar, he says "He's a crook, but he's perfectly honest." And when Hook describes the marriage extortion racket of Jay Otto as "criminal," Malone is amused in the light of Hook's operations, but goes on to reflect that "after all, every man is entitled to his own opinion of what constitutes a crime" (*Midget,* 266).

Weaponry is not a significant element here. Mona McClane promises Jake she will commit murder with the most ordinary weapon she can find (*Wrong,* 21) and she speaks for virtually every murderer in these books. Guns predominate, but there are several knife throwers and wielders of blunt objects. The only exotic weapon is used by Allswell McJackson (*Midget*) who kills his sadistic midget boss (because he has forced the girl Allswell loves into a fake marriage racket) by hanging him from a rope made from the eleven unmatched stockings of the Casino chorus line, then hangs Otto's confederate with the mates.

Despite his fondness for Brooks Brothers suits and Sulka ties, Malone is a sartorial sink—his short, stocky frame strewn with cigar ashes from red, perspiring face to untied shoes. Jake is tall, red-headed and rangy rather than handsome. And Helene is the loveliest creature ever entrusted to humankind, mauve, violet and pale green fragile perfection, immune to the ravages of wine and time. One of the reasons the Malone books almost always take place in deep Chicago winter is to allow Helene to parade her furs (the other is to heighten the dangers of her grand-prix-performance driving).

Helene and Jake are Malone's family; he lives in a Loop hotel and spends his nights in bars and poker marathons. His love-life consists of short-term, expensive flings with chorus-girls. In *Stiff,* however, Malone falls in love tragically—for beautiful singer Anna Marie St. Clair (framed for murder and almost executed) seethes with hatred and is the brains behind a protection racket which is about to cost Jake the Casino. Nevertheless, in a reverse Spade-Brigid confrontation, Malone does not send her to jail but to new fame in Hollywood and with tears in his eyes.

Malone roars frequently but has a very gentle heart. He spends half of *Midget* trying to get a straight story out of faded great singer Ruth Rawlston while spending his last cent on a crash program to restore her splendor. He is fascinated by the cool poise of the Helene-set female—

Holly Inglehart, Elizabeth Fairfaxx, Jane Estapoole. And he is saddened by the police shooting of outlaw "Ma" Lulumay Yandry, whom he has warned because he had drunk her liquor—but whose defense he would never have undertaken (*Wrong*).

The style of the Malone books is uniquely Rice's—a blend of wild action and booze-skewed conversation. The chase scene reaches pinnacles of absurdity with Helene and Jake plunging under and over Wacker Drive and across the rising Chicago River bridge, the police in screaming pursuit and a corpse for company. Rice's bemusement with wordplay begins with her titles—*Home Sweet Homicide, My Kingdom for a Hearse.* Characters' names include Fairr and Justus as detectors and the odd sounding: Hazel Swackhammer, Alonzo Stonecypher, Orlo Featherstone, Abel Skiningsrude, Watchful McGowan, Allswell McJackson and Philomen Ma (May-all-your-enemies-be-confounded) Smith.

Helene, Jake and Malone converse in an exchange of malapropped clichés. "Jake attracts trouble like a magnet attracts flies." "You mean like a honey attracts eyes" (*Wonderful,* 83). Malone "believes in crossing his barn doors after the bridge has been stolen." And "Pride goeth before the spring. I mean, pride springeth into fall" (*Postman,* 237).

There are also similes. The pictures on bohemian Wildevine William's wall, called "Unfinished Symphony" looks like a bright green angleworm between two pale blue fried eggs (*Wonderful,* 264).

Many books feature a recurring gimmick. In *Eight,* Helene relates the art of spinning full glasses of beer down bartops to artful auto skids and practices both zealously. Malone attracts a disreptuable but irresistible dog, whom everyone he meets wants to adopt on sight (*Postman*) and a dollar gin bloodhound (*Fury*). *Wonderful,* laid in New York, has a bartender who reads *The New Republic* and *The Southern Review.* The janitor in *Hearse* reads the *Nation. Wonderful* also presents stylized newspaper headlines: "Model Slaying Not Sex Crime, Police Say," (*The Daily News*), and "Murdered Model Model Union Member" (*P.M.*). Jake, Helene and Malone all suffer from the insight which maddeningly refuses to surface; in the Bingo Riggs-Handsome Kusak novels this is reversed: Handsome has a photographic memory, but Bingo is too preoccupied to listen.

Rice's treatemnt of the police is satirical rather than prescriptive. Homicide Chief Daniel Von Flanagan (he added the Von to escape the Irish-cop stereotype) appears in all but the first Malone book, along with several obtuse ethnic constables. Von Flanagan believes that crimes are committed for his personal frustration and (rightfully) that Malone and company are often at the heart of the confusion. Although his methods and reasoning powers are consistently inept, the overall effect is comic rather than contemptuous. Cops represent the legal impediment to the ongoing investigation, just as Max Hook and his goons throw curves from the underworld.

The worst cop, blustering, corrupt Sheriff Marvin Kling (*Fury*) is found out of town in Jackson, Wisconsin, where Jake and Helene, seeking respite from the Casino, city lights and murder cases, stop to procure a fishing license just in time for Senator Peveley's body to land, quite dead, at their departing feet. This is Jackson's first murder in thirty-two years and the Senator is the richest, most powerful and least loved of its citizens. The Senator's explosively redheaded daughter, Florence, among others, assumes that somebody was sore at "Pa," but Malone argues: "Not necessarily. You don't have to have any feelings about a man, like or dislike, to murder him. There are three reasons for murder: love, money, and fear. And the greatest of these is fear" (*Fury*, 101).

Fear, in truth, dominates the lives of many residents of Jackson—and also infects its visitors. The strictly city-bred Malone and Helene find incomprehensible the prevalent insider-outsider mystique, but it is all too familiar to small-town graduate Jake. As the locals inevitably close ranks, fear of zenophobia in ugly action motivates Jake to challenge the sheriff's retention order, lands him in jail for belting a deputy (back) and transports a reluctant Malone to a backwater so devoid of civilized din that chirping birds can actually awaken the righteous at daybreak.

Fear has engendered the loveless engagement between the decent, if ambitiously confused, District Attorney Jerry Luckstone and the Senator's daughter, Florence: Jerry is afraid of losing the next election and failing to carry on his family's judicial heritage; conversely, Florence, a twenty-nine-year-old virgin, fears entrapment in her father's image and her father's town.

Another father's image sets the train of four murders into motion. Ellen McGowan, popularly known as a remarkable woman, who has followed her father as bank cashier, fears that her father's "borrowing" of bank funds will be revealed and herself embezzles an additional $76,000 to purchase blackmailer Alvin Goudge's continued silence. Goudge, County Treasurer and head of the Brotherhood of Churchmen, sits under a banner in the Courthouse declaring that an honest man is the noblest work of God; he kills Senator Peveley because he is about to expose the embezzlements, a bystander bank teller who happens to stand in the blast path of the bomb which destroys the incriminating records, Ellen McGowan, who confesses the embezzlements revealed by the bomb-inspired audit and Cora Belle Fromm, the slightly disreputable town belle who had been the Senator's unexpected informant.

Goudge also creates the Citizens' Law Enforcement Committee, a respectably-intentioned group roused to civic ire by the sheriff's incompetence, and inflames its rougher members to mob violence with false rape rumors, free liquor and the promise of a large reward for capturing—of course—the current chief suspect, the outsider, namely Jake.

Actually, at this point, Jake appears a likely suspect. Attempting to help out Jerry Luckstone, he engages in an investigative drinking contest with Cora Belle Fromm, loses badly and leaves Helene's robin's-egg-blue convertible conspiculously in evidence in front of the house in which Cora Belle's body is discovered. While Helene and Malone frantically try to find him a hideout from the increasingly hostile mob, Alvin Goudge spirits him away to the County Asylum. Here Malone finally tracks him down with the dubious aid of a dollar-gin bloodhound; and here, against a background of flaming, mob-fired buildings, Malone dissuades the raging lynch mob—a task he describes as little different from convincing a Cook County jury. The exposure of Alvin Goudge follows.

This book is drenched with atmosphere. There are wonderful scenes: Helene, strolling through the dark streets, observing the passions which underlie the Jackson lemonade facade. There are fascinating characters: the portion of Henry Peveley's mind related to alcohol stopped working about 1928, and he believes Prohibition is still in effect, though he carries on his real estate business with contemporary aplomb. *Fury* is probably Rice's most successful book. The plot is ingenious, the characters strongly drawn, and the sentiment well-disciplined.

The Sunday Pigeon Murders (1942) and *The Thursday Turkey Murders* (1943), offer the happenstance detecting of street photographers Bingo Riggs and Handsome Kusak. Bingo is an incurable seeker after the Big Score, despite the honest-toil ethic preached by his Uncle Herman who liberated him from the orphanage at thirteen (by which age a boy might be expected to be helpful around a small grocery). Bingo has dreamtalked Handsome into leaving his newspaper-photographer job to invest his cameras and limited funds, in the International Foto, Motion Picture, and TV Corporation of America. Handsome possesses good looks, a phenomenal memory and the ability to turn a shabby cold water flat into a home; he is credited with an atom-size brain, but his common-sense solutions often save the day. He mickey-finns Mr. Pigeon while Bingo still ponders the problems of retaining this seven-year missing prize, who is about to be declared dead. A half million dollar insurance policy is involved; Bingo (along with assorted gangsters and other interested parties) hopes to con himself into a share.

Bingo is about five feet with sharp features and flaming, standup red hair; he readily understands that any girl would prefer Handsome. Both men are fond of Baby, the landlady's daughter, described as smart, cute *and* beautiful, who, in turn, likes them both and intercedes on their behalf with her unpaid mother. The photography business is very precarious and eviction is an ever-present possibility. Bingo hopes to solve their problems by conning a half share of the Pigeon insurance money from Harkness Penneyth, Pigeon's former partner and beneficiary, as payment for keeping Mr. Pigeon "missing." Mr. Pigeon is quite agreeable to this scheme and settles down to the role of chief cook in their miniscule apartment. Despite the spatial discomforts, Bingo revels in the warm family atmosphere his presence creates.

Outside, however, murders are occurring. Early on, Bingo and Handsome discover a corpse they take to be Penneyth's; they then move on to locate and persuade his "heir," presumably his sister, Leonora. Leonora is an unhappy, faded beauty of considerable business ability. Her no-good brother once "accidentally" tried to kill her under cover of a knife-throwing performance; she is now married to a leeching aristocrat whose two insufferable children she feels helpless to mother except through money. Bingo and Handsome learn to like and pity Leonora and mourn when they find her murdered. Having now lost their second "client," they confess all to Mr. Pigeon, who immediately identifies the murderer as Harkness Penneyth (the first corpse was his butler). This is the man who won the affection of Mr. Pigeon's "treasure" and subsequently drove her to suicide. Mr. Pigeon has left the country in the belief that this is best for his lost love; he returns to seek revenge against his former partner, but instead participates as bait in a police-set trap which ensnares Penneyth, seducer and sister-killer. And Bingo wins the reward.

In *Turkey*, Bingo is after another rainbow, the buried loot from a seventeen-year-old Iowa bank robbery. Along the way, he and Handsome are forced to share their shanty with five escaped convicts toward whom Bingo momentarily feels hunted-animal sympathy. Bingo is constrained from reporting the convicts' whereabouts to Sheriff Judson by chivalry toward a lady acquaintance the cons profess to hold as hostage; his acquisitive propensities are always tempered by his basic good nature and Handsome's expectations of him—which he doesn't wish to disappoint.

Several family portraits emerge from this book: the symbiotic teaming of Bingo and Handsome, the false family of the convicts, and the Sears catalog farm family of Chris Halvorsen. Chris is a respected community member, sometime deputy sheriff, with fried-chicken wife and ginghamed daughter, who is revealed to have been the uncaught inside man in the bank robbery, driven to crime by his mail-order bride's expensive appetites. The wife has also encouraged Chris' daughter, a very ordinarily pretty girl, to believe she is movie-star material too gifted for the local swains. Another nest disrupter is Uncle Fred, brother of one of the convicted robbers, abortionist and Bible-quoter, who terrorizes his niece with prophecies about the bad blood she has inherited from her father.

A principal character in *Turkey* is the best cop in any of the books, Sheriff Henry Judson, a civil servant in every sense of that cliché. Mild-mannered, quietly astute, he welcomes outside help (including Bingo's), shrewdly assesses character, cumulates clues and privately compiles a library on crime detection.

Pigeon and *Turkey* are not among Rice's best books. There are humorous moments and the plots are detectively sound, but the overall effect is rather strained. The reader may like Bingo, but he loves and misses Malone.

Rice authored three non-series books. Of these *Home Sweet Homicide* shares some stylistic similarities with the Malone books. *Telefair* and *Innocent Bystander* are radically different, the one mistily gothic and the other relentlessly hardboiled.

Telefair, The House on the Island, "A Novel of Suspense," is the Gothic fruit of '42, awash with whispering fountains, whispered warnings, deaf-mute servants and hushed-up, homebrewed infidelities, illegitimacies and murders. The setting is a single-family island in Chesapeake Bay whose separation from the "real" world is paralleled by the young hero's deliberately contrived separation from "real" life. Telefair is one of those great fictional houses which takes on a life of its own, as generations of shared names reiterate, even celebrate (and ultimately re-enact) the terrible deeds of its centuries.

Philip Telefair, brilliant, charming absolute maestro of this enchanted realm, tells David, the orphaned great-nephew he has supported since childhood but only now summoned to visit, that the man who owns an island becomes its conscience, its laws and its court of justice. The Telefair ethic holds that all things are permissible to him who loves deeply—even murder, and no Telefair (according to Philip) ever forgets an enemy or forgives an injury, whatever the time or cost.

The story unfolds such an act of revenge, Philip's revenge against David's father, Eugene—who has loved Evangeline, Philip's wife and fathered Edris, whom Philip has reared as his daughter. Philip killed Eugene when David was an infant and has kept Evangeline, now mad, locked up in the old wing of Telefair since the birth of Edris. This is not enough. Like other Rice characters, Philip knows that real revenge is directed against a blameless child—and he determines to make that child a murderer—his own murderer.

To this end, David has been manipulated, ostensibly with love and concern, from school to school, camp to camp, tutor to tutor, forbidden visits to his mother's family, never permitted an anchor, a tie, to any place or person except to the benevolent, unseen great-uncle. Act Two will be the island-indoctrination, instructing David in his heritage, dazzling him with cultured conversation, naming him heir to Telefair, encouraging him to believe that marrying Edris will be the supreme act of repayment—until, in a very ecstasy of gratitude, David requests her hand—only to be coldly refused and to discover that Edris is his sister and Philip the killer of his father. David is then to murder Philip in a mindless rage. But the revenge will not end there; Philip knows David will be protected from prosecution by the island's residents he has so carefully selected: Dr. Von Berger, who has kept him living until revenge-time; Zenobie, who cares for Evangeline—both still-sought convicts whose escapes he has engineered. Instead of going to prison, David will suffer agonizing remorse the rest of his life for killing the one person he has ever loved, the giver of Telefair.

Against this plot stands only Edmund, another nephew, one of the brown-haired mainland Telefairs, whose open, sunny, comfortable home is the antithesis of the fogbound, dog-guarded, secretly malevolent Telefair and whose deformed body is the antithesis of Philip's graceful, classic beauty. But Edmund has been sworn to secrecy by an oath given as a child. And, in the end, Philip defeats himself. He has so blurred David's distinctions between dreamstate and reality that the scheduled killing takes place (very vividly) but only in a dream. Defeated, Philip is killed by Evangeline.

This book is (apparently) Rice's attempt to create a pure Poe tone poem and, indeed, the atmosphere of incipient tragic violence is conveyed very successfully. But there is too much of it—or not enough of anything else. To make the dream-killing feasible, dreamstate description has been protracted to the point of tedium. And the plot, though ingenious, proceeds sluggishly.

And then there is David as hero. His story has *Bildungsroman* prospects, but one feels that David should break away, make Telefair a bird sanctuary, if not grow up, at least get out. But he elects to stay, expecting never again to see Edmund (who returns to the mainland with Edris) and marrying the blind, serene Laurel Stone, herself a Telefair twice-over. Still, *Telefair* is an interesting work in terms of Rice themes (David is certainly the most put-upon orphan of the lot) and versatility.

Home, Sweet Homicide is one of two Rice books listed in the *Haycraft-Queen Definitive Library of Detective-Crime-Mystery Fiction* as best mystery of 1941 (the other, published in 1941, is *Trial By Fury*). *Home* has attracted particular attention because of its semi-autobiographical cast, featuring a widowed mystery author, Marian Carstairs, who writes under three pen-names, pausing for only one day between books, in order to support three precocious children.

A murder is committed next door to the Carstairs. The children think mother should step in and solve the crime, garnering publicity, boosting book sales and gaining a respite from the grindstone. But mother is too busy with fictional mayhem to dally in the real thing (and, besides, she already has a suspect with whom she sympathizes and a victim she despised). So the kids decide to solve the case, using methods gleaned from assorted Carstairs mysteries.

This book was made into a Rice-scripted movie in 1946, with Lynn Barrie as Marian, Randolph Scott as bachelor detective Bill Smith (whom the children decide, while they're at it, to marry off to Marian) and Peggy Ann Garner as April, the conniest of the Carstairs offspring. Sgt. O'Hare, who has nine children of his own, was played with gravel-voiced exasperation by James Gleason.

Besides April, there is Dinah, the oldest, and Huckleberry Archie, the youngest. The children share a private language called King Tut in which all the consonants are words and all the words are spelled out. The most frequently exchanged comment is "Shush-u-tut u-pup." When they are not spreading false clues, April (*et al*) expend a lot of energy kicking one another under the table, trading household chores and trying to raise enough cash to get mother a $3.00 manicure.

Flora Sanford, the murderee, is one of the thoroughly deserving dead. Her blackmail endeavors include half the neighbors and her own husband. She has also been involved in a murder-kidnapping; the victim's father has embezzled army funds to pay the bootless ransom and been cashiered therefore. And this is just one of the many lives Flora Sanford has destroyed.

A quick checklist of ways in which the Carstairs progeny impede the police investigation:

1. April lies about the time of the murder shots—because someone *may* need an alibi (and sure enough, Flora's hapless husband, Willis Sanford, does need one).
2. April removes a second bullet from the eye of a portrait in the guarded Sanford house and Archie gleans ballistics information by flattering Sgt. O'Hare.
3. April tells Sgt. O'Hare an invented story involving a character culled from a Marian mystery which boomerangs when a man by that name turns up. (She is paying O'Hare back for trying to bribe the vulnerable Archie with chocolate malts.)
4. All three hide and feed chief suspect Willis Sanford in Archie's mob's playhouse.
5. April and Dinah discover, under cover of a mob treasure hunt, Flora Sanford's cache of blackmail material and take it home (ultimately they destroy it).

Of course, all of these obfuscations turn out to be boons.

In addition, April and Dinah interrogate, kid-style, the blackmailed neighbors and discover enough to incriminate the neighbor they like best (proving probably, that growing up is painful). In a pint-sized version of Malone's exhausted, reluctant exposure speech, April sobs out her deductions to Detective Smith and Marian, the facts of which are verified by Mr. Cherington, the murderer (and the kidnap-victim's father), as he is dying from a stroke. Thus the "good" murderer and the children will be spared a traumatic trial.

And Marian will marry Bill Smith.

This is Rice's most domestic book, full of double-chocolate-fudge cakes and take-out-the-garbage talk. Marian is a successful writer, but both she and the children feel a void without a man in the house. She also blushes a lot. *Home* won many kudoes and remains humorous and very human reading. Probably the decades between make these children, with their maltshop pleasures and romantic manipulations in aid of mother, indigestibly wholesome today. Yet they were too racy for the 1944 magazine market: one editor turned down the story because April (age 14) used lipstick and another because the children showed an impish disrespect for the police. And the *Time* cover article, which appeared two years after *Home*'s publication, reports that Rice's three children, Nancy, Iris and David (16, 15 and 13) are quite as nice (and as good friends with her) as those in *Home, Sweet Homicide*.[8]

In *Innocent Bystander* (1948) the murder of gambler boss McGurn takes place on the ferris wheel of a waterfront amusement park called the Pier. It is witnessed (but temporarily blacked out) by Amby, a fuzzy-memoried deaf-mute sketch artist who ekes out a living in the Pier's extended carny family life. The subsequent investigation is set against the naturally antagonistic worlds of the carnies—loyal, close (Maritza the fortune-teller feels like a mother to carny garduate Tony Webb, the chief suspect; the owner provides him information and shelter) and the police department—ambition-torn, callous (Chief Investigator Art Smith is despised and conspired against by his ambitious partner, Sgt. O'Mara; their superior knows O'Mara to be a bad cop but calls his brutal beating of the hapless Amby only "a mistake").

Amby is this book's lost child, plot pivot and chief symbol—second only to the carnival itself, that magical touchstone of childhood—all glittering lights and tinkling music and golden promise, however tawdry its daytime aspect. Ellen Haven, the killer, poses for an Amby portrait so that she can observe the body's discovery by Tony, whom she has anonymously set up with the lure of McGurn's payoff for the two-year prison fall Tony has just taken. She then tears the picture in two; one of the severed halves is found by Detective Art Smith, the other by Tony, and each interprets Ellen's split image according to his needs. Smith, an orphanage graduate who retains a belief in human goodness, first reads Ellen as no good; Tony, ex-carnie, gambler, and tough, sees her as a nice kid. The reader learns (52) that she actually looks like the girl both men have imagined, and, *Laura*-like, neither can forget her.

Smith's profession and Tony's survival demand that Ellen's involvement in the murder—in whatever role—be uncovered, yet each is hampered by his personal feelings, Smith to the point of considering framing Tony in order to clear Ellen—a temptation he resists. Amby's actual afflictions serve as metaphors for the deaf ear Smith turns to evidence of Ellen's liaison with the murdered man and for Tony's inability to articulate his conflicting instincts and emotions. Amby is also the key to character: Art Smith rescues him from the brutal assault by O'Mara (but fails to "listen" to Amby's frantic signals that he has remembered Ellen as the killer); Tony, himself born and bred in violence, is shocked by O'Mara's attack and feels that Amby's beaten face symbolizes all the senseless violence in the world. In the confrontation scene with Ellen, Tony tells her he might have forgiven her killing of McGurn and O'Mara, both maneating sharks. But not her killing of Amby.

The book's climax (and best scenes) effectively use the bizarre trappings of the Pier. Amby remembers Ellen on the ferris wheel, Tony and O'Mara furiously battle down the midway and into the Barrel of Fun, Ellen kills O'Mara, then Amby, in the hubbub (blaming Tony for both). Tony hides in the gorilla exhibit, grabs Ellen and descends with her into the Diving Bell, cutting off the air and only using the escape hatch after her admissions are overheard by Smith. Battered, exhausted, Tony then loses his grip on Ellen. She flees into the Fun House. The Midway crowds outside can now watch the mirrored chase as Ellen, Tony and Smith, grope and stumble among thousands of gargoyled images. Finally, as Ellen whirls to stab the real Tony, Smith, reviewing in a flash his many Ellen images, shoots, killing at once the carousel dream and the killer reality.

This book is the most atypical of all the Rice items considered here; it apparently represents an attempt to create a genuinely hard-boiled mystery, sans liquor and wisecracks. Perhaps a film noir was visualized and performances might have humanized the generally unappealing major characters. What *is* appealing—and the most Rice-like—are the caring carny people and their shabby, lit-up world.

Rice wrote three books under the penname Michael Venning, featuring working detective Melville Fairr, whose manner and methods appear calculatedly counter to those of John J. Malone (not to mention

Spade and Marlowe). Gray of hair , complexion, clothes and procedure, Fairr virtually melts into the tapestries, his role undisclosed and often deplored (for he hates inflicting pain) until, at the climax, he reveals his function and findings, accusing, preventing escapes and improvising a script for the police which spares the innocent and punishes the guilty (like Malone) in rather more poetic then legal terms.

The first Venning book, *The Man Who Slept All Day* (1942), is pure English country house in setting, character and clear-cut conclusion. There is a great estate, Ravenswood, the lifework of Frank Faulkner, unique in decor and guestly regalement. There is a one-dimensional villain, younger brother George Faulkner, who is not a suspect in the second murder because he is believed to be the victim of the first. The plot moves by hours through a single Sunday as each of the houseguests searches George's room for the secret the all-day sleeper has ferreted out about him-her, discovers George is dead (a theatrical device) and, believing himself—or one he loves—to be the most likely suspect, conceals the murder in turn. George has hired Fairr (on the pretext that the murder act is a gigantic practical joke) to observe the charade and report to him throughout the day, thereby providing himself with an alibi for his brother's actual murder, which all this planning has been about and which Fairr solves in three or four throwaway deductions at disclosure time.

The murder story, however, is merely the casement for the relationship story, as three couples react and interact and finally confide the skeletons they should have uncloseted years before. The murder-relationship stories come together in the tale of brotherhood—or, better, the tale of the bad brother (George) and his good keeper (Frank). The responsibility for preventing George from seriously harming himself—and others—has been impressed on Frank since childhood, precluding marriage or any other close relationship. Ravenswood and its delightfully entertained guests have become his only family.

But in the event, the real killing turns out to be an anachronism, for Frank has disinherited George only moments before dying. And, doubly ironically, George is not only the rightful heir to Ravenswood, he *is* also the brother he has aspried to be (and hated) all his life. Puny and sickly as an orphaned toddler, George is mistaken by the aunt who reared them for the younger brother; tragically, he *becomes* a mischief maker trying to compete for attention with his larger, healthier and, above all, presumably firstborn and therefore favored brother.

George-Frank might still have beaten the rap and claimed Ravenswood, but he panics, runs and is shot by Melville Fairr, the man he hired as stooge and alibi. Fairr, in fact, has taken the job precisely because he is certain more than a practical joke is afoot and hopes to diminish the damage.

The second Venning book, *Murder Through the Looking Glass* (1943), moves from the country house confinement of *Slept* to the New York mansion of victim Rufus Carrington and adds the contrasting milieus of suspect Jeffrey Bruno's loving farm homeplace and current Greenwich Village apartment and the bordello slum which reared killer Rosalie Gay, presently mistress of Carrington's nephew and neighbor of Jeffrey. Jeffrey, Rosalie, and Rufus are all orphans.

The scope of family betrayal is also enlarged, as several generations of Carrington heirs conspire to expedite their legacies by removing their penurious, long-living *pater familias.*

The book opens into the mind of Jeffrey Bruno waking to groggy consciousness aboard a westbound train, carrying identification papers of one John Blake (which happens to be the name of a long-dead cousin) and a newspaper bearing his picture above the caption "Sought in Murder." Sitting next to him and turning up most everywhere thereafter, sans explanation except an expressed desire to help, is Melville Fairr.

According to the newspaper story, John Blake, who has been employed by Rufus Carrington's nephew, Roger Gunn, and engaged to Carrington's granddaughter, Susan Williams, killed Carrington in a rage when denied a marital blessing. Jeffrey can't believe that he, a mildly successful author of scientific horror stories, fond of parties, girls and Village fellowship, could ever have lived the life of conventional, ambitious John Blake. But Rosalie, whom he believes to be his friend and, later, girlfriend, assures him he has lost whole days out of his recent life, spouts identity theories (split, multiple and *Doppelganger*) and, assuring him that he can't be convicted for a crime another self has committed, urges him to go to the police. Fairr, however, submits that these solutions are merely metaphysical and urges him to investigate logically. Thus Rosalie and Fairr wage a tug-of-war over Jeffrey's fate.

But it is Jeffrey himself, after a night of self-doubt, who realizes from details found in the newspaper story and in John Blake's apartment (the key is in his pocket) that he cannot be the murderer. Nevertheless, thanks to Rosalie, the police are hot behind him. So he first activates the talent for escape he feels is latent in every hunted soul and then the hunter instinct—which leads him to the Carrington mansion, where the Carringtons who have implicated John Blake are assembled—Roger Gunn, Marietta Williams and Rufus Ransom. There follows a virtual suspension of the action while each person present, including the butler, reviews his life story, his relationship with the murdered man and his expectations now that Rufus Carrington is dead. These are blighted lives—self and parent-blighted.

Under Rosalie's tutelage, Roger, Marietta and Rufus Ranson have invented an employee, fiance, murderer named John Blake (chosen by Rosalie who knows of Jeffrey's dead cousin and realizes this will add to the confusion). None of the Carringtons knows that Rosalie has set up Jeffrey as an actual scapegoat; they believe the murderer will remain mythical and that the crime be recorded as unsolved. None would actually have struck the fatal blow; Rosalie does this. But Roger has placed Blake's name on his payroll, rented an apartment in his name and identified him as the man who rushed out of the Carrington house just before he discovered his uncle's body. Rosalie, meantime, has drugged Jeffrey, planted Blake's wallet on him and placed him on the train. Rosalie is now exposed by Fairr, runs and is killed by the arriving police. The police, it seems, know and admire Melville Fairr and accept the story he now presents—that Roalie is the sole person involved in Carrington's murder.

When the police leave, Fairr's full role is finally unveiled. He was hired by Rufus Carrington (who anticipated being murdered by some member of his disgruntled family) to locate the killer—and to let him go. The lasting punishment has been provided by himself—he has left the bulk of his fortune to a small Illinois college. So the Carringtons, unconsoled by riches, are left to their desperate lives and to the sickening truths about themselves and each other. Only Clarke, the butler, receives solace from the will; he is to remain in the mansion until he dies.

Fairr wonders, as he leaves, whether he has done the right thing in not naming the Carringtons as accessories. But he believes there are worse punishments then prison terms. And Rufus Carrington, if not one of the clearly deserving dead, had sown more than his share of misery. It amused Rufus to watch his family's scramblings and ingratiations over the fortune he intended to deny them. Rosalie's death is more depressing to Fairr than Rufus': she was very lovely and full of promise. The murder plan had been ingenious and would certainly have succeeded if Jeffrey hadn't displayed an unexpected reserve of farmbred resourcefulness—a reserve nurtured by the shadowy mentoring of Fairr. Fairr's role has been to gently urge Jeffrey toward the information and courage needed to confront the Carringtons, then to provide the last pieces and "handle" the authorities.

Fairr has said (*Slept*) that he knows how to open a safe, that he has been very wicked. In *Glass* we learn that his heart aches at the thought of sending people to prison—something required in his chosen profession—because he himself has been there (and to reform school, too). Detection is redemption, but this detective knows both sides of the legal system and tempers the letter of the law with compassion and common sense.

Jethro Hammer, third and last of the Venning-Melville Fairr books, begins with a murder, but its true story is the mystery of naming—not so much the problem of who one is, as the importance of what one is called. Jethro Hammer, about age two, abandoned in a small-town Ohio church (apparently by his parents), is taken in by a kindly blacksmith, Will Donahue, who cares for him with the same general love he showers on his own children and stray cats. Rather like a a stray cat, Jethro is simply called "the baby" for months. When naming becomes a necessity, Donahue is curiously reluctant to give this unknown his own name. So, willy-nilly and known to all, he names him Hammer, for the most name-sounding tool in his blacksmith shop. This careless christening is to mold Jethro's life, for, though he is treated generally as a member of the family, he is never quite a member of the family; his name, so bloodlessly fabricated, so absolutely divorced from any human lineage, sets him apart—and this subtle distance is felt and reflected in the community.

In addition to his name, Jethro is handicapped by the superstition that changelings bring bad luck. Lizzie Donahue, his foster mother, blames and hates him—and he knows it—because her daughter Sally is born crippled.

Years later Will Donahue patents a profitable sewing machine attachment and the family moves to New York where Will feels displaced and dies. Will assumes that Jethro, to whom he feels closer than to any of his natural children, will share equally in the estate—but the siblings never even consider this. Jethro is not a Donahue (and neither are they; they have changed their name to the "fancier" *Donohough*, a terrible blow to their father). Jethro walks out and does not return for twenty years, at which time he produces Will's diary which establishes that he, not Will, was the actual inventor. He sues the family for all accrued royalties and wins. Jethro then becomes the Hermit of Wall Street, recluse millionaire, and the Donahues start over.

All of these facts are discovered by the curious Melville Fairr (who has been hired as a bodyguard by Jethro) through interviews wangled with the Donahues, now twenty years older and wiser than on the day of the court case. Losing the money has been their salvation; the common sense of their father resurfaces when they are forced to rely on their own considerable resources. They have flourished and had fun in the bargain. They bear no ill will toward Jethro. Indeed, each expresses a desire to see him and each is extremely inquisitive about why Jethro waited twenty years to sue them. Where had he been?

Shortly after, Jethro is killed and Melville Fairr sets out to discover his murderer as well as the mystery of the missing years and the answer to why, after forty years of silence, Jethro had called each of his foster siblings and asked to see them only the day before he died. The answer to the lost years is supplied by an unknown daughter born in Honduras after Jethro had escaped from twenty years in a Mexican jail (for a murder he did not commit). She never knew her father, but has been expensively schooled by him. Jethro had hoped to find a home in Central America, but the Honduran villagers—who proudly trace their ancestry back to the Mayans—ask Mr. Nadie (Mr. No-Name) to leave. Again, he is the outsider. At this time he had returned to New York and the law suit.

From the contents of Jethro's safe, Fairr unlocks the last tragedy. Jethro had spent the milions he won from the Donahues (the family which denied him a name) trying to trace his real parents—so that he could ask Sally Donahue (still unmarried) to take his name. He has also believed that, as a changeling, contacting his siblings earlier might bring them harm—never realizing that he has already brought them great good by appropriating the money they never earned. Jethro's murderer is an aristocratic friend of Sally's (who hates Jethro because Sally loves him) who learns of Jethro's identity obsession and has cruelly deceived him by claiming to have proof of his true identity. Jethro had called his brothers the day before his death in the belief that he could now introduce himself.

The Donahues try to hire Fairr to find the murderer of the man they now emotionally call their brother—but the killer is already behind bars, put there by Fairr, who, in the book's opening, has been hired by *him* (the killer) to discover how the police made the connection between himself and his perfect crime. Thus Fairr is hired by the victim, the murderer and the family who set the crime in motion. Of course he accepts only Jethro's fee.

The renewal note is struck by Daisy, Jethro's daughter, who will marry young Bob Donahue, but only if their children legally bear the name of Hammer. Thus the union of Hammer-Donahue will begin again, in blood this time and perpetuate a lineage for Jethro.

The Venning books have a yearning, lyrical intensity, a richness and depth not common to many of the others. They lack humor almost entirely—except for the alibis provided by the Donahues (*Jethro*). And they present in fairly naked terms the family relationship themes which run through all the pen names, styles and genres.

Family relationships which recur are the formative ones between children and their mothers, fathers, aunts, uncles and siblings. In addition to poor parenting, there is sometimes poor childrening, but this is mostly confined to *Wonderful* and *Turkey*.

In *Eight,* Aunt Alex is a kind of wicked auntmother, especially to niece Holly. Alex believes she was deserted when her beloved sister married the no-account Miller and is determined to hold on to Holly permanently. Miller has given up his children to a more advantaged life than he can provide, but also for cash. Nellie Parkins, Glen's real mother, has also given up her child, but she (anonymously) takes a job as the Inglehart housekeeper in order to be near him. Both Miller and Nellie make changes in the murder room, but he acts for profit, she to save Glen.

In *Postman*, another housekeepr is revealed to be a caring mother; the silent Violet is the former film star Liza Lavender. She deserted her daughter Elizabeth Fairfaxx to pursue her career but later profoundly regretted her choice.

Susan Williams' mother (*Glass*) is a curious case: she has concocted and been sustained by an *idea* of a child. She finds the actual Susan to fall far short of her dream but cannot cease prodding and plotting to create at least a reasonable facsimile.

Ross McLauren (*Right*) has been reared abroad by an overly devoted mother who aspires to be an artist but cannot finish a single painting. He is devastated by her death and shortly afterwards undergoes a hideous refugee march under Nazi fire (the only mention of World War II in any of the books, fifteen of which were written during its conduct). His rehabilitation is assumed by his mother's friend Mona McClane, who will never be a wet-nurse.

A tragic failure of parenthood unfolds in *Midget*. Jay Otto's father was ambassador to England and his mother a great society beauty when he was born a midget and farmed out anonymously. He was provided with a lavish trust fund and through the years his mother visited and wrote to him without letting him know their relationship. He learns to love only her, while hating everything else in the normal-sized world. Later he discovers his identity, feels doubly deceived and embarks on a cruel crusade of destroying lives. Otto is the most evil of Rice's villains.

Killer Ellen Ogletree's mother (*Wrong*) runs a gossip-mill for gangsters; her father is called Heart-of-Stone Ogletree by Helene. Plain Gay Lacy (*Right*) is a disappointment to both her parents; she kills (partly, at least) to marry her way into the nextdoor Fairfaxx magic circle—so warm, so loving and so close.

Four women in *Fury* are father-scarred. Arleen Goudge has been cruelly deprived of a normal adolescence by her piety-spouting father, Alvin (who is the book's killer). Ellen McGowan, proudly devoted to her prominent father, wishes nothing more of life than to follow in his footsteps. This she (ironically) accomplishes, as first she covers up his embezzlements, then embezzles additional funds (keeping none of the money for herself) to prevent Alvin Goudge from ruining his memory. Cora Belle Fromm had fled town as a teenager because of the social stigma attached to being the bootlegger's daughter. She returns, relatively well off, years later to take up with the husbands of the classmates who shunned her. Florence Peveley, daughter of the meanest, richest, most powerful man in Jackson County, is more resistive to parental domination, but still feels it will take marriage (even to a man she doesn't respect) to get away from him.

It should be noted that only Helene of the Justus-Malone trio has a parent of any kind—amiable George Brand who appears in *Wrong*. Malone apparently sprang full grown from the stockyards and Jake's antecedents are merely placed (Grove Falls, Iowa), not described. Bingo Riggs, Melville Fairr and Art Smith (*Bystander)* are all orphans. Brothers, as noted, are at odds in *Slept;* brothers and sisters are at odds in *Jethro* and *Pigeon*; Philip Telefair *(Telefair)* is the wickedest uncle; Uncle Rodney Fairfaxx (*Postman*) is the best.

There are no bad, bad children in Rice. There are the good-bad Carstairs (*Home*) and a similar few who appear in *Turkey*; others are redeemable with a good swat, like Bugsie Olsen (*Wonderful*) and Alberta Commanday, the brat Malone subdues in *Loop* (and who listens to her mother, in any case). *Wonderful* also depicts Howie Lutts who has been a thief since childhood. His decent father hides him out, but he only steals again. Both Howard and his unpleasant murder-victim cousin Bertha are homosexuals, the only identified homosexuals in any of the books.

The orphanage is the only institution Rice takes a semi-swipe at. (Rodney Fairfaxx even finds the Twelfth Street lock-up quite comfortable [*Postman]*). The orphanage is not presented as a cruel place but as one with a very long arm, which stretches beyond its doors to curtail choices. Sarah White (*Jethro*) is determined to look for the job she wants and runs away at seventeen to prevent being pigeonholed by the state.

The theme of class, per se, is not overt. But clearly there is privilege here. Helene is privileged by wealth and beauty and connections to fracture every traffic law—and never to harm a living soul. Malone is privileged to tilt the scales of justice to include intention and individual worth in their measure. The exercise of power is generally benevolent.

Rice defies categories: conventions were observed, turned inside out and newly created at will. The best books appeared in her most prolific years, with *Fury* at the top of her form, combining and upgrading all the properties. *Postman* and *Corpse* are the most lighthearted, though *Eight, Wrong* and *Right* all have merry moments. *Kingdom* and *Loop*, written the year she died, although they conform to the format and are not without charm, seem curiously vapid.

Part of Rice's explosive popularity was probably temporal: all the boys had gone to war and, in her books, people were killed but no one got hurt. All of her major characters are children: Malone, Helene, Jake, Bingo, Handsome, even that lonely child Melville Fairr. They challenge the establishment by sticking out their tongues; their conduct is excusable because their code is pure.

Notes

The editions of Rice'snovels used for this chapter are listed below, preceded by the original date of publication. All quotations will be cited in the text, using, where indicated for clarity, the abbreviation given after each entry.

Rice's canon is not complete. There are many uncollected short stories. A number of posthumous publications are the results of shared authorship: Ed McBain and Stuart Palmer are both listed as co-authors. These are short stories and have been unavailable, as was the "Daphne Sanders" work, *To Catch a Thief.* This study, then, considers eleven Malone-Justis novels, two Bingo Riggs-Handsome Kusak novels, the three Venning books and the three "singletons": *Telefair, Home Sweet Homicide* and *Innocent Bystander.*

1939 *Eight Faces at Three* (Cleveland, Ohio: World Publishign Company, 1943). (*Eight*)
1940 *The Corpse Steps Out* (Cleveland, Ohio: World Publishing Company, 1945). (*Corpse*)
The Wrong Murder (Cleveland, Ohio: The World Publishing Company, 1944). (*Wrong)*
1941 *The Right Murder* (Cleveland, Ohio: World Publishing Company, 1943). (*Right*)
Trial By Fury (New York: Pocket Books, Inc., 1943). (*Fury*)
1942 *The Man Who Slept All Day* by Michael Venning (New York: Coward-McCann, Inc., 1942). (*Slept*)
The Big Midget Murders (New York: Books, Inc., 1944). (*Midget*)
Telefair, the House on the Island (Yesterday's Murder) (New York: Popular Library). (*Telefair)*
The Sunday Pigeon Murders (New York: Simon and Schuster, 1942) (*Pigeon).*
1943 *Murder Through the Looking Glass* by Michael Venning (New York: Coward-McCann, 1943) (*Glass*).
The Thursday Turkey Murders (Cleveland, Ohio: World Publishing Company, 1946). (*Turkey*)
Having Wonderful Crime (New York: Simon and Schuster, 1943). (*Wonderful*)
1944 *Jethro Hammer* by Michael Venning (New York: Coward-McCann, 1944). (*Jethro*)
Home Sweet Homicide (New York: Simon and Schuster, 1944). (*Home*)
1945 *The Lucky Stiff* (New York: Simon and Schuster, 1945). (*Stiff*)
1948 *The Fourth Postman* (New York: Simon and Schuster, 1948). (*Postman*)
1949 *Innocent Bystander* (New York: Pocket Books, Inc., 1957 (*Bystander)*
1957 *My Kingdom For A Hearse* (New York: Pocket Books, Inc., 1957). (*Hearse*)
Knocked for a Loop (New York: Pocket Books, Inc., 1958). (*Loop*)

[1]"Mulled Murder, with Spice," *Time,* January 28, 1946, pp. 86-88.

[2]"Mulled," p. 88.

[3]"Mulled," p. 88.

[4]"It's a Mystery to Me," *Writer,* 57: November, 1944, pp. 323-24.

[5]"Mulled," p. 86.

[6]E.T. Guymon, Jr., "The Lucky Stiff," *Murderess, Inc.* Editor: Dilys Winn (New York: Workman Publishing Co., 1979), p. 73.

[7]"Wuxtry! Read All About It!" *Time,* July 29, 1946, p. 61.

[8]"Mulled," p. 88.

E. X. Ferrars
(Photo courtesy: Antonia Reen Photography, Edinburgh)

E. X. Ferrars

(Pseudonym for Morna Doris Brown; she also uses the pseudonym Elizabeth Ferrars).

1907	Born September 6 in Rangoon, Burma; daughter of Peter Clouston MacTaggert and Marie MacTaggert (nee Ferrars)
1918-24	Attended Bedales School, Petersfield, Hampshire
1925-28	Attended University College, London
1928	Received University College diploma of journalism
1940	Published first mystery novel, *Give a Corpse a Bad Name*
	Married Robert Brown
1953	Became a Founding Member, Crime Writers Association
1958	Edited *Planned Departures,* a short story anthology
1981	Published most recent mystery novel, *Thinner Than Water*

E. X. Ferrars

Susan Baker

E. X. Ferrars[1] is usually grouped with the classic puzzler or cozy British school of murder mystery.[2] It is true that Ferrars' books share a social milieu with those of such writers as Agatha Christie and Ngaio Marsh, but underlying this classification lurks a wrongheaded assumption: that genre is determined by setting and character rather than by theme, world view and the emotional effect on the reader. Despite her predilection for village and country house settings and despite her skill at drawing characters from the middle and upper middle classes, even despite her gesture toward comedy in ending each book with at least the hint of wedding bells, E.X. Ferrars finally creates a rather grim world, and her books leave a reader uneasy and wary rather than comfortably reassured. For this reason, Ferrars—more than Christie or Sayers—should be seen as a significant predecessor of the new generation of female British mystery writers, such as P.D. James and Ruth Rendell. To think otherwise can stem only from misreading Ferrars or misinterpreting the generic pattern of the classic British mystery novel. To demonstrate why will require, first, a consideration of formula fiction in general, second, an outline of the classic formula and its underlying motives and finally an examination of the several significant ways in which Ferrars violates this formula.

Formula fiction ultimately functions to reaffirm our preconceptions. It does so partly by fulfilling the generic expectations established by our awareness of the formula. More than this, however, formulaic novels soothe readers by reassuring them that the world is what they would have it be. It surely is no accident that, generally, readers strongly prefer one variety of escape literature: some people choose gothics; some choose science fiction or westerns; even those addicted to mystery novels are not equally attracted to both the classic British and the American tough-guy schools. The worlds presented by these two kinds are diametrically opposed: in the classic detective novel, society is finally good, needing only to expel one exemplar of evil to return to a sane and healthy state; in the tough-guy, hard-boiled novel, society is wholly corrupt, unredeemable and only the extraordinary individual can maintain his integrity within it.

In this sense, setting (broadly defined) provides a significant generic determinant, but only insofar as plot and character reinforce the world view.

Some critics will no doubt flinch at examining "world view" with reference to formula fiction. Certainly it is true that readers do not turn to formula fiction for profundity, and indeed too emphasized a theme will detract from the detachment characteristic of formulaic fiction. Not that classic mystery writers of formula fiction never focus their novels around a central notion—Christie's *Death on the Nile,* for example, surely juxtaposes a variety of kinds of love and their destructive or redemptive powers. But this organizing principle never moves to the foreground. When such a principle does, the novel is vitiated as formula fiction and readers justifiably feel their expectations violated. *Gaudy Night* is a splendid book, but as a classic mystery it is a poor thing indeed, the plot overwhelmed by ruminations on women and work. It may seem paradoxical to argue that theme or world view determines the genre of any piece of formula fiction, given the fact that the purposes and effects of such fiction would be disrupted by too much thought (*dianoia*). The point is that while theme must be quite subordinate in *individual* formulaic novels, a single, powerful vision emerges from each formulaic genre and becomes a crucial defining element for that genre.

The classic detective story ultimately projects a benign world—stable, orderly, rational. Murder temporarily disrupts this balance, but typically the discovery of a single murderer—the embodiment of evil—permits his explusion and a return to a healthy normality. W. H. Auden correctly identifies the classic mystery story's villain as a scapegoat, but he is wrong, I think, in calling the genre *tragedy.*[3] The form surely is comic, as George Grella has demonstrated.[4] Hence the characteristic healing that pervades the last chapter of most classic mysteries: rifts in families are overcome, lovers are united or reunited as suspicions clear, routine reasserts itself and the social order triumphs. In this world, violence is aberrant, isolated in one wicked individual. Because society is well-ordered, reason (rational deduction) can identify the source of violence in this one villain and society's justice provides for his orderly expulsion from the society he has disrupted.

The world just described, that of the classic mystery novel, is not, finally, the world of E.X. Ferrars. Some of her books (primarily early ones) fit the classic pattern I've described, but in far more of them something works to undercut it. In a Ferrars novel, the social order rarely triumphs and evil cannot be isolated and tidily expelled. Murder may be followed by healing, but Ferrars emphasizes the lasting scars it leaves behind.

A caveat is in order here. I hope to demonstrate that Ferrars undercuts the central vision of classic murder mysteries while retaining their characteristic milieu, cast and conventions. Much of the evidence for this argument comes from the kinds of murderers she portrays, their ultimate fates and the aftereffects of their crimes on the survivors. Thus, it will be necessary to reveal the solutions to the mysteries of the four novels to be discussed in detail (*The Cup and the Lip, Depart This Life, The Swaying Pillars* and *A Stranger and Afraid*).

In a recent book, *The Cup and the Lip,* virtually every detail works against the scapegoat pattern central to the classic mystery. (I use the term *scapegoat* in its deepest sense, that of an animal made to take on all the evil of a community and then sacrificed to heal that community). The novel opens with an argument between Peter Harkness, the central consciousness from whose point of view the novel is narrated, and his longtime friend, Max Rowley. The two men debate the origins of violence; Peter believes "that violence is an inborn, horrifying evil, to be suppressed at all costs," while Max contends that "if childhood could be happy and free from fear, the young [are] not naturally violent but [have] it instilled into them by the unpleasant example of their elders" (2-3). These views lead Peter into the assertion that all people are capable of violence "given the circumstances" (3) and Max acknowledges the human attraction to violence, at least as reported on the evening news. While similar abstract discussions are not unheard of in the classic mystery novel, placing one at the very begining is unusual; more often, classic mystery writers develop exposition through scenes remarkable for their calm normality, perhaps including only the gentlest foreshadowing of the violent disaster about to erupt in an apparently orderly world. A novel that opens with two key figures acknowledging pervasive violence is hardly likely to project a view of violence as aberrant.

The actual events of the novel begin when Peter and Max's argument is interrupted by a telephone call from Max's wife, Kate. She wants Peter to come to Sisslebridge, where she is staying with friends, and appear on a panel of writers at a meeting of the local Arts League. Kate's host, Dan Braile, was scheduled to participate, but he has been taken ill. Peter refuses, but he then receives a second call with the same request, this one from Gina Marston, Braile's twenty-year-old stepdaughter. She is frightened, but won't say why. Peter agrees to go to Sisslebridge, obviously because he is attracted to Gina. Several of Ferrars' novels begin similarly; the initial action of the plot is the central character's undertaking some sort of errand for a friend, relative, or beloved. (See, for example, *Witness Before the Fact, Breath of Suspicion* and *Neck in a Noose,* or a variant of the pattern in *Blood Flies Upward* and *In at the Kill.*) In a Ferrars mystery, loyalty and generous or helpful impulses may well embroil one in nastiness and danger. It should be noted that this sort of opening makes the central figure an active participant in whatever happens; that is, the protagonist becomes involved with evil, however unwittingly, through his own freely willed actions. The protagonist does not choose evil, but neither does it arise apparently out of nowhere.

When Peter arrives in Sisslebridge he goes not to Braile's home, but to the Manor House Hotel. Despite its name, this is no backdrop for the gracious living typical of the classic mystery. The hotel offers neither luxury, nor quaint charm, nor solid English comfort. Indeed, with its slightly hunchbacked barmaid and halfwitted bellboy-waiter-desk clerk, the Manor House Hotel could serve as the setting for a thoroughly melodramatic gothic novel—except that the details of its description convey dismal seediness rather than foreboding: "A strong smell of mildew surged out at them. The dim, economical lighting of the room showed the source of it, a large, grey, furry patch of mould in the middle of the ceiling" (20). Grey Gables, Braile's house, might seem at first to be a more appropriate setting for a classic detective story; it is large, located at the edge of the village, and houses a substantial number of permanent, semi-permanent and temporary guests. But Grey Gables is neglected and rather shabby, its overall effect austere (52).

So neither the exposition nor the setting of *The Cup and the Lip* is particularly appropriate for a classic murder mystery. The cast of characters and the initial developments in the plot, however, could well fit the traditional formula. The officers of the Sisslebridge Arts League would be comfortable in a Christie novel; they are a country doctor and two women—one giddily enthusiastic, the other blunt and fond of her own unpopular opinions. Similarly, Dan Braile and his household could have been created by Ngaio Marsh, with her fondness for eccentrics and artists. Braile himself is an elderly, gifted and highly successful novelist, with a younger, tense and skittish, rather dowdy wife, Helen. Gina, young, pretty and high-strung, is staying with them, as are Kate Rowley, Max's wife and author of "Sombre Victorian novels about huge families of people who all hated one another" (34), Alice Thorpe, a very elderly poet, the Patons (a young novelist and his wife) and the Weldons. Juliet Weldon seems perpetually vague and distracted, but she writes skilled, if only moderately successful, short stories; Walter Weldon is a critic. Braile's motives for surrounding himself with hangers-on are not clear. Kate says that "He always keeps the house as full as he can of people who need peace and quiet to find themselves in" (43), but Gina believes he's a terrible man, "Yes, really terrible. He only uses other people, he doesn't care for them" (95).

At any rate, this is a suitable cast for a classic mystery. And when it is discovered, first, that Gina believes Dan is gravely ill and that Dan himself believes he is being slowly poisoned, and then that he has disappeared, the reader may well settle into expecting the standard formula. This expectation is reinforced when, just as Grey Gables is filled with tension over Dan's inexplicable disappearance (he was, after all, quite weak from illness), the doorbell rings; enter Adrian Rolfe, an astonishingly handsome, extraordinarily rich young man who has been corresponding with Dan and has arrived at Dan's invitation. And, indeed, for a while *The Cup and the Lip* reads much like a classic formula mystery. There are clues involving such things as who did the washing up and false trails followed from Sisslebridge to London. Peter finds himself jealous as Gina and Adrian engage in flirtation, and Adrian reveals that Dan has suspected Gina of being the poisoner. If this were a novel of the standard formula, Gina would have to be exonerated in preparation for pairing off with Peter, or, in a minor twist, with Adrian. Indeed, Gina turns out to be innocent, but virtually everyone else turns out to be guilty. And at this point, the divergence of *The Cup and the Lip* from the classic formula becomes acute.

First, Adrian Rolfe turns up murdered and Dan Braile turns up alive—Anna, the hunchbacked barmaid, has been hiding him, planning to be his housekeeper when he sells Grey Gables and moves to the Highlands. The plot device of having a supposed victim suddenly appear, alive and well, is typical of Ferrars. (See, for example, *Hanged Man's House* and *The Pretty Pink Shroud*.) More than being a clever turn, I think, this strategy undercuts the traditional formula's preference for appropriate victims. There really is no formulaic logic behind Rolfe's being murdered; he simply has the misfortune to be in the wrong place at the wrong time. Dan Braile is the novel's logical victim and, indeed, the one intended by the villains. Anna has sent samples of Braile's excreta to a cousin to test for arsenic, and when the company assembled at Grey Gables learn this fact, Juliet breaks down. In an hysterical explosion, she reveals that the entire roster of house-guests, except for Gina and Alice Thorpe, had conspired to poison Dan (so Helen could sell Grey Gables and the lot of them live on the proceeds). This development undercuts what's left of the classic formula almost completely. First, the classic villain is rarely "one of us," that is, one of the socially acceptable. Here, the would-be murderers are "all of us"; they are socially acceptable and thoroughly guilty. Moreover, they have been outwitted by the intended victim. How can a scapegoat be expelled and a community healed when virtually the entire community participates in evil and moreover, does so ineptly? Furthermore, nothing is done about this crime of conspiracy to commit murder; the guilty community remains. (One could argue that Christie's truly classic *Murder on the Orient Express* ends similarly with the revelation of multiple murderers who will go unpunished. But, of course, the effect is entirely different. The conspirators in *Murder on the Orient Express* are entirely successful; their victim is a particularly heinous criminal himself; and they are twelve in number, an *ad hoc* jury who avenge society on a vicious kidnapper who would otherwise escape society's punishment.)

The guilty community seems initially to at least be innocent of the novel's actual murder; the halfwitted bellboy confesses to Rolfe's murder. But this explanation is not sustained. Ferrars exploits the established convention of the double twist to give us another very unconventional—in terms of the classic puzzler—solution. The novel ends much as it began, with a conversation between Peter and his old friend, Max. Here, Peter unravels the crime: Rolfe was murdered by Max, who has conspired with the others to prosper through the death of Dan Braile. The would-be murderers surmised that Dan must have been hiding in the hotel and Max had gone to eliminate him and his arsenic-filled corpse. Kate and the others would meanwhile provide each other with impregnable alibis. But by the time Max arrived, Dan had fled to Anna's house and unlucky Rolfe instead became the victim. So *The Cup and the Lip* ends with the protagonist's oldest friend a murderer and most of his social set equally guilty of attempted murder. Moreover, although Peter knows what has happened and believes that Juliet will soon break down and reveal all, the novel itself leaves the numerous guilty parties unpunished. (P.D. James ends her most recent novel, *The Skull Beneath the Skin,* similarly; Cordelia will try to effect justice, but her eventual success is left doubtful.) Justice is not so much thwarted—who would 'scape whipping?—as the idea of justice is abandoned.

Peter simply turns away from the pack of murderers and from Gina who, though innocent herself, is deeply associated with the guilty community. In *The Cup and the Lip,* evil cannot be expelled; it is too pervasive. And society cannot triumph because too many of its members are implicated in the crime. There is a kind of private healing in the protagonist as Peter telephones his long-time girlfriend in the hope of returning "to a world where some values operated and you could count on finding goodness behind the face of apparent friendship" (184). But nothing in *The Cup and the Lip* has affirmed the existence of such a world, the world of the classic mystery novel. Indeed, in his willed effort to salvage some sort of values, Peter rather reminds one of Sam Spade or Philip Marlowe. Like a hard-boiled detective, Peter affirms his own code in a world hostile to all such codes. The mean streets he will walk, however, pass through country villages and the environs of upper-middle-class Londoners.

Virtually every detail in *The Cup and the Lip* works against the deep motive of the classic mystery formula; in so doing, the novel collocates a large number of Ferrars' characteristic plot elements. Many of these involve the identity and fate of the murderer. The villain in a Ferrars' novel, as in *The Cup and the Lip,* frequently evades the course of justice, most often by suicide (e.g., *Skeleton Staff, Blood Flies Upward, Kill or Cure*); sometimes the murderer is murdered in turn by someone avenging the victim (e.g., *The Small World of Murder* and *The Doubly Dead*); occasionally, everyone conspires to hush things up (see, for example, *The Seven Sleepers*). Whatever the method of evading legal justice, it works against the sense of society's ability to expel those who offend against it. Of course, the classic mystery occasionally allows a doomed gentleman suicide as a dignified end, but such conclusions are relatively rare and generally reserved for the truly well-bred who have been driven to murder (out of noble motives or desperation) by a particularly nasty scoundrel of a victim.

So too, *The Cup and the Lip* is typical of Ferrars in that more than one person commits murder, or at least attempts to do so. (Among her numerous novels with more than one killer are *The March Hare Murders, Breath of Suspicion,* and *Drowned Rat.*) Again the multiplicity of villains works against the vision of a community that can be healed by expelling the singular embodiment of evil within it. A similar effect of widespread evil occurs in those novels where several secondary characters are crooks of one sort or another (e.g., *Alive and Dead, Skeleton Staff, Seeing Double*).

This sense of pervasive evil is perhaps strongest in those novels where the murderer is someone much loved by the central consciousness—the killer may be an old friend, a strong romantic object, or even a favorite sibling (e.g.—in alphabetical rather than respective order—*Breath of Suspicion, Foot in the Grave, Hanged Man's House, The Pretty Pink Shroud, Witness Before the Fact*). In other words, close emotional ties with the novel's central consciousness do not exempt Ferrars' characters from guilt. In the classic formula, the shifting of suspicion to each character in turn works to create a sense of relief and reassurance in the reader once the true villain is revealed and punished. In Ferrars' books, however, shifting suspicion simply signals the potential, or actual, guilt of everyone involved, a guilt which is not expiated. The possibility of evil lurking within even those one loves best haunts Ferrars' novels and often becomes a truth the central consciousness must face. Peter's feelings just before the end of *The Cup and the Lip* are significant: "His thoughts are a curious blank. It surprised him vaguely that he felt no anger with Max. His feelings seemed to have gone beyond anger. Perhaps, he thought, true anger requires a kind of innocence, and he had lost it" (183-184).

Loss of innocence is not a comic motif, but it is one that reverberates through the novels of E.X. Ferrars. It is perhaps most explicit as a theme in the 1958 novel, *Depart This Life.* On the surface, *Depart This Life* seems to fit the classic pattern more closely than do many of Ferrars' other novels. The victim, Stephen Gazeley, is perfectly appropriate to the formula: he is thoroughly a cad, the sort of spiritual blackmailer who primarily enjoys holding the lives of others in thrall (cf. P.D. James' *Shroud for a Nightingale);* moreover, he also functions as a typically comic blocking figure, radiating an atmosphere of tension around the engagement of his daughter, Katherine, to Colin Luckett, the only son of Stephen's estranged neighbors. The setting is Gazeley's comfortable home in a quiet English village. And there are numerous secondary puzzles: a beautiful mystery woman, a hostile gardener, an unidentified car and driver. At the novel's end, breaches are healed, the guilty punished.

Despite these congruences with the standard formula, *Depart This Life* characteristically departs from the pattern. First, the murderer is a man who has loved and at least to some extent been loved by Hilda (Stephen's sister), the novel's central consciousness. More crucial, however, is a question of emphasis. *Depart This Life* is less concerned with the solution to Stephen's murder than with his sister's slow and painful realization of her brother's vicious nature. Hilda's emergence from a naive blindness to human evil, her loss of innocence, dominates the novel throughout.

Depart This Life opens with a conversation between Katherine and Hilda. Katherine is fearful that her father will spoil things between her and Colin. Hilda reassures her, saying that "The quarrel, if you can call it a quarrel—" is "with his parents." She explains, "We just don't like the way they've behaved to us" (1). Katherine, more clearsighted than her aunt, scolds Hilda, "You always pretend there's nothing queer about anything. Nothing wrong" (12). In a Ferrars' novel, there is generally something queer about almost everything. Hilda defends Stephen's attitude toward the no longer friendly Lucketts, saying "He said it was just their way. He's really much more tolerant of people's peculiarities than I am" (13). This statement is deeply ironic. Stephen is not tolerant of people's "peculiarities"; rather, he relishes them as a source of the power to torment. And Hilda is excessively tolerant, or more accurately, she is essentially oblivious. As is noted later, "She had preferred to accept people as being more or less what they wanted her to think them, for this had helped to make life calmer and friendlier than it might otherwise have been" (91). (Hilda might be compared to Martha Crayle in *Alive and Dead.*) But Hilda's illusion that one can will a calm, friendly world is shattered—less by the murder of her brother than by the revelation, after his death, of what he had been.

After Stephen is murdered, Hilda and Nelson Wingard have the following exchange:

> "But you were Stephen's best friend, Nelson."
> "Is that what you think?"
> "It's the truth, isn't it?"
> "Doesn't it take two to make a friendship? And what was the truth about Stephen? Well, perhaps we shall find out now. We shall find out a great many things"(55).

And indeed Hilda does. The first shock comes when Katherine tells her that Stephen had learned that Arthur Luckett was not Colin's father and had threatened Valerie Luckett with making this fact known to her husband and to everyone else. Hilda does not want to believe this of her brother. Later that evening she talks with Nelson.

> "The whole world I've lived in has suddenly come to an end this evening. I didn't know that till I'd spoken to Katherine. It didn't come to an end with Stephen's death. Not simply with his death. It's come now because now I don't know what to think about anything or anyone. It's one's thoughts, isn't it, that make up one's world? And mine's gone, because I don't know what to believe about Stephen, about Katherine, about Colin, about you, or about myself either. Have I really been a blind and stupid woman all these years—so blind and stupid that I've been almost wicked?"(73).

As the novel progresses, succeeding revelations force Hilda to acknowledge that she has been "blind and stupid."

She tries to salvage some of her memories of her brother, recalling that he had refrained from using his knowledge of Colin's family to damage Katherine's engagement. But Valerie suggests that "Perhaps the right moment hadn't come yet, the moment when he could inflicit the most pain" (122). And Hilda learns more about Stephen: that he had been blackmailing the gardener into working overtime, that he had taken the first steps toward tormenting the neighborhood mystery woman (Mrs. Frearson) with his knowledge that she once had been accused of murdering her husband. The deepest shock, however, comes when Hilda learns that her brother had blackmailed Nelson for falsifying evidence to save a client. In this case, the price of Stephen's silence was that Nelson should not proceed in his plan to ask Hilda to marry him. Moreover, after an interlude Stephen also had insisted that Nelson resume his visits to keep the pain alive. Hilda responds to this information, "No, that can't be true, that's too much" (163).

But by now she can believe anything. Ironically, she soon discovers that Nelson, too, has lied to her. His visits have been motivated, at least in part, by an affair he had begun with Valerie Luckett. And Nelson also murdered Stephen. This fact, however, in no way exonerates Stephen; there have been, after all, the independent testimonies of the gardener and the mysterious Mrs. Frearson indicating a disposition toward blackmail. Nelson's wickedness parallels Stephen's; it does not justify or replace it. As in *The Cup and the Lip,* there is a pervasiveness to guilt and Hilda is forced to face this uncomfortable fact. It is true, indeed, that her world has ended (see the passage quoted above). Hilda will have to construct a new world and it will of necessity be one that acknowledges the possibility—even the probability—that people may not be what they seem or what one wants them to be.

Ferrars typically insists on this sense that a new world must be created out of the wreckage murder leaves behind. Unlike the classic mystery formula which treats murder as a puzzle and its solution as the expiation of guilt for the community, a novel by E. X. Ferrars more often presents murder as the catastrophe that not only uncovers all the weak spots in the social fabric but also weakens them further. Her books rarely portray a society healed and affirmed; rather, they plunge their protagonists into a disaster that destroys their innocence.

So far, I have focused on the ways that Ferrars' novels, despite their social milieu, diverge from the pattern of classic murder mysteries. Because the elements of the standard formula project a reassuring vision of the social world as redeemable and ultimately able to restore order within itself, to alter these elements significantly and repeatedly is to alter the projected world view. The question remains of precisely what vision of the world the novels of E. X. Ferrars imply. Her titles are suggestive. Frequently they hint at lurking danger (*Fear the Light, Sleeping Dogs*) or at tenuousness and instability (*Foot in the Grave, The Cup and the Lip, The Swaying Pillars*). In a dangerous and uncertain world, one may well choose to narrow horizons, to retreat into the known security of home and friends, but other of Ferrars' titles signal her rejection of such security as illusory: *Murder Among Friends, Murder Moves In, Furnished for Murder, The Small World of Murder.* The vision adumbrated by these titles is paticularly developed in two novels: *The Swaying Pillars* and *A Stranger and Afraid.*

The Swaying Pillars opens, as do so many of Ferrars' mysteries, with an encounter between two old friends. Purely by chance, Helena Sebright (the novel's central consciousness) meets her old friend, Cleo Grant, in the Underground at Picadilly. Over coffee, Cleo suggests that Helena might be interested in a most unusual job—escorting a seven-year-old girl, Jean, to her grandparents' home in Tondolo, capital city of the recently independent African nation of Uyowa. Jean's father, Denis Forrest, is going to give a three-month series of lectures in America, and her mother, Marcia, is very busy as an actress, so sending the child to her grandparents for a while seems the best plan. Helena accepts the job, but not before Denis warns her that there recently has been some political unrest in Uyowa. As noted earlier, the gambit of a friend's request is typical of Ferrars and here it has the effect of placing a cast of very British characters in a most exotic setting. The central figures in *The Swaying Pillars* could have been transplanted to Tondolo from an English village. Jean's grandparents are Hugh Forrest, a calm and sensible former headmaster, and Forrest's wife, Judy, who resents her daughter-in-law (Marcia). Their son Paul is a physician who has been very much in love with Cleo Grant. The Forrests' social circle includes the following people: the superintendent of police, Robbie Meldrum, and his wife Barbara; Vernon Elder from the British consulate; and the Passfields—Jim a journalist and his wife, Peg, a rather vulgar and social-climbing woman who is loudly racist.

Here, again, Ferrars exploits a standard convention of the classic mystery. Agatha Christie, for example, could transport her village murders to archeological digs in Mesopotamia (*Murder in Mesopotamia*), to luxury conveyances (*Murder on the Orient Express, Death on the Nile*), even to ancient Egypt (*Death Comes as the End*), without altering the basic formula. Ngaio Marsh, too, could have Roderick Alleyn detecting in New Zealand (*Colour Scheme, Died in the Wool*) as well as in England. In these and similar cases, the classic mystery writer still assumes a well-ordered society—one with a defined social hierarchy, shared values and an efficient police force. Ferrars uses the convention similarly in *No Peace for the Wicked* and *Skeleton Staff*, for example. But in *The Swaying Pillars*, Ferrars moves her British characters into a society in turmoil. As the novel's title suggests, the social structure in Tondolo is verging on collapse; it cannot provide a stable order to be restored by the expulsion of a localized evil.

The plot of *The Swaying Pillars* is convoluted. Against a background of public violence, as first an assassination attempt and then a military coup take place in Tondolo, Helena and the Forrests face private terror when Jean is kidnapped. After various twists and turns, the kidnapper turns out to be Cleo Grant; her dismembered hand, with its characteristic silver nails and still wearing a ring Paul had given her, is dredged up from the crocodile-ridden river on whose banks Jean was last seen. Cleo has conspired in the kidnapping with Jim Passfield, who is actually Petrzelka, the Czech to whom Cleo was once engaged and with whom she remained obviously in love. Cleo has betrayed the Forrests, old friends with whom she had lived after her parents' deaths, and she in turn has been betrayed by Petrzelka; it is he who has pushed her into the river. Petrzelka also kills his vulgar wife (whom he has brought into the scheme), and he himself is found shot—apparently a random victim of the violence attending the Uyowan military coup. Fortunately, Jean is found drugged but unharmed; Helena and Paul fall in love, although the novel undercuts projections of a happily-ever-after future for them by hints that Paul will never completely recover from his doomed passion for Cleo. The last paragraph of the novel should be quoted in full:

> [Paul] started to say something else, then stopped and [Helena] saw a shadow on his face. It was the look that she had come to think of as the Cleo look, and she knew it might be a long time before it finally faded. Meanwhile he never spoke of Cleo. Nobody spoke of her. When they mentioned, which was rarely, the time when Jean had been missing, it was as if they felt that the agony of it had been brought about by some natural disaster, a hurricane or an earthquake, not a human betrayal. Cleo was lost, gone, drowned deep, left to the river (192).

Here, I think, Ferrars portrays the human will to revise the past so that one can bear to go on with the future. Actually, nothing that happens in *The Swaying Pillars* can be attributed to "natural disaster." Rather, the entire novel is woven of human betrayals. Cleo and Petrzelka, as suggested earlier, betray nearly everyone. Moreover, they succeed in the kidnapping, insofar as they do, because the Forrests are also betrayed by their native servants who withhold knowledge of the crime in order to protect Gilbert Kaggawa, the deposed president of Uyowa. Kaggawa is an old friend of the Forrests—he and Denis were at University together—and the servants hide him in the Forrests' home. (He is, perhaps not incidentally, wanted for treason; the charge arises, of course, simply from the political turnover.) Neither the servants nor Kaggawa wish to harm the Forrests—but they do. One could excuse these betrayals as unfortunate but necessary given the higher loyalty to one's country—or what one wishes for one's country. But Ferrars neatly undercuts this rationalization by having neither Kaggawa nor his rival triumph; rather, there is a military coup, and Uyowans rally around the new ruler in jubilation. The commentary on this outcome is sardonic: "Almost no one had heard of General Ighodaro before, but suddenly he was known to be the man who would put everything right.

And you demonstrated, you shouted slogans, because after all you were alive" (186). So much for higher loyalties.

Indeed, in *The Swaying Pillars* both the public and private worlds are radically unstable. Certainly, justice can hardly be said to prevail. As noted earlier, none of the three criminals comes to trial. Such an outcome is typical of Ferrars, of course, but here the impotence of public justice is underscored. When Superintendent Meldrum is told of the sequence of events, he replies, "You'll have to make an official statement about this Passfield business, of course, but at the moment I don't think anyone would be much interested in it" (189). Private violence is essentially irrelevant in a world of public violence; in the midst of revolution, there simply is no real social order to triumph reassuringly. One exchange between Helena and Passfield is particularly interesting in this context. Passfield is speaking of some recent ritual murders: "Very nasty, all the same, because, apart from anything else, to our minds they seem quite motiveless" (164). Helena contends the reverse, "I think the more nearly rational it seems, the worse it is" (165). And Passfield responds, "I've always put it the other way round. The more rational the motive, the nearer the murder gets to—well, warfare, revolution and other normal human activities" (165).

Of course, comments by the evil Passfield/Petrzelka are suspect, and the novel does seem to attribute many of Uyowa's problems to British Imperialism. When contraband arms (hidden by the servants) are discovered buried beneath the pergola Hugh Forrest had been trying unsuccessfully to construct, he observes the following:

> "And I thought it was because I hadn't learnt enough about building, hadn't troubled enough with the foundations. And perhaps it's true in a sense that I hadn't.... We came along, we British, with unpractical ideas of building a society on all sorts of unsteady pillars—parliamentary government, justice, law and order—but we left the foundations to look after themselves" (132).

So one perhaps could contend that the novel contrasts Uyowan instablity with British stability and thereby affirms the latter. But I don't think so. *The Swaying Pillars* finally questions the ability of *any* society to restrain the violence intrinsic to its members; were social order "natural," it wouldn't require such extensive foundations to remain intact. Imperialism, then, may exacerbate flaws inherent to all social systems, since it arbitrarily imposes one inadequate order on another. And I would argue, further, that while *The Swaying Pillars* addresses certain doubts more overtly than other of Ferrars' novels, its skepticism toward the efficacy of social order is absolutely typical of Ferrars. And it is absolutely antithetical to the collective vision of classic detective stories.

On this subject, Ferrars stands between the classic and the hard-boiled worlds. The social order portrayed in classic mysteries is benignant, reliable and efficacious against intrusions of particular evil; above all, society permits decent and civilized people to lead decent and civilized lives. In hard-boiled novels, society is wholly corrupt and indecent. Even people who would behave well cannot; the social order ultimately taints and corrupts them. In Ferrars' world, however, evil resides in human beings rather than in the world around them. The social order functions moderately well as long as people behave themselves, but it is utterly inadequate to restrain, contain, or expel wickedness when it erupts into violence, as it sometimes will. For Ferrars, the veneer of civilization is real and to be valued, but it is fragile.

The Swaying Pillars epitomizes E. X. Ferrars' skepticism about the ability of social orders to prevent violence and disorder. It is true, however, that many of her books do project a private healing or regeneraton in their protagonists. (See the earlier discussion of *The Cup and the Lip,* for example.) And, of course, failure of the larger social world to order and secure life can encourage a shrinking of one's horizons, a deliberate narrowing of emotion and concern into a focus on a small, intimate, known community—particularly one's family and longtime friends. Yet Ferrars continually undercuts this specialized private realm as a source of reassurance, security or certainty. Her books abound, for example, with siblings who don't like each other very much (e.g., *Skeleton Staff*)—even to the point of murder (e.g., *The March Hare Murders, Murderers Anonymous*). It isn't that, in Ferrars' world, family members never manifest love and loyalty to each other; rather, one simply cannot rely on familial bonds alone to assure stability or trustworthiness. So too, as discussed earlier, established ties, long-standing friendship, and passionate love provide no guarantee against betrayal or against the discovery of evil in those one knows best.

One of Ferrars' most interesting treatments of this theme—perhaps her best—occurs in *A Stranger and Afraid,* which indeed collocates many of Ferrars' characteristic themes. The novel opens as Holly Dunthorne, a graduate student in English Literature, returns to Roydon St. Agnes, a village that is essentially part of Helsington, where several of Ferrars' novels are set. Holly has cut short her vacation in Portugal after receiving a letter from Andrew Meriden, the object of her first and lasting girlhood crush. Although through the course of the novel Andrew and Holly grow into mature love, it is clear that her early fondness for him was inextricably tied to her infatuation with his entire family. Holly's own parents were usually traveling, so she had grown up at boarding schools, spending holidays with her aunt, Judy Dunthorne, a neighbor of the Meridens. Given Holly's rather distant family, one can easily understand her attraction to the colorful Meridens. Ben Meriden is a genius and artisan, a designer and builder of handcrafted furniture. He can afford to practice his art because his wife, Isobel, is wealthy; she is also high-strung, often swept away by her predilection for petty and unnecessary economies, and quirkily determined to permit her three children to fulfill their personalities. (They all attended Helsington's progressive school, which Ferrars mentions in several novels—never very favorably.) Andrew, the oldest Meriden child, is a talented mathematician; Kate is Holly's age, lovely but directionless; the younger son, Marcus, is described as extraordinarily beautiful, but he is a habitual liar and in trouble with the police (unjustly, it turns out) as the novel opens.

The Meridens and Holly's attraction to them may well remind readers of Ngaio Marsh's eccentric Lampreys and their admiring Roberta (in *Death of a Peer,* published in England as *Surfeit of Lampreys*). And, indeed, the initial situation is similar: a young woman returns to the family which has enchanted her. But the resemblance does not extend to the plot. In Marsh's novel, the murder victim is an obnoxious uncle whose death solves the Lampreys' perpetual financial problems and the murderer is, conveniently and cheerfully, a servant. In *A Stranger and Afraid,* however, the victim is Holly's likeable and harmless aunt and the murderer turns out to be Ben Meriden, who thinks Judy Dunthorne has been blackmailing him about his affair with Lisa Chard, a local celebrity. In an odd twist, however, the blackmailer is Isobel. Deeply hurt by Ben's infidelity, she has wanted to make him suffer. (One could ask whether murder or blackmail was the greater betrayal; both Ben and Isobel ultimately kill themselves, usurping society's responsibility for judgment and retribution.) Once again, even this brief comparison indicates Ferrars' divergence from the classic pattern where murderous evil so often correlates with inferior social status and the exposure of a murderer generally purges and heals a community.

A further comparison with *Death of a Peer* is pertinent. When murder intrudes on Marsh's Lampreys, they close ranks, resorting to all sorts of foolish lies and evasions to protect one another. Disaster does not weaken the family ties; if anything, it revitalizes them. (One could compare Christie's *Mysterious Affair at Styles* or Dorothy Sayers' *Clouds of Witness.*) So, too, in Josephine Tey's *Brat Farrar,* familial bonds are strong enough to withstand even the deep guilt of one member. But in *A Stranger and Afraid,* the family structure collapses under presssure. Here, as elsewhere (see, particularly, *The Small World of Murder*), Ferrars seems to view families as microcosms of society; superficially, they work to order and sustain life, but under the pressure of violent death their structural weaknesses are exacerbated, even to the breaking point and the damage is irrevocable.

As is typical of Ferrars, *A Stranger and Afraid* does not portray the healing of a community but rather reveals the inability of human affections and bonds to sustain stability under pressure. The fragility of friendship and the potentially destructive stress of family relationships reverberate throughout the novel. Indeed, like Peter in *The Cup and the Lip* and Hilda in *Depart This Life*, Holly is compelled to surrender her naivete about people and their ties to one another. After the murder, Holly learns that Judy and Ben had once been in love, that Ben had married Isobel primarily for money, that Ben and Lisa had had an affair, that Ben was a murderer and Isobel a blackmailer (motivated by vengeance rather than greed). There is a very real terror here, characteristic of Ferrars' work, grounded in the extent to which we can be ignorant about those closest to us. This theme is anything but reassuring. As Lisa Chard says, "Better the devil you don't know than the devil you do. That's true, you know. It's finding yourself intimate with the devil that's so frightening" (140).

Moreover, Holly's realization extends beyond the shattering thought that someone she has loved could murder her aunt, a woman that he himself once loved. She also must surrender her idealized vision of the Meridens as a family. Early in the novel, Stephen Floyd, a visiting architect and a reasonably detached observer, tells Holly that Marcus Meriden never "had a chance, growing up in that family." He continues, "A father who's a genius, granted, but totally unresponsible. A hopelessly permissive but wildly possessive mother. An elder brother who simply clears out to Canada and doesn't help. And a lovely but brainless sister" (13). Floyd's comments outrage Holy—"What would she not have given herself to have belonged to a family like the Meridens?" (14). She remembers the Meridens as "all, in their different ways, unlike anyone else whom she had ever met" (15). Later, her beloved Andrew, the most stable member of his family, is even harsher than Floyd: "And you know, I think, in our family, we're all monsters of some kind. We're all exaggerations of something or other. Something in each of us has got over-size and out of proportion. Ben's exaggeratedly dedicated to his non-commercial art, Isobel to the welfare of the family, Kate to desperation and boredom and drink—increasingly drink. Marcus too and he can't carry it as Kate can" (88-89). This is the family Holly always adored and perhaps more significantly, felt she knew well. And it is a family typical of Ferrars—closer to those of Ross

Macdonald than to those of Marsh, Tey or Sayers. Ferrars' most recent novel is significantly titled *Thinner than Water* and its protagonist observes, "I know that the real life of any family is always a puzzling, secret thing and that hatred and jealousy can be under the surface, sometimes all mixed up with genuine love" (15).

Hollys most explicit realization occurs while she is staying with the Meridens after her aunt's murder. Ferrars' description of Holly's feelings at this point should be quoted at length.

> The feeling had been almost the same as she had had in Judy's study the evening before when Ben, Lisa and Stephen had been there together, a feeling that they were all concentrated on one another in a way that meant nothing to her, a feeling that she did not belong there. It hurt her a good deal to recognize this. She had always taken for granted that she meant more to the Meridens than, plainly, she did.... But somewhere she had gone wrong.
>
> She thought of Ben's almost contemptuous definition of friendship. '...the odd meeting from time to time, the occasional helping hand held out, a limited sort of trust...' And she began to think that perhaps that was all it was for people as they became older, compared with the ardent thing it was for a child (133).

This kind of realization may be necessary if one is to grow up, but it would be out of place in a classic formula mystery where the solution of a murder heals breaches and reunites a community. Here, as elsewhere, Ferrars emphasizes the inevitable gulf between people rather than affirming the more inherently comic possibility of bridging that gulf with community and affection. Holly will be like Cam in *Skeleton Staff;* accused of taking everyone at face value, Cam replies, "Not after today.... Never again" (141).

Set more than six months after the murder has been solved, the final chapter of *A Stranger and Afraid* represents Ferrars at her best, subtly complicating the thematic emphasis of the rest of the novel. Holly and Kate are sharing a flat in London. Kate has finally found her metier as a magazine editor and writer of minor love stories; Holly is preparing to meet Andrew at the airport—for the first time since the central events of the novel. Superficially everything has returned to normal, just as we might expect in a classic mystery. Two things, however, complicate the sense of tidy resolution characteristic of the traditional formula: first, those truly responsible for the catastrophe are left unpunished; and second, Ferrars emphasizes that rebuilding one's life after disaster is inevitably a painful, tentative and slow process.

As mentioned earlier, the villains in Ferrars' novels frequently evade justice, undercutting any sense of society's ability to regenerate itself through expelling those who violate its tenets. Ben's and Isobel's suicides are typical in this respect. But in *A Stranger and Afraid,* the subject of legal justice or even of some other sort of retribution is complex. For although Ben is a murderer and Isobel a blackmailer, they perhaps bear less moral guilt than the two other characters who break no laws at all. As described above, the Meridens are all obsessive in some fashion and thus vulnerable on the subjects of their obsessions; moreover, what the young Holly saw in them as delightfully different seems to have involved an emotional intensity that finally became explosive. Yet it required an outside catalyst to bring the explosion about.

Early in the novel, Kate calls Lisa Chard "a force of destruction" (31). And indeed she is. Lisa, a successful playwright always alert to and making notes on potential material for her plays, not only had an affair with Ben, but also casually left her notes about the affair lying around to be discovered by Loraine Gargrave, an aspiring actress Lisa had taken up (again, to mine for dramatic material) and then dropped. Loraine's "death-dealing work" (188) was to take revenge by tattling to Isobel, thus setting the subsequent disasters in motion. In reading *A Stranger and Afraid,* one senses that although Ben and Isobel are likely instruments for evil, the real sources of evil in the novel are Lisa and Loraine, who emerge absolutely unscathed. Not only is society unable to expel or punish them, at the novel's end, they are, in effect, being rewarded: Loraine's career as an actress is thriving and Lisa's most recent play is still running in London. As in Ferrars' other works, evil here cannot be isolated and expelled—it is too pervasive.

This reminder of pervasive evil would alone be sufficient to thwart a reader's desire for a comforting conclusuion, but Ferrars' depiction of Holly also works against a sense of tidy resolution in the novel's final chapter. Superficially, of course, she is a typical comic heroine, about to be united with her beloved. But Holly and Andrew have learned too much; they have reservations. (Compare the tenuous but real relationship between Virginia and Felix Freer that Ferrars is developing in *Last Will and Testament, Frog in the Throat,* and *Thinner Than Water.*) In their letters, they have "soberly and thoughtfully" agreed that "after the sort of events that had shaken them all last year, no one, of course, should do anything impulsively or purely emotionally" (188). They know that after disaster, rebuilding a life takes time, so time is "to be allowed for Andrew to settle into the new job in Edinburgh and for Holly to finish working for her Ph. D., and for the two of them to get to know one another again in a normal atmosphere" (188). This passage points to something at the heart of Ferrars' divergence from the essentially reassuring comic formula. In the classic mystery pattern, a society's infection erupts as murder and thus can be cured once the scapegoat/villain is expelled. Life then goes *back* to normal; a healed society returns to its previous equilibrium. In Ferrars' world, on the other hand, there can be no going back. Murder changes things. The survivors rebuild their lives, of course, but they must do so without the innocence and illusions which formerly sustained them.

Notes

[1]Ferrars' novels are listed below, preceded by the original date of publication. All quotations will be cited in the text and are to the American edition:

1940 *Give a Corpse a Bad Name* (London: Hodder and Stoughton).
1940 *Remove the Bodies* (London: Hodder and Stoughton; New York: Doubleday, 1941). (*Rehersals for Murder*).
1941 *Death in Botanist's Bay* (London: Hodder and Stoughton; New York: Doubleday, 1942). (*Murder of a Suicide).*
1942 *Don't Monkey With Murder* (London: Hodder and Stoughton; New York: Doubleday, 1942). (*The Shape of a Stain).*
1942 *Your Neck in a Noose* (London: Hodder and Stoughton; New York: Doubleday, 1943). (*Neck in a Noose).*
1945 *I, Said the Fly* (London: Hodder and Stoughton: New York: Doubleday).
1946 *Murder Among Friends* (London: Collins; New York: Doubleday, 1946 (*Cheat the Hangman).*
1948 *With Murder in Mind* (London: Collins).
1949 *The March Hare Murders* (London: Collins and New York: Doubleday).
1950 *Hunt The Tortoise* (London: Collins; New York: Doubleday).
Milk of Human Kindness (London: Collins).
1952 *The Clock That Wouldn't Stop* (London: Collins and New York: Doubleday).
Alibi for a Witch (London: Collins and New York: Doubleday).
1953 *Murder in Time* (London: Collins).
1954 *The Lying Voices* (London: Collins).
1955 *Enough to Kill a Horse* (London: Collins and New York: Doubleday).
1956 *Always Say Die* (London: Collins; New York: Doubleday, 1956). (*We Haven't Seen Her Lately*).
1956 *Murder Moves In* (London: Colins; New York: Doubleday, 1956). (*Kill or Cure*).
1957 *Furnished for Murder* (London: Collins).
Count the Cost (New York: Doubleday; London: Collins; 1958). (*Unreasonable Doubt*).
1958 *Depart This Life* (New York: Doubleday; London: Collins; 1959). (*A Tale of Two Murders*).
1960 *Fear The Light* (London: Collins and New York, Doubleday).
The Sleeping Dogs (London: Collins and New York: Doubleday).
1962 *The Busy Body* (London: Collins; New York: Doubleday, 1962). (*Seeing Double*).
1962 *The Wandering Widows* (London: Collins and New York: Doubleday).
1963 *The Doubly Dead (*London: Collins and New York: Doubleday).
1964 *The Decayed Gentlewoman* (New York: Doubleday; London: Collins; 1964). (*A Legal Fiction*).
1965 *Ninth Life* (London: Collins).
1966 *No Peace for the Wicked* (London: Collins and New York: Harper).
1967 *Zero at the Bone* (London: Collins; New York: Walker, 1968).
1968 *The Swaying Pillars* (London: Collins and New York: Walker).
1969 *Skeleton Staff* (London: Collins and New York: Walker).
1970 *The Seven Sleepers* (London: Collins and New York: Walker).
1971 *A Stranger and Afraid* (London: Collins and New York: Walker).
1972 *Breath of Suspicion* (London: Collins and New York: Doubleday).
Foot in the Grave (New York: Doubleday; London: Collins; 1973).
1973 *The Small World of Murder* (London: Collins and New York: Doubleday).
1974 *Hanged Man's House* (London: Collins and New York: Doubleday).
Alive and Dead (London: Collins; New York: Doubleday, 1975).
1975 *Drowned Rat* (London: Collins and New York: Doubleday.)
The Cup and the Lip (London: Collins; New York: Doubleday, 1976).
1976 *Blood Flies Upward* (London: Collins; New York: Doubleday, 1977).

1977 *The Pretty Pink Shroud* (London: Collins; and New York: Doubleday).
Murders Anonymous (London: Collins; New York: Doubleday, 1978).
1978 *Last Will and Testament* (London: Collins and New York: Doubleday).
In at the Kill (London: Colins; New York: Doubleday, 1979).
1979 *Witness Before the Fact* (London: Collins; New York: Doubleday, 1980).
1980 *Frog in the Throat* (London: Collins; New York: Doubleday, 1981).
Experiment With Death (London: Collins; New York: Doubleday, 1981).
1981 *Thinner Than Water* (London: Collins; New York, Doubleday, 1982).

Short Story Collection
Designs on Life (New York, Doubleday, 1982).

Uncollected Short Stories
1959 "The Case of the Two Questions" (*Ellery Queen's Mystery Magazine*, October).
"The Case of the Blue Bowl" (*Ellery Queen's Mystery Magazine*, August).
1960 "Playing With Fire" (*Ellery Queen's Mystery Magazine*, January).
"The Case of the Auction Catalogue" (*Ellery Queen's Mystery Magazine*, March).
1964 "Suicide?" (*The Saint*, October).
1965 "Look for Trouble" (*The Saint*, May).
1972 "The Long Way Round" (*Winter's Crimes 4*, London: Macmillan).
1976 "Ashes to Ashes" (*Ellery Queen's Giants of Mystery*).
1977 "Sequence of Events" (*Winter's Crimes 9).*
"The Rose Murders" (*Ellery Queen's Mystery Magzine*, May).
"A Very Small Clue" (*Ellery Queen's Mystery Magazine*, June).
1978 "The Forgotten Murder" (*Ellery Queen's Mystery Magazine*, January).

[2]See, for example, Jessica Mann, *Deadlier Than the Male* (New York: Macmillan, 1981), p. 241; or Hanna Charney, *The Detective Novel of Manners: Hedonism, Morality, and the Life of Reason* (London and Toronto: Associated University Presses, 1981), p. xxiv; or, indeed, the cover blurbs on any of the recent spate of paperback reprints of Ferrars' novels.

[3]"The Guilty Vicarage," *The Dyer's Hand*, (New York: Random House, 1962), pp. 146-58; reprinted from *Harper's*, May, 1948.

[4]"Murder and Manners; The Formal Detective Novel," in Larry N. Landrum, Pat Browne, and Ray B. Browne, eds., *Dimensions of Detective Fiction* (Bowling Green, Ohio: Popular Press, 1976), pp. 37-57.

Patricia Highsmith

(Photo copyright © Stern, Hamburg, reprinted with permission)

Patricia Highsmith

1921	Mary Patricia Highsmith, born 19 January in Fort Worth, Texas; daughter of Jay Bernard and Mary Coates Plangman; adopted stepdaughter of Stanley Highsmith
1942	B.A., Barnard College
1949	*Strangers on a Train,* first novel
1951	*Strangers on a Train* filmed by Alfred Hitchcock in somewhat different form
1952	Published non-crime novel, *The Price of Salt* (NY: Coward McCann, c1952) as Claire Morgan
1955	*The Talented Mr. Ripley* introduces series character Tom Ripley
1957	Mystery Writers of America Scroll and Grand Prix de Litterature Policiere, both for *The Talented Mr. Ripley*
1961	*The Talented Mr. Ripley* filmed as *Purple Noon* by Rene Clement
1964	Crime Writers Association Silver Dagger (best foreign crime novel) for *The Two Faces of January*
1966	*Enough Rope* filmed by Claude Autant-Lara, based on *The Blunderer* (1954)
1981	*The Black House,* twenty-second crime book

Patricia Highsmith

Kathleen Gregory Klein

I

In her refusal to be limited by the conventional considerations of the genre, Patricia Highsmith is, quite simply, one of the best and most significant crime writers working today.[1] Critic Blake Morrison notes that "[T]o call her a 'crime writer' sounds limiting, even patronising, since, like Chabrol, Highsmith is less interested in the mechanics of crime than in the psychology behind them;"[2] while Brigid Brophy extends the praise, "as a novelist *tout court* she's excellent.... Highsmith and Simenon are alone in writing books which transcend the limits of the genre while staying strictly inside its rules: they alone have taken the crucial step from playing games to creating art."[3] What characterizes Highsmith's work beyond attention to character development and atmosphere is a way of examining human beings which unnerves and disquiets the reader. She takes a grim look at the darker side of human nature, revealing the innate capacity of everyone for violence, even murder. While some readers might deny this assessment of themselves, escaping to the classical puzzle novel with its neat definitions of villainy and while others, preferring those "mean streets," erroneously believe that they are facing death as it really can happen, Highsmith, both obviously and subtly, recognizes a common personality trait. Equally present in everyone, the propensity for evil is inescapable; its execution depends on circumstances, not the will or public posture of the individual.

In accenting dualities, Highsmith futher comments on the universal inclination to violence. Her characters' duets of love and hate, power and powerlessness, order and disorder, guilt or guiltlessness never really display the expected results. All virtue can not reside within a single character, nor can it invariably triumph. Blended in such a way that lovers hate, ordering disorders, or powerlessness empowers, the dualities are charged with intensity and mystery. Like sexuality, a persistent challenge in Highsmith's works, opposites and pairs reverberate discordantly.

Like only a few of her colleagues, Highsmith has written critically and instructionally about crime fiction. While undoubtedly exaggerating some of her advice and conclusions, nonetheless, she acknowledges the craft involved in writing popular fiction ("popular" is used here to identify that which is widely read and praised, not to make any unnecessary artificial distinctions between "literary" and "popular" fiction). The title of Highsmith's non-fiction, "how-to" book, *Plotting and Writing Suspense Fiction,* provides a significant indication of one approach to her work. It implies that organization of plot elements, development of action and concern for the overall structure of the work are central among Highsmith's concerns. Even a casual consideration of her novels and short stories verifies this obvious fact as the opening paragraph of each work exemplifies perfectly. Succinct, but action-filled, each opening forces itself upon the reader's attention. Four examples from the novels and short stories easily demonstrate the point:

> Coleman was saying, "My only child, she was, but it doesn't mean she'll be your only wife. Your last wife."
>
> *Those Who Walk Away*

> "There's no such thing as a perfect murder," Tom said to Reeves. "That's just a parlor game, trying to dream one up. Of course you could say there are a lot of unsolved murders. That's different." Tom was bored. He walked up and down in front of his big fireplace where a small but cozy fire crackled. Tom felt he had spoken in a stuffy, pontificating way. But the point was he couldn't help Reeves, and he'd already told him that.
>
> *Ripley's Game*

> Greta showed Ed the letter as soon as he opened the door. "I couldn't help opening it, Eddie, because I knew it was from that—that creep."
>
> *A Dog's Ransom*

> When Mr. Peter Knoppert began to make a hobby of snail-watching, he had no idea that his handful of specimens would become hundreds in no time.
>
> "The Snail Watcher"

Like other famous first lines in literary works (eg. *Pride and Prejudice* or *Anna Karenina),* they orient the reader not merely to characters or plot but primarily to atmosphere, the prose setting. Tightly organized yet never hurried, Highsmith's novels and short stories compel the reader's attention through her careful delineation of contrasts between realistic and improbable detail.

Although *Plotting and Writing Suspense Fiction* is extremely varied in its approach—concerned with choosing an agent, expecting advertising of a publisher, recognizing the germ of an idea, or organizing the first page—it is generally chatty and personal in style. Highsmith uses her own ideas and works, her failures as well as her successes to focus the details of her advice. For the reader rather than the writer of fiction, the volume's greatest appeal lies in the important clues it provides to Highsmith's thinking and the perspective on her own work which it articulates; as a volume of criticism of the genre, it is generally unfocused and limited in its concerns.

At the outset, Highsmith claims to accept the trade definition of suspense: "stories with a threat of violent physical action and anger, or danger and action itself" (1). But she refuses to concede the usual limitations ascribed to the genre, believing instead that "the beauty of the suspense genre is that a writer can write profound thoughts and have some sections without physical action if he wishes to, because the framework is an essentially lively story" (1). This contrast between the usual expectations and the expanded form of the genre is at the heart of Highsmith's talent and success. More widely praised in England and Europe than in the United States, she is not limited abroad to a narrow category, rigidly defined and briefly reviewed. Instead she is accorded serious consideration; as a result, she encourages young writers to "keep as clear of the suspense label as possible" (142). She indicates her own limitless conception of the possibilities, free of formulaic blandness of gore and brutality, by citing *Crime and Punishment* as a perfect example of the genre's possibilities.

The centrality of character formulation and development as a subject in this book belies the title's insistence on "how" to focus on "why;" not being formulaic mystery or detective novels, her works are never concerned with teasing the reader about "whodunit." In fact, the tantilizing question of why crime is planned or committed is seldom answered with satisfying finality. Instead, the reader is treated to a progress report on the criminal's mind and emotions at work. People, then, rather than plots, are at the center of Highsmith's suspense-filled universe. The crucial pair—character and atmosphere—are both defined and placed through a "bit of action" which is focused at the center or the climax of the story. Although this action—such as an imitated murder (*The Blunderer*) or an exchange of victims (*Strangers on a Train*)—may often first occur to her without the appropriate characters attached, Highsmith notes, its direction and thrust later serve to identify a major facet of the characters' personalities or wills.

As action determines her characters, Highsmith explains, point of view affects her tone. She abandoned first person narrators as a novelistic device when she "got sick and tired of writing the pronoun 'I,' " (82) and recognized that her scheming characters seemed more sympathetic when filtered through the authorial consciousness. Because Highsmith varies her novels' point of view, moving from limited to absolute omniscience, even using two different perspectives in a single novel, most of her works, despite their similarities, have a fresh and unique appeal. She is adamant about the importance of good and careful writing, critical of the gimmickry which pervades many novels and most short stories. Nonetheless she is not tediously serious; the writer must acknowledge the game-playing element in his work, she notes.

Highsmith is thus led to acknowledge the recurrent theme in her own works, which she sees in six of her first ten books—the relationship between two men, frequently strangers, occasionally mismatched friends. These two do not always divide neatly into categories of good and evil, right and wrong, criminal and victim; their relationships, whatever overtones of these they may contain, are based on a real or perceived inequality which Highsmith manipulates, blurs, or emphasizes. She reuses this theme easily, believing that "[U]nless one is in danger of repeating oneself, they should be used to the fullest, because a writer will write better making use of what is, for some strange reason, innate" (146).

Because puzzles and mysteries bore her and because she finds "the public passion for justice" artificial, Highsmith believes in the inevitably interesting and dramatic criminal: "I rather like criminals and find them extremely interesting, unless they are monotonously and stupidly brutal" (50-1). Naturally, then, she is careful to recognize the necessity of suspending moral judgments and even shutting off one's mind to certain strictures and proscriptions which she would unquestionably acknowledge in daily life. Moralizing and censorship are equally unacceptable to her; recognizing the use the artist makes of experience, she rejects artificial judgments.

When all the subjects on which she cautions other writers to take care are considered in view of her own fiction, Highsmith's concern for character presentation, development and unfolding is clearly at the center of her work. Carefully she builds one detail after another, aiming at a portrait of the person himself. His inclinations are probed; his secret musings revealed; his sudden and often unexplained plunge into criminality is charted. The atmosphere and actions which encourage and reinforce him are painted in. Not only the character alone but also the character in contrast draws her attention; in the recurring thematic pattern of pairs of men, the influence of one upon the other is explored. In the recurring pattern of couples of man and woman, the questions of power and powerlessness are presented and reversed, challenged and enacted. Finally, the pattern of the criminal's interaction with his second, sometimes unknown, self is considered.

Highsmith acknowledges an exclusive use of the masculine

perspective in her own fiction: "women are not so active as men and not so daring." Not only are her protagonists male (with only one exception), but also their attitudes toward women are conventionally stereotyped. Almost unconsciously Highsmith validates the concept of women as appropriate victims of murder or violence; they are presented as having deserved punishment for being too available or unavailable sexually, too domineering or insufficiently independent, too loving or too hateful. The short stories collected in *Little Tales of Misogyny* with their stereotyped titles ("The Fully-Licensed Whore," "The Wife," "The Breeder," or "Oona, The Jolly Cave Woman") are the most openly anti-women. Inasmuch as women are easy victims, violence and crimes against them are easily justified and rationalized.

II

Highsmith's first novel, *Strangers on a Train,* later filmed by Alfred Hitchcock in his characteristic style, is a model for the rest of her fictional canon; in theme and attitude, action and characters it announces her chief concerns and the direction her work will take. Highsmith's concept of the thriller, its attitude and moral posture, is clearly enunciated here; her concern is not with uncovering the roots of a crime already committed in either the classical or hard-boiled style. She does not accept the legalistic notion of justice; detectives, though both private and official ones are included in many of the novels, are not memorable characters, but are overshadowed by the protagonist himself. In a similar way, detection is overshadowed by criminal activity; despite the presence of both, the focus is skewed. Neither the classical detective story with its focus on the investigated nor the hard-boiled with its concern for the detective's interaction with those he chases forms the basis for Highsmith's novels. Instead the criminal, his mind, and emotions, are minutely dissected. His perspective dominates the novels and comes to dominate the reader as well.

A focal concern of this and Highsmith's other novels is the ordinary individual's capacity for violence and murder. Anyone, the characters come to recognize, can commit murder; it is not that the individual must be right for the task but that the circumstances make anyone right. As Guy Haines comes to realize, contrary to his childhood beliefs in the goodness of human nature, love and hate as well as good and evil live side by side in every human heart. There are not different proportions of each depending on the person's temperament; all good and all evil coexist. To find them, it is only necessary to look a little for either one; anyone can be pushed over the brink. As Anne Faulkner expresses it, "Amazing what goes on in people's lives" (195).

The action and situation of *Strangers* are typical of Highsmith. Two men, meeting accidentally, find themselves, almost without knowing how, caught in a love-hate relationship which puzzles them. As they are almost ignorant of its beginnings, they are unaware of how to bring it to a conclusion even if they were certain they wanted to. The action arises from a simple proposal by Charles Bruno: he will kill Guy Haines' wife if Haines will return the favor by killing Bruno's father; both will be able to escape suspicion since there is no link between them. In conception the plan is successful; its failure comes from both of the men who are to execute it: Guy cannot agree to the plan but can be manipulated five or six months later into meeting his obligation while Charley Bruno cannot keep himself from contacting Guy and trying to be friends. Thus both aspects of the plan's success—mutual consent and complete separation—are jeopardized.

The dualistic male pair is matched in two other all-male combinations: Guy finally confesses his share in his first wife's murder to her lover Owen Markman; Bruno is dogged consistently by Gerard, his father's detective, who eventually overhears Guy's confession. The Guy/Bruno pair thus splits into two less intense and less destructive segments—Guy/Owen and Bruno/Gerard. This is mirrored in the two wives of Guy Haines—Miriam, a redheaded southern girl with limited education, few social graces and too much interest in other men, contrasts with Anne, an intelligent, talented, wealthy woman of tact and sincerity. For all his vacillation, Guy can abandon neither; for all his determined gentlemanliness with Anne, Bruno wants to dispose of both. A pair of mothers, pair of murderers, pairs of houses, parties and hotels carry the point a bit too far in this first novel, but the crucial focus is well-developed and carefully maintained.

Charley Bruno is hardly an appealing character; his physical appearance, personal habits, tendancy to whining and self-pity, not to mention his plan for murder, do not appeal to the reader. Yet Guy's tie with him is partially affectionate in nature; not only shared crime and Guy's guilt keep them together. Guy reveals his private feelings and problems believing that Bruno, as a stranger, is an unthreatening listener, but is forced to admit later that this is no ordinary stranger on a train but rather a cruel and corrupt one. Bruno seems incapable of being surprised; details only encourage him to probe for more information. Deciding to kill Miriam, his half of the "deal," he experiences neither guilt nor remorse, only a kind of excitement which gives direction to his life. Afterward he imagines his responses to a radio interview: She was like a rat to be killed; he couldn't say whether he would ever do it again; yes, he rather liked killing her. In the murder, in his plot to have his father killed so he and his mother would be free to live, in his drinking to constant drunkenness and in his reckless pursuit of Guy, Bruno reveals a man who always wants more, who cannot be sated. Although he claims to love Guy like a brother, he fantasizes being rid of Anne so the two men can really be close. His deficiency, Guy notes, is that Bruno does not know how to love, though he needs to learn. "Bruno was too lost, too blind to love or to inspire to love. It seemed all at once tragic" (188). Bruno's only response is to equate love with sex or women and to think that he has never liked either.

Bruno quotes Guy as once having talked about opposites, saying that every person has an opposite, unseen part of himself which is lying in ambush waiting to attack unexpectedly and dangerously. This is clearly how Guy sees the two of them related; and to some degree, Bruno does also. Only metaphorically is it possible to understand the link between these two. Guy Haines is a well-respected young architect who seems to almost fall under the hypnotic spell of another man and his own innate decency. The latter, as much as the former, leads him to murder; because he is racked by guilt for not having prevented or accused Bruno in Miriam's murder, he equalizes his guilt by murdering Bruno's father. Guy is persistently haunted and reassured by the idea that his destiny, which he has always trusted, holds the answer to his guilt. He is convinced, for example, that atonement is part of his destiny and will find him without his searching for it; or, that the murder he's committed might have been part of his destiny—an improbable mixture of arrogance and humility which compels him to obey only the laws of his own fate.

A key to both *Strangers* and Highsmith's inversion of the standard techniques of the genre can be found in Guy Haines' profession. As an architect he is concerned with design, order, harmony and honesty. When he rejects a beach club commission because of Miriam's new entanglement in his life, Guy is genuinely pained to think of the imitation Frank Lloyd Wright building which will replace his perfect conception; in designing his own Y-shaped house, he refused necessary economies which would truncate the building. His work is, for him, a spiritual act, defined by unity and wholeness; it rejects disorder, fragmentation and shallowness. Contrasted in the two sections of the book are his description of the bridge he hopes to build as the climax of his career and his inability to accept the commission when telegraphed an offer. His dream of a great white bridge with a span like angels' wings is shattered when his feeling of corruption keeps him from his talent.

In Highsmith's fictional world, issues of order, harmony or civilization—whatever it is called—are seldom so simple and traditional.

Contrasted with the more stereotyped perspective which Guy accepts is her series character Tom Ripley. His notions of order are equally predictable; Bach, or classical music in general, provide the right stimuli to focus his attention, distill and concentrate his mind. Ripley uses these devices, however sincerely he may value them as entities in themselves, as personal preparations for crime: fraud, theft, murder. Not so amoral, Guy uses them as avoidance mechanisms; he refuses to consider trying to create perfect order out of his own disordered mind. These attitudes toward order mark Highsmith's vascillating and threatening challenge to oversimplified theories of order and disorder, harmony and chaos. Never committing her fiction to either the triumph of order or the inevitability of chaos, she creates worlds which misuse both, locations in which both are equally and simultaneously present; in fact, she suggests that they may be indistinguishable. Highsmith's manipulation of these dualities suggests closer parallels with contemporary absurdists and existentialists than with her colleagues in crime or suspense fiction. Challenging the either/or structure of human thinking in a work ostensibly about a pair of murders and murderers is part of Highsmith's conscious expansion of an established genre into a new and provocative form.

Like *Strangers on a Train*, Highsmith's masterful novel, *The Blunderer* charts the intersecting lives of two men who plan similar murders. Also filmed, this novel qualifies as one of the 100 best detective novels of all time, according to Julian Symons in the *NYT Book Review*. "Unworthy friendships" is how Walter Stackhouse defines the subject of a book he considers writing: "A majority of people maintained at least one friendship with someone inferior to themselves because of certain needs and deficiencies that were either mirrored or complemented by the inferior friend" (8). Coming across a newspaper report of an unusual death, Walter saves the clipping in his scrapbook of notes for his essays; later, he begins to consider how the murder might have been committed by the victim's husband. Miserably unhappy with his own wife Clara, he begins to fantasize committing a similar murder. Like Walter, Clara easily recognizes unworthy friends: she considers most of her husband's companions and even their neighbors in that light. Her critical, unfriendly, insulting manner costs Walter many friendships which he cherishes; he simply cannot forgive her.

Walter's fantasy life is rich and full. Because the world in which he lives does not meet his expectations, he creates an alternate reality in which the ordering of both events and motives are within his own command. Having convinced himself through reading newspaper clippings of Melchior Kimmel's guilt, he travels to the man's bookstore just to meet him, scrutinize him and reaffirm his verdict. Circumstances identical to those surrounding Helen Kimmel's death arise for the Stackhouses; Walter behaves exactly as he believes Kimmel had done, except that he does not kill Clara, although she dies. Initially, Highsmith's intermingling of Walter's fantasy with his actions implies murder; gradually, it becomes clear that Clara's death is truly not his responsibility.

The novel's irony develops from this confusion of reality and questions of responsibility. Kimmel has been a very careful killer; the police cannot prove his crime. Although they are suspicious, they cannot charge him. Nonetheless, he is guilty. Walter, not even sufficiently inventive to create his own mode of murder and then not sufficiently calculating or clever to go through with it, is a blunderer. He has left clues and suspicious evidence everywhere for the police to discover. Yet, he is innocent. The police are only reinforced in their unprovable thesis about Kimmel by the plethora of evidence they find against Stackhouse.

Bonding the two men further together in a strange alliance is their response to the police investigation. Initially both protect each other from Corby, a brutal, driven cop who tries to intimidate both Walter (psychologically) and Kimmel (physically). When their mutual protection breaks down, both men rush to betray each other to Corby; only the liar is believed. In a final irony and gesture of angry frustration, Kimmel kills Walter, taking great satisfation in his death: "There was Stackhouse, anyway! Enemy number one!" (288). Captured immediately, Kimmel is caught killing the man who, he believes, murdered him by the blundering imitation which convinced the police.

Ironically, Walter's inability to acknowledge all the truth about his activities to either friends or the police leads to his being shunned. Neighbors too often questioned by the police avoid him; his respectable housekeeper quits; his friend and intended law partner withdraws from the arrangement; finally, his new girlfriend, a sensitive and affectionate violinist and children's music teacher, frustrated by his persistent evasions and new stories, begins to suspect him and ends their relationship. Even as Clara alive had alienated his friends, he too, responding to her death, achieves the same effect. His alienation is both the cause and effect of Walter's being forced into an isolated position where he feels compelled to create his own reality, ordering events which have no apparent basis in fact.

Walter Stackhouse's almost compulsive fascination with his counterpart is part of his cycle of "unworthy friendships." The ones he had documented for his essays clearly invoked an aura of power whereby the superior friend maintained his status through this relationship. And yet, in the pairing of Stackhouse and Kimmel, Highsmith challenges the foundation of so-called friendship which Walter establishes. The surface of an unworthy friendship implies all power and prestige to the superior partner; yet his dependence on the socially, economically, or morally inferior partner puts him under the second man's power. Should the weaker person withdraw even the slightest, the ostensibly stronger personality would be left without a framework in which to judge himself. Kimmel and Stackhouse articulate this exactly; the imaginative, amoral, clever Melchior Kimmel cannot evade Walter Stackhouse's blundering imitation or undesired attachment. Walter's fascination with this unwilling companion alerts the police and marks his power in the relationship. However, prior to this, his similar fascination had so engaged Walter that he felt compelled to imitate Kimmel's supposed wife-murder, implying that he is actually as powerless to resist Kimmel's subconscious, hypnotic influence as he later is to avoid Kimmel's enraged revenge.

Inverting and reversing concepts of power and powerlessness between the two men, Highsmith here indicates even more clearly her view of human conflict. Frequently, the same issue is raised more covertly in the novels and short stories, shown as male-female struggle. Both men in this novel insist on the unreasonable power which their wives have over them; the extent is more fully described in the Stackhouses' marriage but is implicit also with the Kimmels'. The temporary appearance of female power is shattered, however, when the women are threatened by the power-seeking men. Both women, the novel implies, are justifiably punished; Kimmel shares this attitude when he murders Walter. This parallel suggests a second: in establishing "unworthy friendships," men are looking for the male equivalent of a wife—someone whose inferiority is unquestionable, whose "power" can be manipulated, whose defined existence reinforces the ego of the man who chooses him/her. In Highsmith's novels, true and positive frienships are seen as impossible. Characters feed parasitically off each other, destroying the "friend" for their own needs, having sought someone whose destruction they will not really regret. Even when a character, such as Charley Bruno, sees the relationship as symbiotic—mutual rather than one-sided—he does not recognize how enormously different the intentions of the two friends are. As a result, the same alienation and destruction are inevitable.

The link between power and sexuality is clearly enunciated in *The Two Faces of January*, recognized in England as the best foreign crime novel of 1964 by the British Crime Writers Association. Ostensibly based on the criminal-accomplice alliance between Chester McFarland and

Rydal Kenner, their relationship actually begins with Rydal's surprised recognition of Chester's physical resemblance to his recently dead father, an archaeology professor at Harvard. Seeing Chester in this context, Rydal vascillates between relating to Chester himself or to Chester as a shadow of his father, with Rydal alternating between his fifteen-year-old self and his current adult stage. The novel is told from the alternating perspectives of the two men filtered through a central consciousness so that their reservations and curiosity about each other are both documented. Meanwhile, the authorial voice is weighing both. This pairing is further complicated by Chester's wife's (Colette) resemblance to Rydal's first love, Agnes, who had accused him of raping her, initiating Rydal's serious conflict with his father. Rydal's attraction to Colette generates his conflict with Chester, the father substitute.

The dual identities which these characters have in Rydal's mind are matched by their multiple aliases, assumed under a variety of circumstances and for different reasons. Chester's phoney stock dealing has led him to use various names in the U.S.; his flight from murder in Greece forces him to purchase two false passports. Colette, deciding at the age of fourteen that she did not like her given name Elizabeth, renamed herself; marriage changes her name again as does flight with Chester. Suspected of murder, Rydal not only obtains a false passport but also poses as an Italian, his fluency in languages allowing him to blend into crowds in Greece, Crete and Paris also.

Similar to their manipulation of names—accurate and false—is the author's and characters' dealing with truth. Rydal has a juvenile criminal record because of Agnes' accusation of rape and an attempted grocery robbery in bitterness and anger at being disbelieved; nonetheless, he is no criminal. Chester McFarland, who has escaped suspicion, owes his income to deception and fraud, his continued freedom to murdering a Greek police officer, and his conflict with Rydal to the killing of his own wife in an attempt to murder Rydal. However, they both protect and expose each other in the police investigation triggered anew by Colette's death; the unspoken and unacknowledged between them keeps each committed to the other. Finally, in his deathbed confession, Chester continues to lie, freeing Rydal from all voluntary participation in either murder or flight to escape arrest.

It is continually clear that Chester's parental resemblance persists in its influence. Chester's protection of him, clearing him of complicity in any of Chester's crimes, demonstrates a faith in Rydal's essential decency and reverses his father's harsher judgment on that same point twelve years earlier. Rydal considers his own behavior, perhaps also reflecting on the past:

> He did not by any means emerge a hero, nor did his behavior appear very intelligent, but none of his actions was labelled criminal (283).

The final note of reconciliation with his past, father, and himself is signaled in Rydal's decision to attend Chester's funeral although he had deliberately bypassed his own father's, because "Chester deserved more than that." In this, Rydal rounds off his adolescence and frees himself to return to the States. As his paternal grandmother's money, willed as a sign of her belief in him, had freed Rydal to escape to Europe, Chester's money, extorted in exchange for silence and freedom, sends Rydal back home.

In himself, Chester McFarland is not an especially interesting character. A petty criminal in terms of his types of crime if not his financial success, his only complexity comes from Rydal's interest in and confusion about him. Before the police official's death, he is friendly and fairly easygoing; he kills almost by accident, shows little remorse or fear and is surprised by his wife's more emotional response. His attempt to murder Rydal comes from male sexual jealousy and possessiveness over Colette and Rydal's mutual attraction; though he fails to eliminate his rival, Chester does break up the flirtation by killing his wife instead. His reaction is proportionally more one of anger at Rydal for having escaped than of sadness or self-directed anger.

On the other hand, Rydal Kenner is a psychologically complex and even confusing character. Throughout the novel, his actions and reactions are based on a mixture of feelings of anger and betrayal at fifteen and his adult attempt to feel reconciled with his father through an intense attraction to and rejection of Chester McFarland. Immediately involved in Chester's criminal activities, the reverse of his relationship with his own stern father who had him sent to reform school, Rydal begins to confuse the two men, superimposing the image of one over the other. No longer the less knowledgeable child, Rydal assists the unprepared McFarlands, through his knowledge of Greece and the language, to obtain false passports and escape notice; this knowledge is ironically the result of his father's disciplined teaching in Rydal's childhood. Rydal's response to Colette's flirtation because she reminds him of his first love offers him the opportunity to justify his adolescent behavior, avenge the rape charge, punish his father for being wrong, and take advantage of Chester. The mutual seduction of young Rydal and Agnes is superseded by the flirtations seduction of Colette; when she changes her mind, Rydal's acceptance of that decision despite his aroused feelings vindicates his former claims of innocence. Because they never slept together, although

Rydal taunts Chester with the idea that they did, he is able to manipulate the sexual situation as Agnes had done, hurting the father substitute/husband.

In most of Highsmith's works sexuality correlates with power and possessiveness. Men generally don't like women as people; Charley Bruno merely speaks more openly than most about the opposite sex as a whole rather than a specific individual:

> ('What significance did it have for you that your victim was female?')... Well, the fact that she was female had given him greater enjoyment. No, he did not therefore conclude that his pleasure had partaken of the sexual. No, he did not hate women either. Rather not! Hate is akin to love, you know.... No, all he would say was that he wouldn't have enjoyed it quite so much, he thought, if he had killed a man (*Stranger,* 96-7).

This unadmitted hatred is tied to possessiveness in two ways: jealousy and envy. Men wish to possess both women themselves and what women seem to have simultaneously. To do this, it becomes necessary to destroy women physically or psychologically. Chester McFarland insures permanent ownership of his wife through her death and from this he also gains Colette's possession—Rydal Kenner and his fascination. For Rydal, who had never possessed her in either sexual or legal terms, her murder had to be avenged not so much for her loss as for his own.

This stereotyping of male-female relationships as little more than potentially destructive sexual encounters is typical in Highsmith's fiction. Several causes are worth considering: first, she has totally absorbed social attitudes and is unconscious of the anti-woman tone; second, she is acknowledging a mind-set on the part of her readers which is too strongly ingrained to be easily overthrown; third, having challenged the boundaries of her genre in so many other arenas, she is unwilling to force the issue. Certainly not arguable in most cases is the theory that the portraits of women are ironically inverted as critic Tom Paulin notes of *Misogyny* (and the point is valid elsewhere): "[I]t would be wrong to read these stories as indirectly feminist satires on dependancy because the real centre of their inspiration is the delight Patricia Highsmith everywhere shows for the brutal ways in which these unlikely women are first murdered and then 'thrown away as one might throw away a cricket lighter when it is used up.' "[4] Paulin's "everywhere" must, however, be modified, as must any judgment of Highsmith's treatment of women, to acknowledge her 1977 novel *Edith's Diary*. Even here, however, the revisionist treatment of women is covertly presented.

Not usually considered a suspense novel, *Edith's Diary* is unique in Highsmith's canon for its female protagonist. The novel is ostensibly the story of a former New York housewife and writer's move to rural Pennsylvania and of the years which follow during which her son drinks, fantasizes and can't hold a job; her husband divorces her and remarries; his invalid uncle finally dies and Edith's favorite great aunt and supporter dies. Throughout, Edith records these events and others which never happened in a large leather-bound diary she has had since college. It is her confidante and her escape. Finally, her friends and ex-husband accuse her of mental instability and an incomplete grasp of reality; trying to disprove them, she is accidentally killed. In fact, the novel is anything but what it appears to be. Unlike her counterparts in other novels, Edith is never acknowledged as a victim nor is her death seen as murder. While no single individual is actually responsible for killing her, Edith dies as a result of society's pressure to conform to a female stereotype urged on her by her ex-husband. As a representative of the larger community, Brett Howland stifles Edith's psychological life and contributes to the circumstances which lead to her physical death.

In *Edith's Diary,* Highsmith is following in the tradition of nineteenth century women writers who disguised their tales of anger and frustration in the more conventional and acceptable cloak of punishing women for their independent behavior. As recent feminist literary criticism has noted, a pattern of action was developed in which the assertive, strong-willed, intelligent female character suffered one of three inevitable fates: insanity, suicide, or death, as apparently logical outgrowths of and altogether commendable punishment for their behavior. What critics have also noted, however, is the way women writers have used these surface stories to hide their more subversive underlying message. Certainly, Charlotte Bronte and Charlotte Perkins Gilman provide perfect examples of this; Jane Eyre and the nameless narrator-writer of "The Yellow Wallpaper" are Edith Howland's literary ancestors. They write their own stories because they are unable to create their own lives; Edith's diary becomes a novel, like Highsmith's, in which the woman writer tells two stories.

The surface story of Edith's growing madness and apparent personality change is told in two ways: by her ex-husband and her friend, Gert Johnson, and through her diary entries. The people who know her become convinced that she is changing, that she is no longer in control of her own sanity. They verify this change by pointing to four specific activities which they cannot understand and do not wish to accept. Edith, they say, has become unusually and excessively argumentative to the point where she is willing to alienate friends and acquaintances; she has become increasingly conservative in her attitudes and proposes more authoritarian institutions in her writings; she has published parodies or fantasies in underground newspapers. Finally, she has refused a $10,000 check from her husband who offers it as part of the estate of his dead uncle. For the casual reader, Edith's diary entries reinforce the charges of instability: she invents a happy, successful marriage and life for her son Cliffie whose amoral and lazy behavior has remained unchanged since his childhood; and, after their divorce, she writes of her ex-husband Brett's death, not his actual remarriage and new family. In emphasizing her happiness and satisfaction, Edith's diary entries seem directly contradictory to her reality in which anger and frustration surface daily over the divorce and having to continue to care for Brett's invalid, incontinent Uncle George while Brett and his new family avoid the daily responsibility and expense.

If this evidence seems weighted against Edith, it rapidly becomes apparent that the submerged story, carefully revealed and concealed, makes a different point. At the novel's opening, Edith is a young married mother. Her husband wants to live in the country which he believes their child needs and deserves. Although Edith agrees to move, she is not sure she accepts Brett's rationale. Apparently happy in their new home, Edith becomes more tied to her family; even the local newspaper they try to start jointly has Brett, the professional, as the final authority. And, although he delegates the responsibility for their son Cliffie, Brett's advice and criticism make it clear that he still wishes to control how she handles the boy. The pattern is continued when his Uncle George comes to live in the extra room which was to have been Edith's study; almost alone, she cares for the selfish old man. Nonetheless, she has some illusions of control over her own life; she believes she participates in the decisions which direct her life. When Brett divorces her, leaving George and Cliffie behind, pressing money and, later, psychiatrists on Edith, she begins to recognize how few of the decisions reflected her own choice.

Unable to change the divorce, Cliffie, or George, Edith takes control of her life in two logical ways: her social opinions alter and her diary records a better life. It is certainly plausible that the liberal Edith should gradually become more conservative and even propose stricter, more authoritarian measures in some of her articles. Even as others have controlled her life, she is demanding a place to control also. Having lost power in her own actual world without being aware of it, she gropes for another part of the world where her knowledge, experience, talent or mere presence will offer her some escape from a powerless position. Yet she also continues to write for *Shove It,* an underground magazine, which accepts a fantasy deliberately more extreme than her actual beliefs, almost as though to demonstrate how varied her opinions are. In this, she seems to believe that by constantly changing the grounds of her argument, by persistently refusing to be forced into any mold, she can avoid the judgment and limitations society—in the pernicious form of family and friends—seeks to impose upon her.

The diary entries, which seem to demonstrate Edith's decline, are actually very carefully introduced, making clear her awareness of the life she is creating for herself in exchange for the one others would like to force on her:

> Edith had in the last month decided that Brett should be dead since about three years now. It didn't matter that this conflicted with George's demise and funeral service. Edith was writing her diary for pleasure, and was taking poetic license, as she put it to herself (278).

While she does not consistently insist on this fictive approach, occasional reminders do surface to alert the aware reader of her deliberate and conscious creation of an alternative reality. Aware that her husband and friend know that she mistrusts their plotting to get her to see a psychiatrist, Edith, nonetheless, tries to placate them—"make a gesture of goodwill!" Offering to show them a piece of her sculpture, she trips carrying it down the stairs, hits her head and dies. While falling she "thought of injustice, felt her personal sense of injustice combined now with the crazy complex injustice of the Vietnam situation..." (345).

Parallels with the Vietnam war are not inappropriate in this covertly feminist novel; at issue is the repeated question of power and superiority. The traditional American male, secure in the knowledge that his point of view is always accurate, saw himself rushing to defend the smaller and weaker nation of Vietnam as he sees himself hurrying chivalrously to assist the weaker sex, all the time despising these "gooks" and "broads." In unconsciously deliberate power plays, he destroys both. Edith's attempt to placate society, to convince it to leave her alone, are the gestures of the subordinate; her failure to achieve even understanding or an independent life is inevitable. The demands she makes challenge the established order's view of itself and threaten the hierarchical arrangement of power and status.

If *Strangers on a Train* is the model for Highsmith's later work, then *The Storyteller* presents a paradigmatic overview of her non-series novels. Highsmith must have enjoyed writing this compendium of good and bad murder-detective-suspense tales enormously. In a short story, "The Man Who Wrote Books in his Head," she creates a protagonist who so completely wrote and polished his novels mentally that he felt no need of committing them to paper; even on his deathbed he is able to quote passages accurately, although he has obviously remembered only some of his works. It is certainly true that, with the exception of Walter Stackhouse, all of Highsmith's characters are inventive and imaginative; however, in no other work as compared with *The Storyteller* do their stories intersect and yet so completely miss the mark since, after all, the murder they describe here never happens.

The victim is Alicia Bartleby whose accidental death actually follows the investigation of her suspected murder. Accused by a neighbor and his partner is Sidney Bartleby, a novelist and television scriptwriter. Complicating Sid's defense is the diary he kept after Alicia's departure for a secret rendezvous with her lover. Wishing to experience guilt in order to use the material in his writing, Sid has fantasized Alicia's murder and recorded the details in his diary. Hoping to clear himself, he tracks his wife; when she later dies, Sid forces her lover to commit suicide, believing him guilty of Alicia's death.

The novel is an unusual one in Highsmith's canon with far less of the overt brooding and dark atmosphere which marks most of her work; it is even more striking for its apparent lack of or interest in violence until the very end. These factors combine to give a misleading surface impression of the story and the author's intentions. Although the work seems more benign, even positive and relatively harmless, it is actually more negative and critical of human inclination to crime and violence than her more blatant murder novels. Couched almost entirely in stories, fantasies, inventions, novels and TV scripts, the substance of the book seems distinct but unthreatening; the characters seem inventive but non-violent. In fact, the very complex and satisfactory quality of their fantasies seems, through eighty percent of the book, to replace the need for action. Insidiously, Highsmith makes the reader laugh, approve, even easily identify with the story-makers, especially Sid; for who has not imagined what he would never wish to do?

Because Sidney and Alicia Bartleby have marital problems, they decide to separate briefly, she deliberately not telling him that she's going to Brighton where she hopes to meet a new lover, Edward Tilbury. A writer with a growing sense of hostility, Sidney has little success selling his ironically named novel *The Planners.* Having often imagined the details of murdering many people, including his wife, Sidney decides to use Alicia's departure as an opportunity to visualize her dead and himself the murderer. He even keeps a notebook to help him feel like a real criminal, noting actions and reactions as if for a novel: "Sidney thought automatically and as impersonally as if he were thinking about the actions of a character in a story" (32). When the police find the notebook, Sidney explains his view of it: "The narrative—descriptions in the notebook—is not true. You might say the ideas in it are true. I mean, it's not a diary of facts'' (209).

Including Sidney's, which is the most elaborate and most imaginative, six different stories intersect throughout this novel, delighting the reader by Highsmith's adroit parallels. The Bartlebys' neighbor, Mrs. Lillybanks, constructs hers around having seen Sid carrying a rolled carpet over his shoulder out of the house at dawn on the day after Alicia had left. Carrying the carpet as though it contained a heavy body, Sid is fantasizing murder; Mrs. Lillybanks suspects him of just that. Sid's partner in writing TV scripts has a much more self-centered version of the story; Alex Polk-Faraday blackmails Sid for a larger share of their joint royalties when the police are investigating. Refused, he tells a version of Alicia's murder story which claims to take seriously his and Sid's joking repartee about wife-murderers. Unlike Mrs. Lillybanks who has cause for suspicion and remains silent, Alex accuses Sid to the police. Meanwhile, Alicia, under an assumed name, and her lover are deliberately hiding out, refusing to respond to police information requests in the newspaper. Alicia's version of events is based on embarrassment at having to admit where she's been and what she's done; the longer she hides, the deeper this difficulty goes. Edward Tilbury, on the other hand, commutes weekly to his office in London where he tells the false story of his weekend whereabouts over several months. Concerned primarily for his reputation, he urges Alicia to respond to the police; she, with the same concern, refuses. Overlying all these inventions is Sid's newest TV character, The Whip:

> The Whip would be a criminal character who did something ghastly in every episode.... The audience saw everything through the Whip's eyes, did everything with him, finally plugged for him through thick and thin and hoped the police would fail, which they always did. He wouldn't carry a whip or anything like that, but the nickname would be suggestive of depraved and secret habits.... He has no police record, because he has always been too clever for the police. And he started young, of course. No, that couldn't be conveyed, because The Whip had no intimates with whom he talked. That would be part of the fascination: the audience wouldn't know what was on The Whip's mind until he started doing things (33-40).

Sidney thinks about his journal of Alicia's ''murder'' and episodes of The Whip: the former ''gave Sidney a pleasant feeling of both creating something and of being a murderer'' (82); the latter undoubtedly reinforced it.

Eventually Sidney becomes a killer but not as he had expected, nor is Alicia the victim. Instead, he seems to be responsible for Mrs. Lillybanks' heart attack; he believes she may have died from fear of him. He also forces

Edward Tilbury to commit suicide, inaccurately suspecting him of having pushed Alicia off a cliff. Neither death is a conventional murder; neither can be attributed to him. Like The Whip, he eludes capture and is more clever than his detractors; he even recognizes that he could safely write the facts of Tilbury's death in his notebook without attracting police suspicion.

Sidney's claim and belief that he is punishing Tilbury is debatable. It seems far more likely that his actions result from sexual jealousy, guilt for suppressed hostility against Alicia, revenge for the difficulties their hiding out cost him and anger for Tilbury's apparently having done, in supposedly murdering Alicia, what Sidney himself is able only to fantasize doing. Finally, moving confidently and aggressively against Tilbury, he is able to become his own character, to create himself.

Rootless or disatisfied, Highsmith's characters often need, like Sidney Bartleby, to create themselves. In one of two ways, Highsmith defines this self-creation or re-creation through the concept of dualties which regularly appears in her novels. First, two characters are bonded together in a love-hate relationship as one tries to absorb the essential qualities of the other so that the two seem as one. Charley Bruno does this with Guy Haines in *Stranger*, leading both of them to murder and rejection; Walter Stackhouse imposes himself on Melchior Kimmel with both success and failure. Otherwise, a single character, equally unsettled about his own nature and personality, divides into two, becoming both what he was and what he hopes to be. Colette McFarland (*January*) changed her name as a teenager to feel like a different person; Edith Howland writes a second self. In *This Sweet Sickness*, David Kelsey functions normally in his work world while simultaneously constructing a fantasy-marriage, decorating a home and having conversations with his imaginary bride. With unsatisfying self-images, these characters require an alternative mirror to the one which reflects reality. They remake the world to conform to their needs, even if that leads to murder and violence.

In certain ways, they would all like to emulate Sidney's creation, The Whip. Defined in a phrase—"The Whip acts" (35)—this character serves as a standard against which all Highsmith's characters measure themselves. The reader feels much like the projected TV audience; in the latter case motivation is unknown because The Whip shares none of his thoughts with friends. In the novels, psychological and emotional attitudes are presented and analyzed but no conclusion is ever clearly and incontrovertably reached. Characters often seem to act and especially to kill, for reasons other than those articulated by the text. If The Whip is a model of the unknowable killer-of-action, then his direct and mirror images among Highsmith's protagonists are like him in the acting and unlike him in being as unknown to themselves as to their audiences. Too few see themselves clearly; their self-images are informed by fantasy and desire.

III

Highsmith's only series character, Tom Ripley, appears in four novels published between 1955 and 1980: *The Talented Mr. Ripley,* which won both the Mystery Writers of America Scroll and the Grand Prix de Litterature Policiere, *Ripley Under Ground, Ripley's Game* and *The Boy Who Followed Ripley.* Because even the first novel is based more on character alone than on the combination of character development within a self-ending plot and because Tom himself is likeable despite his criminal actions, the Ripley character is one of the few Highsmith creations who can continue. He bears some resemblance to Rydal Kenner in *The Two Faces of January;* in fact, both Ripley and the young man he befriends in *The Boy Who Followed Ripley* are like Rydal in their attempts to escape and yet understand the past, to know themselves and comprehend their own often implausible actions. The Ripley novels are also made more interesting in having the usual traits of a series: the recurring cast of supporting characters including his wife, housekeeper, criminal associates and even his first murder victim, Dickie Greenleaf; familiar and new aspects of the protagonist are developed as former episodes and established traits are woven into each additional novel—music, art, the American-in-Europe character. Tom Ripley remains recognizably familiar yet develops interesting aspects as he matures.

The young Tom Ripley introduced in *The Talented Mr. Ripley,* is gauche, uncertain and not quite immoral or guiltless; he has a strong sense of inferiority and an intense desire to change his lifestyle and himself. Several typical patterns are established here and continue with slight variations in the subsequent novels: the mixture of sympathy and justification Tom feels, his desire to get and then protect exactly what he wants and feels he deserves, his isolation which is not loneliness, and his wilingness to kill. The last is the least interesting in itself. The reader's real fascination with Ripley comes from the mixture of all his other tendancies with that one, from questions about the absence of guilt and of any ordinary pangs of conscience.

At the novel's opening, Ripley is reasonably worried about being followed from one bar to another by a stranger since he has been operating an IRS scam. Although the potential difficulty works out well, in accord with Tom's philosophy that "something always turned up," the Ripley status and attitude are established. First, he has cause to be always on guard; secondly, he manages to escape detection. The meeting he has with Dickie Greenleaf's father and the subsequent commission to convince his distant acquaintance, Dickie, to return home from Europe give Tom what he hopes will be an opportunity for a new life. He dwells on his rejection, deprivation, modest and unfulfilled childhood desires and hopes to succeed. Like Lambert Strether in Henry James' *The Ambassadors,* Tom fails completely in his assignment, the results satisfying him and disappointing his employer. Ironically, this "job" does lead him to a new life, but not as he had anticipated—he does not become the smart, well dressed, clever and successful American in Europe.

Perhaps the results of his trip ought to have been apparent from his interview: he lies to the Greenleafs about how well he knows their son, his education, his former jobs and tells them the truth only about having been orphaned and raised by an aunt. Yet, "he had felt uncomfortable, unreal, the way he might have felt if he had been lying, yet it had been practically the only thing he had said that *was* true" (18). Feeling rejected by Dickie and his girlfriend and also by Mr. Greenleaf's businesslike letters when he cannot convince Dickie to return home, Tom assuages his genuinely hurt feelings by imitating Dickie, wearing his clothes and mimicking his voice. Caught at it, he is embarrased and his hurt, angry feelings grow:

> He hated Dickie, because however he looked at what had happened, his failing had not been his own fault, not due to anything he had done but to Dickie's inhuman stubbornness. And his blatant rudeness! He had offered Dickie friendship, companionship, and respect, everything he had to offer, and Dickie had replied with ingratitude and now hostility. Dickie was just shoving him out in the cold (87).

For this, he feels justified in murdering Dickie.

Although Tom occasionally, and once in particular, regrets having killed Dickie and wishes he could change what had happened, he is more often pleased with his cleverness in evading discovery by Dickie's friends and family or the police, in masquerading successfully as Dickie and in forging a will making himself Dickie's heir. It is this last success which finally frees Tom from his early awkwardness, feeling of inferiority and needing the world to approve of him; it gratifies his desire for luxury, importance, self-justification and getting away with something.

When he reappears in *Ripley Underground,* Tom has married the daughter of a wealthy businessman and provided himself with an income by participating in an art fraud where forgeries are passed off as the work of a reclusive painter who actually has committed suicide. Disguise is again an important motif as Tom impersonates the painter Derwatt as he impersonated Dickie Greenleaf. Determined again to protect his possessions, he poses successfully and kills where necessary. In this novel, Ripley's material acquisitions and personal taste form an important part of the development of his character; the opportunity to create himself and his life has been used in ways which satisfy him:

> Tom loved his leisure, however, as only an American could, he thought—once an American got the hang of it, and so few did. It was not a thing he cared to put into words to anyone. He had longed for leisure and a bit of luxury when he had met Dickie Greenleaf, and now that he had attained it, the charm had not palled (93).

As well as any other example in the novel, this clarifies his state of mind. He is complacent and self-satisfied, almost a bit smug and superior about others who can not achieve as he has; while the stated goal is appreciation, the means to it was murder—which presumably others could also not handle. He demonstrates no pangs of conscience or remorse; his pleasure is not dimmed by the memory of how it was obtained. Like Sid Bartleby, David Kelsey, and Edith Howland, he has assumed another identity in which his actions are reasonable and logical, his rewards deserved and justified.

The three legal and ordinary pleasures which he enjoys are introduced here and developed in subsequent novels: gardening, music and art. His illegally obtained incomes help him build a greenhouse, purchase a harpsichord and collect fine paintings, both real and forged. Music especially becomes a leitmotif as Ripley uses different types or even individual pieces in varying circumstances to alter or improve his mood. Preparing to impersonate the painter Derwatt, he sends his colleague out to purchase a copy of *A Midsummer Night's Dream* to inspire him. Jazz, on the other hand, does nothing for him in crucial moments—"only classical music did something. . . because it had order, and one either accepted that order or rejected it" (177). After a successful shootout with the Mafia and destruction of the bodies, he discusses Bach with his dazed companion, describing the composer's work as instantly civilizing.

Because he is not so frantic for acceptance or affection as he had been with Dickie Greenleaf and because he is now more mature about his role in relationships, Tom can be more introspective about his marriage. Neither sex nor his wife Heloise's family money concern Tom as much as their shared disrespectful partnership, their ability to laugh together at conventional attitudes, their similar though not equal amorality.

However, no matter how important she is to him and how much confidence he has in her, he does not tell her what he does or where his money comes from, although she suspects both. Even in lovemaking he preserves a certain separation which might be "shyness or puritanism...or some fear of (mentally) giving himself completely" but may also be a positive pleasure experienced from the "inanimate, unreal, from a body without an identity" (151). And yet, humanly contradictory, he does not want to be rejected, salving his ego when people who've heard rumors about his reputation withdraw by the knowledge that most people really liked him when they got to know him better in his own home where he has created an ambiance of culture, taste and friendliness which charms them. The reader shares his neighbors' vascillating judgments of Tom, subtly drawn to like him despite distaste and revulsion for his actions by Highsmith's refusal to relinquish these contradictions in his portrait.

Ripley's contradictions certainly extend to his crimes and murders: while he gives the impression of being willing to bypass violence and additional crime so long as he can protect his safety and income, he also kills without squeamishness or regret and commits minor crimes virtually without thinking about them except when the arrangements inconvenience him. There is a strange quirk of logic in all but the first novel which allows his actions to seem finally justifiable. The cruelest of Ripley's actions is no crime at all: because cancer victim Jonathan Trevanny had, Tom thought, sneered at him, Ripley begins a cruel game in *Ripley's Game* to drag the cancer victim into a scheme to murder two Mafia men. He wants to "make Jonathan Trevanny who Tom sensed was priggish and self righteous, uneasy for a time" (26). Ripley succeeds, but Trevanny, who kills one Mafia man alone and three more in Ripley's company, becomes estranged from his wife and child, confused and guilty and finally dies in another shootout. Although Tom recognizes the role of his own curiosity and later tries to help Trevanny accomplish the murders and make peace with his wife, the casual manner in which he sets all this trauma in motion and his suggestion that medical records be falsified to prod Trevanny to further action are thoughtlessly and needlessly callous. In the end, Ripley can even feel virtuous because the victims were Mafia—"there were people more dishonest, more corrupt, decidedly more ruthless than himself" (115)—and because Trevanny's wife, having not helped the police, seems as corrupt as "much of the rest of the world" (267).

Mixed motives regularly dog Ripley's decisions. To protect the Derwatt forgery schemes, he believes that he would "*lay my soul bare, show him the poems I've written to Heloise, take my clothes off and do a sword dance. ...*" (*Under Ground*, 60); instead, he murders. Death and deception are justified in the name of Bernard Tufts, Derwatt's close friend, admirer, and forger whose conscience drives him toward suicide. Telling himself that he's going to help Tufts, Ripley half consciously urges him toward death, making Tufts doubt his vision and sanity. With this death, two of Ripley's problems seem solved: Tufts cannot now reveal the forgery scheme and his burned corpse can be falsely identified as Derwatt. Though he thinks he might have preferred another outcome, Tom knows he consciously worked the situation out as he really wanted. Even Ripley's apparently generous offer to help runaway Frank Pierson in *The Boy Who Followed Ripley* return to his family and reject his own feelings of guilt at having pushed his crippled father off a cliff is motivated, in part, by Tom's seeing himself in the boy and wanting to recreate and thus justify his own behavior. How far apart the two are is registered in Tom's attitude about guilt:

> How was Frank ever going to achieve the big justification, which would take away all his guilt? He might never find a total justification, but he had to find an attitude. Every mistake in life, Tom thought, had to be met by an attitude, either the right attitude or the wrong one, a constructive or self-destructive attitude. What was tragedy for one man was not for another, if he could assume the right attitude toward it. Frank felt guilt, which was why he had looked up Tom Ripley, curiously Tom had never felt such guilt, never let it seriously trouble him. In this, Tom realized that he was odd. Most people would have experienced insomnia, bad dreams, especially after commiting a murder such as that of Dickie Greenleaf, but Tom had not (*Boy*, 95).

Yet, in taking Frank to Berlin, giving him time to plan, rescuing him from kidnappers and flying home to the States with him, Ripley shows understanding and compassion which almost no one else could. However, his inability to understand Frank's guilt and need for personal salvation eventually contribute to the boy's suicide. Tom's sympathy and recognition of his failure to comprehend leave him as vulnerable as he had been with Dickie Greenleaf's rejection and no more certain how to cope with it.

Tom's guiltlessness and apparent inability to comprehend guilt feelings in others are among the strongest impressions a reader receives from the Ripley series. In the four books Tom participates in over a dozen murders, three extended fraudulent schemes, four major betrayals of trust and dozens of minor crimes. Only infrequently and briefly is he ever even willing to consider the morality of his decisions or the ethical nature of his behavior. Highsmith's conception of the criminal-hero as a superior person (expressed in *Plotting*) is manifest in Tom Ripley's creation of himself. Once he has justified, however briefly and inadequately, lying to

Dickie Greenleaf's father in order to secure the trip to Europe, he recreates himself. Rejecting his unpleasant childhood, all the memories and all the lessons learned in it, he becomes a new-born. His schooling both on the ship and in Italy convince Tom of the futility of moral behavior. Not immoral but thoroughly amoral, he accepts no standards of judgment which would undermine his new status and freedom. In the clear-cut contrast between himself and Frank Pierson, Tom is genuinely bewildered. Intellectually, he knows that some people feel guilty; he takes advantage of this in dealing with them. Emotionally, he no longer comprehends the feeling. Self-serving and self-protective, Tom recognizes that to atune himself to guilt would inhibit his financial and criminal success; so he perseveres in his chosen ignorance of guilt and rejects circumstances which would force the sensation upon him.

Because Tom Ripley, like few other Highsmith protagonists, is a calculating criminal whose behavior is both conscious and deliberate, he poses a dilemma for the reader. On the one side, his actions and their consequences are vicious and destructive; he can be neither enjoyed nor admired in that light. On the other, his motivations and choices are clearly and logically debated; there is a certain fascination to the way his mind works which can intrigue and attract a reader who is simultaneously repulsed. Tom's criminality seems to fit him; it is a part of his everyday life. Side by side in his living room hang two "Derwatt" paintings, one real and the other—"in the place of honor"—forged. He recognizes his preference for the forgery despite his judgment that the other is better art. This image may also represent his life where ordinary activities stand next to criminal ones, the latter usurping the primary place in his life. For the reader, the disconcerting blend of real and ordinary with forgery and crime may discompose; but, at least here, readers understand how Tom operates and where his priorities intersect.

IV

Having considered the extraordinary talent and vitality which Highsmith brings to the genre, as well as the innovations and expansions she uses to extend its limits, the conclusion to this essay is an appropriate place to speculate on her reception by readers. Julian Symons, who admires her work, calling her "the most important crime novelist at present in practice," also recounts an annecdote about mystery publisher and fan Victor Gollancz regarding Highsmith's novels.[5] Having read *The Two Faces of January*, Gollancz declined to read her works further. Symons wryly remarks that Highsmith is an acquired taste which some never manage. It is possible to analyze, admire and value her contributions to fiction without having acquired the taste and, even, without particularly wishing to read her next published work. While admiration and pleasure need not always go hand-in-hand, some consideration of the divergent feelings her work provokes illuminates her intention.

In establishing the novels' frameworks, atmospheres and, often, characters, Highsmith seems to be providing a realisitic perspective. Details are sharp and accurate; settings are reliable, characters behave in ways observable in society at large. While readers of classical puzzle-mysteries look for an intellectual challenge and fans of the hard-boiled expect psychological truth and action, no reader of crime or mystery fiction anticipates deliberate violations of realism. In such circumstances, puzzles cannot be solved or criminals' moves anticipated. Nonetheless, Highsmith violates this convention; unbelievable details, actions, psychology or motives sit side-by-side with realistic elements. If the readers were merely confused, disoriented, or annoyed by these juxtapositions, the novels could be rejected as failures. However, although these reactions are shared by Highsmith's audience, this response must be separate from the judgments. Perhaps one of Highsmith's great strengths is in making readers nervous and uncomfortable with her talent.

Chief among Highsmith's deviations is her presentation of psychological motivation. The characters seem so much like known and understood people in the everyday world that their decisions to kill are unanticipated, unpredicted and baffling. Because the murderers are such ordinary people, the readers initially identify and emphathize with them. Highsmith uses the narrators' varieties of omniscience to create sympathy for the protagonist; she manipulates readers to like her characters and understand their lives and feelings. She draws her readers into recognizing themselves in most of the characters' action and behavior. Then a character murders; the readers are faced with accepting Guy Haines' discovery that anyone has the capacity for killing given the right circumstances. Rejecting this idea, which would force them to see themselves as potential murderers, the readers attempt to retrace the character's psychological state, mental attitude and reasoning patterns which led to the decision to kill. Frequently, there are none; or, more accurately, none really matter. Only the intersection of victim, killer and circumstances make this occasion different from others. The crime-solution game of conventional detective novels becomes a new kind of psychological scavenger hunt in which all the clues either mislead or direct the readers to vacant lots. Without the explanations which allow the readers a comfortable place from which to contrast themselves and the murderer, their avoidance mechanisms are employed for self-protection. They become irritated with the character, seeing ways in which circumstances could have been avoided, loopholes sought and danger eluded. In this process of criticism and distancing, readers often confuse their dislike for the characters and discomfort with the criminal activity for a valid critique of the novel and its author.

In challenging the readers' self-image of safe innocence and protective, benign behavior, Highsmith risks alienating her audience. Her canon of twenty-two crime books indicates more clearly than any single evaluation how willing she is to take such risks. Her characters are too much like and yet too unlike her audience to be attractive and appealing; their behavior is too close to the dark ruthlessly hidden side of human personality; their actions, however, much they may correspond with readers' fantasies, are too disruptive to be allowed. In showing us ourselves, Highsmith takes the elements of her given genre and creates a sharp, new fictional form.

Notes

[1]The editions of Highsmith's novels and short-stories used for this study are listed below, preceeded by the original date of publication. All references will be included in the text using, where necessary, the abbreviation given after each entry.

1950 *Strangers on a Train*, New York: Penguin Books, 1979 (*Strangers*).
1954 *The Blunderer*, New York, Coward McCann, 1954 (*Lament for a Lover*).
1955 *The Talented Mr. Ripley*, New York: Coward McCann, 1955.
1957 *Deep Water*, New York: Harper, 1957.
1958 *A Game for the Living*, New York: Harper, 1958.
1960 *This Sweet Sickness*, New York: Harper, 1960.
1962 *The Cry of the Owl*, New York: Harper, 1962.
1964 *The Two Faces of January*, New York: Doubleday, 1964 (*January*).
1964 *The Glass Cell*, New York: Doubleday, 1964.
1965 *The Story-Teller*, New York: Doubleday, 1965 (*A Suspension of Mercy*).
1966 *Plotting and Writing Suspense Fiction*, Boston: The Writer, 1966 (*Plotting*).
1967 *Those Who Walk Away*, New York: Doubleday, 1967.
1969 *The Tremor of Forgery*, New York: Doubleday, 1969.
1970 *Ripley Under Ground*, New York: Doubleday, 1970 (*Under Ground*).
1970 *The Snail-Watcher and Other Stories*, New York: Doubleday, 1970.
"The Snail-Watcher," "The Birds Poised to Fly," "The Terrain," "When The Fleet Was in at Mobile," "The Quest for 'Blank Claveringi'," "The Cries of Love," "Mrs. Afton, Among Thy Green Braes," "The Heroine," "Another Bridge to Cross," "The Barbarians," "The Empty Birdhouse."
1972 *A Dog's Ransom*, New York: Knopf, 1972.
1974 *Ripley's Game*, New York: Knopf, 1974.
1974 *Little Tales of Misogyny*, London: Heinemann, 1977 (*Misogyny*). "The Hand," "Oona, the Jolly Cave Woman," "The Coquette," "The Artist," "The Middle-Class Housewife," "The Fully-Licensed Whore, or, The Wife," "The Breeder," "The Mobile Red-Object," "The Perfect Little Lady," "The Silent Mother-in-Law," "The Prude," "The Victim," "The Evangelist," "The Perfectionist."
1975 *The Animal Lover's Book of Beastly Murder*, London: Heinemann, 1975. "Chorus Girl's Absolutely Final Performance," "Djemal's Revenge," "There I Was, Stuck with Bubsy," "Ming's Biggest Prey," "In the Dead of Truffle Season," "The Bravest Rat in Venice," "Engine Horse," "The Day of Reckoning," "Notes from a Respectable Cockroach," "Eddie and the Monkey Robberies," "Hamsters vs. Websters," "Harry: A Ferret," "Goat Ride."

1977 *Edith's Diary,* New York: Simon and Schuster, 1977.
1979 *Slowly Slowly in the Wind,* London, Heinemann, 1979.
"The Man who Wrote Books in his Head," "The Network," "Something You Have to Live With," "Slowly, Slowly in the Wind," "Those Awful Dawns," "Woodrow Wilson's Neck-Tie," "One for the Islands," "A Curious Suicide," "The Baby Spoon," "Broken Glass," "Please don't Shoot the Trees."
1980 *The Boy Who Followed Ripley,* New York: Lippincott, 1980 (*Boy*).
1981 *The Black House,* London: Heinemann, 1981. Short stoires.

[2]Blake Morrison, "Hot Stuff," *New Statesman,* 30 March 1979, p. 454.

[3]Brigid Brophy, "Highsmith," in *Don't Never Forget: Collected Views and Reviews* (New York: Holt, Rinehart and Winston, Inc., 1966), p. 149.

[4]Tom Paulin, "Mortem Virumque Cano," *New Statesman,* 25 November 1977, p. 745.

[5]Julian Symons, *Mortal Consequences* (New York: Schocken Books, 1973), p. 182.

Shirley Jackson

1919	Born December 14
1940	B.A. from Syracuse University
	Married Stanley Egar Hyman; 2 sons, 2 daughters
1965	Awarded an Edgar by Mystery Writers of America for Best Short Story of the Year: "The Possibility of Evil"; Died August 8

Note: *NY Times*, May 1, 1965, p. 24, has MWA awarding the best short story Edgar to Lawrence Treat's "H as in Homicide."

NY Times, April 23, 1966, p. 29, has MWA awarding Posthumous Edgar to Jackson for this story.

Shirley Jackson
Carol Cleveland

Shirley Jackson[1] is one of the most haunting, and haunted, figures in American literature. In the spring of 1948, a young housewife was pushing her baby up a hill in a stroller. She conceived the idea for a story, went home and wrote it and in twenty-four hours mailed it in all but published form. The story was "The Lottery." Outwardly her life was one of energetic normality, involving the production of four children, numerous birthday parties and thousands of brownies. Inwardly she constructed and executed a scathing moral analysis of American society.

***

Stanley Edgar Hyman has described his wife's warmth and motherliness and readers of her two family chronicles, *Life Among the Savages,* and *Raising Demons,* realize that they are dealing with a dedicated and talented comedian. But the same mind that was driven to domestic frenzy by "The Birthday Party" was also meditating on horrors, both familial and universal. When the first of her six novels appeared in 1948, she had been publishing stories in national magazines for seven years. In all the novels and many of the more than ninety stories she wrote, she deals with serious, not to say grim, themes. She explores psychological horror and literal murder. She delineates the iron laws of society untempered by morality and her best work mixes these sources of terror inextricably and inimitably. The family chronicles are notable for their non-corrosive irony, for the funny surprises and awful revelations that life has in store for the unwary mother. But the only form of derangement that appears in these books is the metal fatigue that a mother of four is subject to. These memoirs are early and admirable examples of an American literary subgenre: the diary of the mad housewife. Jackson was among the first to admit publicly that, while motherhood might be a useful institution for children, it was not conducive to serenity in the mother.

Jackson's serious work, while shot through with comic episodes, is suffused with a sense of individual peril and cultural catastrophe. The irony in her fiction is dramatic, and bleak. The surprises her characters face are not funny, and the revelations are liable to be pure hell. "The Lottery," for its economy of means and dramatic impact, is a classic American short story. Set in the present day, it shows us a perfectly ordinary town full of good citizens preparing for their annual lottery. Not until the final moments of the action does it become clear that the "winner" of the lottery will be stoned by the rest of the village. The story can serve as an important focal point for an analysis of Jackson's vision of the modern world and its terrors because sociological horror, including murder, is one of the two mainsprings of Jackson's serious work. "The Lottery" is the quintessence of this part of her vision. In "The Lottery," society murders literally. In her longer fiction, society takes more indirect means to the same end.

In Jackson's work, as in all good detective fiction, the universe in which the story takes place is a profoundly moral one. In the classic detective story, society is seen as basically good—productive lives are being lived, the innocent are protected, love flourishes the better for having overcome obstacles. In the superficially cynical view of the hard-boiled school, society is a collection of more or less rapacious individuals who are restrained from thorough mayhem only by the fragile structure of law and individual codes of conduct. In both subgenres, murder is the essential crime. When murder is committed, the innocent suffer, decent lives are disturbed and those ties of dependence and trust by whose existence we define community are weakened. In the classic detective novel, the uncovering of the culprit restores the torn fabric of social order. In the hard-boiled mystery novel, where there was no very civil order to be restored, the solution to the crime at least validates the irreducible moral value, truth.

But traditionally, neither of these subgenres supplies a formal resolution for the investigation in which society itself is found to be the culprit. And this is doubtless why Jackson did not use these forms. In the classic detective novel, society at large is assumed to be capable of telling right from wrong and of administering justice. In the hard-boiled novel, the detective himself assumes the post of moral arbiter and often administers justice personally if a corrupt or clumsy legal system cannot. In Jackson's world, the guilty are not greedy or crazy individuals, but society itself acting collectively and purposely, like a slightly preoccupied lynch mob. In Jackson's fiction, there are no ties of trust or dependence to be weakened. Like the villagers in "The Lottery," her characters speak of trivia while someone collects a pile of stones. Crime, even murder, is constantly being committed in her world, but there is usually no one innocent enough to bring the guilty to justice. The crimes being committed here are not illegal, and therein lies their terror.

In tone and moral purpose, Jackson's world most closely resembles those created by a contemporary school of hard-boiled detective novelists for whom social commentary is just as important as the excitement of the chase. Influenced by both Ross Macdonald and Margaret Millar, this school has often used an interesting variation on the traditional search for a murderer. They use the search for a child who is missing or has run away as a means of exploring the hypocritical, chaotic underside of a superficially successful society. Jackson uses the search for a lost child more than once and for similar purposes. But she aciduously avoids the tone of moral superiority usually taken by the central consciousness (or conscience) of the hard-boiled detective. In her world, the lost children aren't found unless they can find themselves, and no one comes to close the lottery.

In "The Lottery," Tessie Hutchinson's last words are "It isn't fair, it isn't right" (219). What is about to happen to her is, of course, perfectly fair and right by the logic that has guided her life up to that moment. Victims are always chosen "fairly," by blind chance, and it is eminently "right" not to risk crop failure, possibly the rationale for the Lottery. Tessie has, like the rest of the town, steadfastly refused to imagine the lottery from the victim's point of view until forced to. Tessie pays a heavy penalty for her share in her society's lack of vision, of sympathetic imagination. The penalities inflicted on the victims of prejudice, another symptom of lack of imagination, are often subtler than stoning, but they can be just as effective. These subtle stonings, or brutal blindnesses, are significant themes of the five novels that will be treated here.

Jackson was concerned with prejudice in college, long before the publication of her first *New Yorker* story, "After You, My Dear Alphonse," which speaks lightly but tellingly of racial prejudice. "Flower Garden" (1949), cogently discusses prejudice as part of a long emotional suicide, and "A Fine Old Firm" (1944), delicately points out the anti-Semitism on the American home front. In these stories, the victims of prejudice are either black or Jewish or tolerant. And the bigots are busy inflicting their prejudice on their own children. In four of the five books I will discuss, the children of the morally blind are particularly susceptible to psychological damage.

In *Raising Demons* and *Life Among the Savages,* Jackson gives the reader portraits of four egregiously healthy, imaginative children. The oldest, Lauri, creates an imaginary classmate for his first months at school, a child who conveniently absorbs all the punishment Laurie's own misbehavior calls down. The second child, Jannie, creates an extended family more to the liking of her romantic nature than the boring people she lives with. The last two children, Sally and Barry, frankly practice magic and actually disappear physically into an imaginary kingdom for several hours. All of Jackson's children return to the fold of reality when imagination has served their temporary needs. The youngest brilliantly captures the healthy child's sense of security and identity when he responds to his father's question "Where did you go?" by explaining "You are the daddy. . . and I am the Barry, and Sally is the Sally, and Jannie is the Jannie and Lauri is that Lauri and Mommy is the Mommy" (*Demons*, 657). A healthy child can wander into imaginary kingdoms and come back in time for dinner because he knows he is standing safely within the circle of his family's love and attention.

In *The Haunting of Hill House, The Bird's Nest* and *Hangsaman,* Jackson gives the reader portraits of three young women in various degrees of mental and emotional disarray, which has been caused or exacerbated by their families. Eleanor Vance, Natalie Waite and Elizabeth Richmond are all entering on the same crucial phase of their growth—the last step into the adult world as independent people. All find themselves coming seriously apart when confronted with this task.

Jackson had a strong penchant for mixing genres and reversing conventional expectations. In *The Haunting Of Hill House,* she takes a tired formula from the gothic romance and turns it inside out to tell a genuine ghost story with strong roots in psychological realism. The classic gothic formula brings a vulnerable young girl to an isolated mansion with a reputation for ghosts, exposes her to a few weird happenings to heighten the suspense, then explains the "supernatural" away by a perfectly human, if evil, plot and leaves the heroine in the strong arms of the hero. In *House,* the heroine is exceedingly vulnerable, the weird happenings quite real, the house really haunted.

Eleanor Vance, as unmarried daughters have been expected to do, has spent her youth taking care of a bedridden mother. This has "left her with some proficiency as a nurse and an inability to face strong sunlight without blinking" (7). Eleanor's sister and brother-in-law have rewarded her for this long and faithful service with a cot in their daughter's bedroom and half interest in a car. The "strong sunlight" that Eleanor blinks at is normal life; she is incapable of relaxed adult conversation; she is desperate for an independent, satisfying life, and she is almost completely without the means of achieving it. She has so little experience that she will take anything offered.

What fate offers is Hill House, which is mad. She is summoned by Dr. John Montague to be part of a ghost-hunting house party. She has been chosen because of a poltergeist incident dating from her adolescence. Jackson assumes that poltergeist phenomena happen, that they are the result of repressed emotion and that Eleanor is author and victim of the increasingly frightening events that follow the installation of the party of four at Hill House. Jackson also assumes that houses and other locales can be the centers of evil associations—wells of misery and agony waiting for suitably tenuous human beings to drink from them. What Eleanor needs in order to have any hope of survival is a place to belong, where she is welcome for herself, not suffered as a duty. Hill House welcomes her. She is exactly the personality it has been waiting for.

It is the house, with its doors that shut by themselves, rendering the casual guest simultaneously trapped and lost, that drives Eleanor past her ability to understand or cope with her own emotions. Her fellow ghost-hunters are very ordinary people, ill equipped to understand the despairing love affair that develops between Eleanor and the perverse house. What they can understand is her need for human relationship and they reject it. Their responses, individually and as a group, to Eleanor's deterioration constitute another social sacrifice, less violent than the conclusion of "The Lottery" but just as effective. John Montague, their leader, is an ineffectual academic who hopes to make his reputation by careful measurement of any occult phenomena that a benign fate might drop into his hands at Hill House. Luke Sanderson, heir to the house, is a charming moral coward, and Theodora is a clever, witty, utterly selfish young woman who can give a surface affection if it costs her nothing, but who closes like a trap if asked for anything more.

Eleanor passes by stages from her first terrified revulsion at the house to basking in what she feels to be its warmth and acceptance of her. From horror at the scrawled message that appears in the hall one morning, "Help Eleanor Come Home" (103), she progresses to a state of intimate awareness of the life and breath of the house, including its older ghosts. She has almost reached this stage when Mrs. John Montague arrives for the weekend, a stock comic treatment of the insensitive battle-ax. Mrs. Montague's system of belief in planchette messages is so perfect that she is impervious to the real manifestations of Eleanor's progress from a living, if fragile, human being, to genuine ghostliness. To Mrs. Montague is given the task of summing up, with detailed dramatic irony, the process of Eleanor's dematerialization. She addresses her husband:

> Perhaps you do not feel the urgency which I do, the terrible compulsion to aid whatever poor souls wander restlessly here; perhaps you find me foolish in my sympathy for them, perhaps I am even ludicrous in your eyes because I can spare a tear for a lost abandoned soul, left without any helping hand; pure love—(153).

A few hours later, when Eleanor has been rescued from probable suicide at the invitation of the house, Mrs. Montague asks, "with great delicacy," "Does anybody agree with me. . . in thinking that this young woman has given us quite enough trouble tonight?" (167). A few hours later, Eleanor is dead. She crashes her car into the tree at the bottom of the drive, happy that she has found a way to stay at Hill House—happy except for a few questions that flick through her mind at the end: "*Why* am I doing this? Why am I doing this? Why don't they stop me?" (174).

One of Jackson's favorite devices is to give her characters tags from nursery rhymes or ballads that run like refrains through their minds and may also comment upon plot or theme. Eleanor's refrain is "journeys end in lovers meeting." This is the last reversal of gothic convention, but not the final irony. Eleanor has met her lover; the house has desired her far more than her family or society as represented by her fellow ghost-hunters. As elsewhere in Jackson's world, those whose death society finds convenient do in fact die, having been sentenced to it long before by lethal inattention. As long as Eleanor had some slight use as nurse or psychic sensitive, she was tolerated. As soon as she began to demand full attention, to disturb the peace, it became necessary to dispense with her completely.

The most poignant treatment of this theme occurs in an uncollected story titled "The Missing Girl" (1957). Young Martha Alexander goes missing from the Phillips Educational Camp for Girls Twelve to Sixteen on a Monday, but her disappearance is not reported until the Thursday because it is so very hard to tell that she is gone. After a thorough search of camp records and an interrogation of its teachers, it is found to be impossible to prove that she was ever there. Indications there certainly are, but no *proof*. Seen only as a face in a crowd, peripherally and glancingly, Martha has made dangerously little impression on her world. If she ran away (if she was ever there at all), she was never found and if found, not recognized.

Martha was missing before she disappeared. Eleanor lived for over thirty years as a convenience to someone else and ended as a ghost. Identity is extremely fragile in Jackson's world and it can be as dangerous to have too much of it as to have too little. Those whose gifts and energy make them stand out from the crowd may be criminally mishandled because of their visibility.

The ordeal of Natalie Waite in *Hangsaman*, a novel of psychological detection, stems from having too much of the wrong kind of attention. Like Eleanor Vance, she is vulnerable, and for reasons that are only superficially different. Eleanor's family used her as a nurse, or unpaid personal servant, while totally neglecting her emotional and social development. Natalie, at seventeen, is the daughter of an overpowering, overbearing father, a professional critic, and a mother who has been bullied into submission by him. Natalie, like Eleanor, has played an indispensable role for her family. She is Arnold Waite's protegee, his eager and accomplished student, the daughter of his mind as well as of his body. When they discuss the weekly papers she writes for him, he speaks to her as an intellectual equal. But under the polished performance she gives her father, she hides an adolescent personality in chaos, no more noticed by her family than Eleanor's was.

Leaving the hothouse environment of her home for her first year at college, she finds herself trapped in the claustrophobia of the sensitive. Every encounter she has at college is a nightmare of self-consciousness and other-consciousness, whether it is an ordinarily stupid initiation ceremony or a drink at the home of an admired professor. From being the center of a concentrated, demanding attention, she becomes a face in the crowd and a misfit when noticed. Her room is her only retreat from the demands for a secure personality, or a seamless facade, either of which would come in handy and neither of which she has.

Increasingly depressed and isolated in her room, she begins to find herself haunted by an imaginary "friend." Like any adolescent, she has a deep need to be loved for her singular, irreplaceable self. All the real people in her world fail miserably to give her any attention that is not a reflection of their own needs. Her father needs critical companionship and he has no talent for offering simple, uncomplicated affection. Her mother, trapped in her own frustrations, gives her daughter, as her only heritage, an earnest warning not to repeate her own mistakes. The young English professor Natalie admires proves to be more enamoured of the sound of his own voice and of her father's critical reputation than aware of Natalie's separate existence. He is also developing, in his panicky young wife, a second Mrs. Arnold Waite. And Natalie's classmates seem to be either frightened nonentities or malicious nonentities. Natalie does not know precisely who she is, but she is sure she is tired of being a perfect student with no friends. So she creates an imaginary friend named Tony. One critic took Tony to be a real person and a Lesbian.[2] Tony is something much more dangerous, a creation of Natalie's hyperactive imagination, an imagination fed by loneliness and disappointment that life on her own is even more emotionally unrewarding than life at home.

The conclusion of *Hangsaman* is, by contrast with Eleanor Vance's fate, a happy one. But to emerge victorious from her struggle with the forces of darkness, Natalie must first identify her enemy and then defeat her. Another Jackson character reflects that "...recognition is, after all, the cruelest pain..." (*Nest*, 317). Like Eleanor, Natalie falls in love with her enemy. Her soul mate Tony embodies Natalie's vigorous imagination, her growing but unfocussed sense of mastery and her total rejection of the common herd. As Natalie's withdrawal from society progresses, she has an hallucinatory episode in which she takes possession of the college grounds and its population. By quick, easy steps, Natalie has soon made herself into a cruel and spiteful god, stripping the clothes from the tiny mannikins who have tormented her, packing them into one room of a tiny house and eating them, "chewing ruthlessly on the boards and the small sweet bones" (153).

It does not surprise the reader to find Natalie capable of this ugly vision, since a pronounced paranoia is part of her painful adjustment to adulthood. Natalie's father has a tendency to consume the people around him, either by squelching their individuality or by remaking them in his own image. Arnold Waite's scornful and arrogant style is the only form of mastery that Natalie knows until she can find her own. The creation of Tony dramatizes her desperate effort to distinguish herself from her father. The climax of the novel follows Natalie's and Tony's attempt to escape from the dull, maddening, threatening world of the ordinary. In it, Natalie imagines that every person she sees is part of a conspiracy to entrap her: the whole world has become a stage, and all the automata on it merely actors in a play whose purpose is to destroy her. This fantasy is a more elaborate version of an earlier series of interrogations by an imaginary detective who has tried to make her admit guilt for some unspecified crime, probably murder. Both fantasies reflect the extreme pressure of her father's attention: in his love and his demand for perfection, he scrutinizes every letter, every sentence.

And so Natalie and Tony flee the eyes of Arnold Waite and the leaden mass of the mundane. Near the end of their journey, Natalie reflects on the state of her universe, which is also the progress of her illness:

> If *I* were inventing this world,. . . I would gauge my opponent more accurately. That is, suppose I wanted to destroy the people who saw it clearly, and refused to join up with all my dull ordinary folk, the ones who plod blindly along. What I would do is not set them against numbers of dull people, but I would invent for each a single antagonist, who was calculated to be strong in exactly the right points. You see what I mean? (178).

Tony, as usual ahead of Natalie, replies grinning:

> The trouble is. . . that you've got this world, see? And you've got enemies in it, and they're enemies because they're smarter. So you invent someone smart enough to destroy your enemies, you invent them so smart you've got a new enemy (178).

Natalie recognizes here what will soon be dramatized: that Tony is such a masterful creation, such a perfect complement for Natalie, that she is dangerous. Tony is socially assured where Natalie is not; forthright where Natalie is paralyzed by indecision; she is a natural leader and a powerful storyteller, and she faintly resembles Arnold Waite. After she has led Natalie to an isolated wood, she begins to paint with words the worlds she and Natalie can dominate and soon puts an imaginary foot down on the sands of the tropical island that is sometimes a sign of danger in Jackson's world. The warm sands of that island tempt the visitor to stay forever, casting off all ties to the real world. But that world, though ugly and depressing, is necessary to sanity.

The real world reasserts its importance in Natalie's consciousness by the most unromantic of means: cold feet. The more concscious she becomes that she is cold, damp, far from home and frightened, the greater her awareness that Tony demands absolute trust, absolute allegiance and the most intimate love. And Tony is finally brought to admit the truth of Natalie's realization that there is "Only one antagonist...only one enemy" (186). Tony admits that she herself is the enemy, the queen of Natalie's personal world of madness.

Tired, bereft, but self-possessed, Natalie hitches a ride back to town with a couple who warn her of the dangers awaiting young girls alone in the woods, another example of the multiple levels of dramatic irony that Jackson likes to assemble. Natalie *has* had a nasty sexual encounter, but it was not in these woods. It was with a guest at a party given by her father. The metaphorical woods she has been lost in, her own distorted imaginative world, she is carrying back to town with her. But Natalie has found her way out of those woods. The last sentence of the book summarizes Natalie's personal victory and perhaps Jackson's only vision of salvation: "As she had never been before, she was now alone, and grown-up, and powerful, and not at all afraid" (191).

Natalie has solved the mystery of her enemy's identity, a feat that very few people in Jackson's world accomplish. At first she had mistakenly identified her enemy as no less than the rest of the world—every stupid, malicious, futile human being in it. Only by a determined effort to separate herself from them, to define herself, does she discover the enemy's real identity: her own mockery and arrogance, her own passionate desire to dominate her fellow creatures—herself. Although the climactic scenes with Tony suggest a separation from her, a desertion of her alter ego, in reality Natalie has dominated Tony by assimilating her, by recognizing that she is part of her own nature. And by recognizing her own evil, she has at least a hope of minimizing its impact on others. Since the vast majority of Jackson's characters assume themselves to be innocent, they can quite easily project their own fears and hostilities onto their less powerful neighbors.

For Elizabeth Richmond in *The Bird's Nest,* Natalie's ordeal would have seemed simple. There are six major characters in *Nest* and Elizabeth is four of them. Here too, the heroine's family bears major responsibility for her failure to grow up whole. From an emotionally difficult childhood, culminating in the traumatic death of her mother, Elizabeth has emerged in literal fragments. There is *Elizabeth,* sober, repressed and dutiful; *Beth,* who is sweet, affectionate, and dumb; *Betsy,* gleefully unrepressed and malicious; and finally *Bess,* cold, calculating, and defensive.

The book opens with a familiar symbolic motif, the crooked house. *Elizabeth* works in a museum at the opening of the novel, and the breaking out of her other personalities is signalled, or triggered, by the appearance of a gaping hole in the wall next to her desk. The hole's purpose is to correct a pronounced list in the building. When one of the four walls that enclose *Elizabeth's* neat life becomes an open shaft to the foundations of the building, another side of her intrudes into her work life, the mocking *Betsy. Betsy* begins to remind *Elizabeth* that she too is a rickety structure and one with depths which exist whether *Elizabeth* admits it or not.

Elizabeth's four selves are the expression of a logical campaign for survival among the peculiarly difficult conditions of her life. The daughter of a beautiful, very careless woman, Elizabeth grew up alternately smothered by her mother's attention and desolated by her emotional vagrancy. At the beginning of her own sexual maturity, an encounter with the last of her mother's lovers left her hopelessly confused about betrayal and adulthood. Her mother's death seemed to follow immediately upon a fit of anger at her and at that point Elizabeth buried her confused emotions and turned them into discrete selves. Each of her four selves knows part of the truth about herself and her mother, and none of them can bear to know the whole truth.

Jackson's mixture of forms in this book is original and daring. She mixes medical mystery with social comedy. The drama of the battle between the heroine's four selves for control of her life is perfectly serious and includes a convincing attempt at murder. But Jackson uses the book to remind us that mental health, if it can be achieved, must function in a world of very imperfect people. Dr. Victor Wright is ostensibly the detective in the mystery of the origin of Elizabeth's multiple selves. Actually, with his passion for Thackeray and his distaste for evidence of evil and sexuality in young girls, he is a figure of fun. Nor is Elizabeth's slow groping toward full consciousness noticeably hastened by her Aunt

Morgen, a figure of fine comic dimensions.

Morgen's life has been devoted mainly to cleaning up her sister's messes, of which Elizabeth is the last and least comprehensible. Plain and masculine-looking where her sister was beautiful, Morgen has offered explanations, listened to other people's problems, seen the disaster she might have foretold come to pass, and been rewarded only with independence, rather than the love and child that were wasted on her sister. Morgen's life at the time we meet her is centered around food, liberal doses of brandy in the evening, and the pleasures of honesty—mainly on the subject of her dead sister's character. Morgen notes practically every evening that: "She was a lovely girl, my sister Elizabeth, but mud clear up to the neck" (158-9). Morgen has established this view of her sister with such force that *Elizabeth* is incapable of contradicting any part of her aunt's analysis. Much less is she capable of being rude, loud, selfish, or honest in her aunt's house.

An unconscious conspiracy develops between Morgen and Dr. Wright. Neither Morgen nor Victor Wright is really prepared to meet a whole, integrated Elizabeth Richmond, because that woman has a mind of her own. She also has normal sexuality, about which Morgen is ambiguous, fearing it may turn out to be her mother's promiscuity. And finally, Elizabeth has a sense of the ridiculous which, as *Betsy,* she exercises on Dr. Wright, contributing to his dislike of her. When Dr. Wright first meets *Betsy,* he perceives only the mask of a demon. With characteristic male prejudice and a total lack of scientific detachment, he rejects *Betsy,* wanting to deal only with the charming, ingratiating *Beth,* the weakest of Elizabeth's four selves. *Betsy* calls him "Dr. Wrong," and threatens that "someday,. . . I am going to get my eyes open and then I will eat you and Lizzie [*Elizabeth*] both" (197). Dr. Wright refuses *Betsy,* under hypnosis, permission to open her eyes and in so doing, may contribute to the emergence of a fourth personality, the crude, ruthless *Bess,* whose one object is to take possession of her inheritance. The crisis is finally brought on when Elizabeth's four selves are alternating so rapidly that Morgen concludes she must be institutionalized. *Betsy* helps bring on this decisive threat, with nice irony, by making her aunt a mud sandwich, served shortly afterward by the dutiful *Elizabeth.* Jackson is not afraid to milk multiple personalities for laughs: another episode has Elizabeth's four selves taking four successive baths under her aunt's weary eyes.

But Morgen and Victor Wright are dogged and brave, if sometimes misguided, and they are rewarded by the beginning of Elizabeth's healing, the coalescing of her four selves. She and Dr. Wright agree on the proper way to describe this event when he reminds her that "you have just eaten your four sisters" (364). That this metaphor is an important clue to Jackson's understanding of human society and psychology is confirmed by a reflection of Dr. Wright's at the comic soiree that closes the book: "Each life, I think,. . .asks the devouring of other lives for its continuance; the radical aspect of ritual sacrifice, the performance of a group, its great step ahead, was in organization; *sharing* the victim was so eminently practical" (378).

There must be a victim, Jackson suggests. It is not whether one eats people that makes the difference between health and illness, but whom one eats and the degree of recognition the victim is accorded. The villagers of "The Lottery" simply sacrifice one another without recognizing an intimate relationship. They take life without even tasting it imaginatively. Arnold Waite, Dr. Wright and Aunt Morgen all nourish themselves by partially consuming other people. Natalie's father has consumed her mother whole, but not Natalie. His demands on her are the product of his love as well as of his perfectionism. Aunt Morgen has digested her sister's life as a means of maintaining her own strength and identity. Dr. Wright's vanity has been nourished by the *Beth* in his patient, and he must learn painfully that if he wants any *Beth* at all, he will have to swallow some *Betsy* too.

But those who achieve the soundest health are the ones who learn to eat themselves. Natalie Waite, in the course of her illness, eats her world and its inhabitants. Later she devours herself to gain the necessary strength to keep from being eaten by others. Elizabeth Richmond and Natalie first personify the evil, the anti-social, in themselves as other people. Then, having come to know their enemies from a (relatively) safe distance, they painfully recognize their own complex and frightening identities, and assimilate them.

In Jackson's world, a healthy and complex moral growth is possible for individuals, but almost never for large groups of people. In *The Road Through the Wall,* Jackson worked out her strong feelings on the subjects of class insularity and racial prejudice. *Road* surveys the life of the twelve families who live on Pepper St., which runs through a moderately affluent suburb in California. The wall which runs along intersecting Cortez Road is the major symbol of their isolation, not just from the ugliness of the world, but from the consequences of their own lives. On one short block of Pepper St., a microcosm of WASP society, there is an aristocratic enclave, an upper and lower middle class, a Jewish ghetto, a lower class and a couple of isolated old women. When the wall is torn down at the beginning of the summer that is the book's time span, things begin to fall apart, at first subtly. The destruction of the wall is the beginning of a process that will render the neighborhood less protected from the poverty, and the appearance of poverty, that these people fear. Jackson tells the reader in the Prologue that the WASP men of Pepper St. "thought of their invulnerability as justice" (5). Then she demonstrates just how invulnerable they really are and how much justice they have in them.

The Desmonds are the aristocracy, upwardly mobile, conscious of it, gracious and well-mannered, completely vacuous. They are the parents of an adopted son, chosen for his physical perfection, and of a long-awaited, cherished daughter of their own. The Roberts, the Donalds, the Ransom-Joneses and the Merriams represent the upper middle class. The lower middle class is composed of the Catholic Byrnes and the first-generation immigrant Martins. The Perlmans live in an invisible ghetto that only their daughter Marilyn seems conscious of at the beginning of the summer.

At school, lower-class Helen Williams has made it clear to Marilyn Perlman that she is different and had better remember it. Helen is precociously forward with boys, malicious and a bit vicious with her younger sister. She's not a nice child and the mothers of Pepper St. know it, but none of them makes Helen off-limits to her own children. This sanction is reserved for Marilyn, after she and Harriet Merriam strike up an acquaintance and become "best friends" in the middle of the summer. Harriet's feverishly proper, ludicrously "cultivated" mother explains Harriet's transgression to her and one of the few human contacts in the book is broken. Some of the children on the street have picked up their parents' prejudices easily, but some have to learn the hard way.

The Williamses, Shaw's "undeserving poor," move out in the middle of the summer. Their replacements in the rented house are, on the level of realism, both pathetic and admirable. On the level of symbol, they complete the scathing analysis of American society that Jackson makes in this book. Into the rented house moves Frederika Helena Terrel, a child of great awkwardness and little beauty, who is apparently the major caretaker for her retarded and unruly younger sister Beverly. This job she performs faithfully and imaginatively. She is one of the best mothers on the block.

Among the children, the adult social hierarchy is being reproduced as faithfully as they copy their elders' prejudices. The aristocrats are those boys who are athletic and attractive to women (even if the women are twelve-year-old girls and Helen Williams). Some of the most fatuous conversations in the book take place between the heads of the Desmond, Roberts and James households, as the fathers congratulate each other on the promise of their teen-aged sons and patently on their own achievement in producing them.

Not all the young men show the same promise, however. Fourteen-year-old Artie Roberts is "puny" (a euphemism for bookish), and his younger brother is already a more sought after athlete than Artie, who has been ghettoized by his entire family for his oddness. An even more serious case of ostracism within the family is young Tod Donald, whose fate it is to be the inept younger brother of a member of the football team and victim to the pernicious Virginia Donald, who has nearly ignored her brother out of existence. Virginia is precociously mean, more than ready to assume the mantle of the departing Helen Williams.

Like their parents, these children have no sense of morality, only a loosely fitting set of manners. Besides Frederika Terrel's faithfulness, the one solidly moral act in the book belongs to Marilyn Perlman. When she finds herself part of a group of children baiting Frederika, she turns to Virginia, the ringleader, and says "You shut your fat mouth" (121).

The climax emerges in a series of disjointed, telling vignettes. Three-year-old Caroline Desmond is found to be missing after a party which most of the block attends. (It is one of Jackson's eerie parties at which some people seem to have a good time, but not with each other, and other people have a terrible time.) Hasty inquiries are made and a search organized. Old Miss Fielding has not seen her. (But the reader remembers that Beverly Terrel had been missing a few days earlier and that Miss Fielding had denied seeing her because her tea was getting cold.) Fourteen-year-old Pat Byrne turns down Tod Donald's urgent (and puzzling) request to buy his bicycle. Pat remarks on Tod's strange behavior. (And the reader remembers that Pat has let Tod treat him to the movies, since Tod can assure himself of company only by buying it.) Frederika is willing to help, but can only form an analogy with Beverly's behavior: Beverly's sole joy is to steal money from her mother's purse and wander off to the store for candy while her sister searches frantically for her. And the reader realizes that Beverly has been regularly, constantly lost since she moved to Pepper St., and that Fredrika has gotten less than no help in finding her. Beverly is not an *important* lost child.

The manners which seem to hold this world together are fragile: they disintegrate at a touch. Since there is not enough real community for a Greek chorus, odd figures stand about commenting on the action in perfect isolation. Mr. Merriam is found sitting quite alone in the pantry during the party, with drink and cigarette and music, apparently having a wonderful time. Mr. Donald has visited Miss Fielding several days before the party and, in a sort of double monologue, revealed his passive alienation:

> They expect me to watch,... They just sit there and expect people to watch

them and be interested. They think everything is important and necessary (166).

Mr. Donald, Virginia and the football hero James are Tod Donald's family. When the search for Caroline Desmond comes up empty, the adults congregate and Pat Byrne mentions Tod's strange behavior and his absence. It is immediately assumed that the two children are together and that Tod must know something. While the mob of public opinion stands on the village green letting a stray remark from Pat Byrne coalesce the guilty verdict around Tod, Mr. Donald stands at the door of his house, with a finger in his book. He moves toward the group and then retreats, awash in the tide of his own estrangement. Tod has delayed returning home for fear of being laughed at for thinking anyone was looking for him. When he does return, he finds that *everyone* is looking for him and that all the authority in the world (in the figure of a policeman) is asking, then demanding, that he confess. After a lifetime in the shadows, Tod is unable to bear this spotlight. He hangs himself. And "Hanging, his body was straighter than it had ever been in life" (214).

Caroline Desmond's death is not so much solved as it is swept under the rug. She is found in a creekbed, her head crushed by a rock, clad in her yellow party dress. Mr. Merriam and Mr. Perlman, both ineffectual but kind, discuss the matter and doubt that Tod had the strength to pick up the rock. Mrs. Merriam feels that Tod got off too easily and is sure that he was up to no good with Caroline (rape of a three-year-old by a thirteen-year-old is what she has in mind). The truth is stranger than even Mrs. Merriam can imagine. Early in the book, Tod, who "rarely did anything voluntarily, or with planning, or even with intent acknowledged to himself" (74), had wandered into the Desmond house after watching Mrs. Desmond and Caroline leave. Inside, he finds his way to the closet that holds their clothes, sits down at the back and repeats all the obscenities he knows. Leaving the house and lying on the lawn, he crushes the delicate yellow blossom from a shrub.

An earlier incident suggests that Tod's subconscious mind is as active as his conscious one is passive. One evening when he has been pushed out of a group of girls and rejected by a group of boys, Tod is "possessed of as strong a desire for punishment as he had ever achieved" (43), and throws a handful of rocks at the girls. This gesture fails of its object when no one is seriously hurt and Virginia inquires whether he was aiming at a window. Clearly Tod envies Caroline, the most cherished child on the street. Clearly he has had at least one impulse to destruction in order to be repaid in the commodity he is starving for—attention.

It is possible that Tod did kill Caroline in a sort of moral accident. If he did, on impulse or by accident, crush her in her yellow dress as he had crushed the blossom, he apparently goes to his death unaware of what he is being punished for. His thoughts that night, as Jackson reports them, show a total ignorance of what has happened to Caroline.

Road is a sociological horror story wrapped around a mystery. The book is full of lost children: Caroline Desmond is the object of an instant, massive search which cannot change the fate that has already overtaken her. Beverly Terrel, although often lost (and invisible to most of Pepper St. because of her extreme neediness), is always found because her sister is always looking. But Tod has been lost for his entire thirteen years and has been starving slowly. Caroline's death may have been an accident, a murder by a vagrant, or the act of a person of diminished capacity.

Jackson leaves the question both unanswered and unanswerable on the evidence she gives us. Because no one in the Pepper St. community has cared enough to find out what happened, with unerring mob instinct, they have picked the weakest among them as the scapegoat. Caroline's death might or might not have been preventable. But Tod Donald's suicide could have been prevented by any number of people—by someone saying, at the right time, "You shut your fat mouth."

Pepper St., hiding behind its wall of imaginary invulnerbility, will never admit its individual or collective guilt. A moral miracle of this order begins to happen only once in Jackson's work—at the conclusion of *We Have Always Lived in the Castle*, perhaps the finest of her novels. The main forms involved here are the moral fable and the crime novel, in which the study of character and motivation are more important than the solution of the crime. Six years before the novel opens, four members of the Blackwell family had been poisoned at dinner one night. Three Blackwells survive, living reclusively in the "castle," their beautiful, isolated home. Eighteen-year-old Constance, who had cooked the dinner, was prosecuted for the crime and acquitted. Twelve-year-old Merricat (Mary Katherine), had not been at the table and their Uncle Julian, although he survived, was poisoned, his health ruined.

The identity of the Blackwell poisoner is not hard to guess. The reader soon realizes that it is far more likely that Merricat poisoned her family than that Constance poisoned anyone at all. The book is chiefly a tour-de-force: a story told through the eyes of a mass murderer and told so that the reader comes to feel affection, understanding and even respect for her by the conclusion of the novel. Merricat, eighteen when the novel opens, narrates the second chapter of the Blackwell drama, whose climax is the burning and pillaging of the castle by the vengeful villagers, who still believe that Constance was guilty. At the end of the novel, Merricat has achieved just what she wanted, the exclusive company of her sister Constance "on the moon," that is, completely cut off from all normal contact with the rest of society. Stuart C. Woodruff has argued that in this novel, "...it is Jackson's purpose to convert us, to make us feel the moral superiority of 'life on the moon' to a drab and mean existence in the village."[3] But the moral situation is perhaps a little more complex than Mr. Woodruff suggests. The state of Constance and Merricat at the end of the book is undeniably presented as the best of a limited number of solutions for the two sisters. But their isolation is already all but complete when the story opens and Constance, who has borne the burden of guilt for the murders for six years, does not need much further proof of the malice and pettiness of the villagers. The only important change at the end of the book is in the relationship between the two sisters and the villagers. It is a profound change and needs to be taken into account in a statement of the book's theme.

The fundamental assumption of Jackson's serious work is that any social group will, for its own convenience or pleasure, sacrifice a victim. This constitutes an attempt to deal with the universe by magic, of course. As a method of dealing with reality, Jackson would probably not quarrel with it, except to hope that white magic rather than black would be used. It is not clear whether Merricat started using white magic after, or before, she murdered the rest of the family. What is clear is that the magic has enabled her to deal with the suffering caused by her realization that she has done wrong. Although she never betrays any remorse for killing her family, she has suffered keenly for bringing pain to the only person who loves her unreservedly, or indeed at all, her sister Constance. Magic has given her a form with which to express a moral and intellectual response to her crime, a type of response which the villagers are incapable of at the beginning of the story. Merricat has made up a number of rules for herself which have the effect of protecting the household from a repetition of her crime. And it is Merricat who makes up the rules; Constance merely notes and respects them. Merricat's first rule is prohibition from preparing food (since it was she who poisoned the sugar six years before). There are also numerous ritual occasions for being nicer to Uncle Julian. Also, at some cost, she protects Constance from the malice of the village by running the gauntlet of the twice-weekly trips for groceries.

Although Constance, with her great capacities for love and self-sacrifice, has certainly protected Merricat since the murder, she has also been protected *by* her in real ways. It is, after all, Merricat who takes an instant and immovable dislike to cousin Charles. Cousin Charles appears one day professing family feeling and a desire to help the girls. He soon moves into the house, in on Constance, and obviously wants the family fortune more than anything except his own comfort. It seems at the beginning that Merricat's dislike is motivated solely by her fear that Constance will marry and move back into the world, subjecting Merricat to a society she cannot cope with. Whatever her initial grounds, Charles soon justifies all her hatred. Merricat's great victory in the novel is that she uses only magic, *symbolic* poison, to remove Charles, rather than actual poison. Nevertheless, when her magic accidentally starts the fire that brings on the climax of the book, she exposes Charles' greed and insincerity very effectively.

Actually, Charles' full poverty of soul should have been obvious to Constance long before the fire. Not to look for evil in others may be a virtue, but to ignore clear evidence of it is at least to lack a practical survival skill. Though a very good person, Constance is highly specialized and needs a protected environment as much as Merricat. Constance has been swayed by Charles' arguments to leave the castle not because this would mean a more normal life for her, but because it might improve life for her charges, Merricat and Uncle Julian. On the night of the fire, Constance asks Merricat whether she had put the poison in the sugar bowl and Merricat confirms that she did. The next morning, Constance apologizes for having intruded so far on Merricat's privacy as to ask her about her guilt for the crime for which she has borne the blame for six years. In short, Contance tries to eat all the guilt in her immediate neighborhood. From the pen of Shirley Jackson, she is an astonishing creation. She needs Merricat's suspicious nature to protect her from herself.

In fact, *Castle* depicts a functioning relationship between two moral oddities, a murderer and a saint. But the most startling development in the novel is not that Merricat sticks to white magic in a moment of temptation, or that Constance learns some caution, which she does. It is that for the first time in Jackson's work, the mob reveals that it, too, is capable of repentance, moral growth, regeneration. On the night the fire breaks out at the castle, the villagers behave just as readers of Jackson's work would expect them to. The fire department arrives trailing crowds of onlookers, come to feed on the misery of their enemies. Once the fire is out, fire chief Jim Donell removes his fire hat with ceremonial deliberation and casts the first stone. The orgy of destruction that he permits leaves the house a shambles and Uncle Julian dead, probably just forgotten to death.

What happens next is astonishing. As Merricat and Constance rebuild their lives together, the villagers begin, one by one, to reveal that they are individually capable of recognizing their corporate guilt. Under cover of darkness, they come singly to offer food and confession: "I broke one of the chairs and I'm sorry" (164). "This is for the dishes,"... "We apologize about the curtains,"... "Sorry for your harp" (166). They cannot leave their own names, but they have recognized their capacity for envy and destructiveness. Repentance and atonement have begun here. This is Shirley Jackson's world and so the relative hopefulness of this resolution is heavily qualified. Some of the villagers use "the ladies" to threaten their children with. And the last reported contact between the villagers and the castle suggests that a mythology has begun to grow up that says that "the ladies" can "see everything that goes on," (172) and will punish further transgressions. As Merricat atones by magic, so do some of the villagers; a bowl of eggs is a token of their repentance (and may protect their children from retribution). But Merricat has wisely chosen a good god in Constance, while the villagers are stuck with the wounded, dangerous creations of their stunted imaginations.

What Jackson brought to each of the popular genres she used was an insistence that for every gaudy crime committed, there are a hundred drab social murders and domestic dismemberments that we watch unmoved. If sanity and social responsibility are represented by the Desmonds and the Donalds, by John Montague and Arnold Waite, then it is a kind of sanity that costs too much in the suffering of children and other innocent bystanders.

The protagonists of three of these novels are young women, and the ordeals they undergo are intensified, if not caused, by that fact. Natalie Waite has been singled out for attention by her father as much for her intelligence as for her gender, but certainly the obsessive quality of his love is partly explained by the fact that he assumes a high degree of malleability in Natalie. The imaginary friend she creates is female, perhaps as partial replacement for her broken reed of a mother, who has set a long and discouraging example of submission to her father. Elizabeth Richmond's transition to adulthood would have been less agonizing without the attention of her mother's lover. And her recovery would perhaps have been smoother without the conventional expectations of her physician as to what constitutes a healthy woman. As for Eleanor Vance, the chances are near zero that society would expect a man to devote his youth to the care of his mother simply because he was not married. Eleanor's nearly total lack of experience and self-confidence is surely the result of her gender.

Jackson was not on record as a feminist, but she undoubtedly noticed that girls are more easily imposed upon, if not murdered, than boys. From the family chronicles, we know that she found life as a wife and mother entertaining, exhausting, and well worth doing. From her treatment of certain dessicated "career girls" in her short stories, we know that she envisioned one of the alternatives to conventional family life as fearful. All the more unexpected, then, is the fragment of a novel Jackson was at work on when she died. In it she gives us as narrator a woman in the process of liberating herself totally from duty and convention. She has paid her dues to society in marriage to one Hughie, a nice man and a bad painter, and at his death, which she feels as a relief, she sets out for a suitably anonymous city to discover a new identity more or less by feel. She decides to call herself Mrs. Angela Motorman, reports that she "dabbles in the supernatural," and tries out her skill at shoplifting in the last chapter. This fragment has humor, verve, an undercurrent of eeriness, an appreciative echo of Flannery O'Connor, and is quite unlike any novel Jackson had yet published. *Come Along With Me* demonstrates that from the beginning to the end of her writing career, Shirley Jackson was at work mixing genres, confounding the expectations of the self-righteous and the placid, examining the lot of women, and exploring the differences between crime and evil.

Notes

[1]The editions of Jackson's novels used for this study are listed below, preceded by the original date of publication. All quotations will be cited in the text using, where necessary for clarity, the abbreviation given after each entry:

1948 *The Road Through the Wall* (New York, NY: Popular Library, 1976). (*Road*)
1949 *The Lottery* (New York, NY: Fawcett Popular Library, 1975).
The Intoxicated
The Daemon Lover
Like Mother Used to Make
Trial By Combat
The Villager
My Life With R.H. Macy
The Witch
The Renegade
After You, My Dear Alphonse
Charles
Afternoon in Linen
Flower Garden
Dorothy and My Grandmother and the Sailors
Colloquy
Elizabeth
A Fine Old Firm
The Dummy
Seven Types of Ambiguity
Come Dance With Me in Ireland
Of Course
Pillar of Salt
Men With Their Big Shoes
The Tooth
Got A Letter from Jimmy
The Lottery
1951 *Hangsaman* (New York, NY: Ace Books). (*Hangsaman*)
1953 *Life Among the Savages* (in *The Magic of Shirley Jackson,* New York, NY: Farrar, Straus and Giroux, 1966).
1954 *The Bird's Nest* (in *The Magic of Shirley Jackson,* New York, NY: Farrar, Strauss and Giroux, 1966). (*Nest*)

1957 *Raising Demons* (in *The Magic of Shirley Jackson,* New York, NY: Farrar, Straus and Giroux, 1966). (*Demons*)

1957 Uncollected short story, "The Missing Girl," in *Fantasy and Science Fiction,* Vol. 13, No. 6 (December, 1957), 42-52.

1959 *The Haunting of Hill House* (New York, NY: Fawcett Popular Library). (*House*).

1962 *We Have Always Lived in the Castle* (New York, NY: Fawcett Popular Library). (*Castle*)

1968 *Come Along With Me* (New York, NY: Viking Press, 1968).

[2]John O. Lyons, *The College Novel in America* (Carbondale: Southern Illinois University Press, 1962), p. 63.

[3]Stuart C. Woodruff, "The Real Horror Elsewhere: Shirley Jackson's Last Novel," *Southwest Review,* 52 (Spring, 1967), p. 155.